26 in 26
Neighborhood Resource Centers
26 Neighborhood Strategies in a 26 month time frame
A Grant Funded by the LSTA
(Library Services & Technology Act)

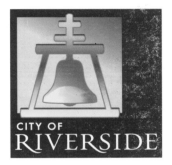

CITY OF
RIVERSIDE

Riverside Public Library

Read This Book . . .

• • • if you serve in a leadership role in a nonprofit organization as executive director, development director, controller, financial manager, or marketing director, or as a member of the board of trustees.

• • • if you're contemplating a fundraising, development, or membership-building program for your organization.

• • • if you contribute money or time to a public interest group or a charity.

• • • if you're managing a political campaign or running for public office.

• • • if you're involved in public relations or advertising for nonprofit organizations or political campaigns.

• • • if you've taken an interest in the activities of a public interest organization or a political campaign as a reporter, news producer, consultant, or student.

• • • or if you simply want to understand better what direct mail fundraising is all about.

Revolution
in the
Mailbox

Revolution in the Mailbox

Your Guide to
Successful Direct Mail Fundraising

MAL WARWICK

JOSSEY-BASS
A Wiley Imprint
www.josseybass.com

Published by Jossey-Bass
A Wiley Imprint
989 Market Street, San Francisco, CA 94103-1741   www.josseybass.com

Jossey-Bass books and products are available through most bookstores. To contact Jossey-Bass directly
call our Customer Care Department within the U.S. at 800-956-7739, outside the U.S. at 317-572-3993,
or fax 317-572-4002.

Jossey-Bass also publishes its books in a variety of electronic formats. Some content that appears in print
may not be available in electronic books.

Readers should be aware that Internet Websites listed in this work may have changed or disappeared
between when this work was written and when it is read.

Library of Congress Cataloging-in-Publication Data
Warwick, Mal.
    Revolution in the mailbox : your guide to successful direct mail
fundraising / Mal Warwick.— 1st ed.
        p. cm.
Includes bibliographical references and index.
  ISBN: 978-1-118-10511-5
  1. Direct-mail fund raising. I. Title.
  HV41.2.W3788 2004
  658.15'224—dc22

                                        2003025427

FIRST EDITION
HB Printing   10 9 8 7 6 5 4 3 2 1

Contents

Tables, Figures, and Exhibits

Tables

Figures

Exhibits

Preface

In the years following World War II, the Easter Seal Society and a few other big American charities began making extensive use of the mails to meet their increasingly ambitious fundraising goals. With little cash outlay, they mailed millions of inexpensive fundraising letters and consistently reaped huge profits. So successful were these early mass-mail fundraising efforts that some charities simply banked the proceeds without bothering to record the contributors' names and addresses. It was cheaper to send out virtually the same appeal again the next year to the same millions of addresses.

That was more than half a century ago. A great deal has happened since: a more than twenty-fold increase in charitable contributions, the advent of ZIP codes, fundraising scandals featured on network news, extraordinarily powerful personal computers, 1,000 percent inflation in nonprofit postal rates, and a similarly huge rise in printing costs—and, above all, *competition* in the form of appeals mailed by thousands upon thousands of nonprofit causes and institutions both large and small.

In 2002, the U.S. Postal Service distributed more than 14 *billion* pieces of mail for nonprofit organizations—most of them appeals for funds. (Those 14 billion letters constituted approximately 16 percent of all the bulk mail delivered in the United States that year, or nearly one out of every six pieces of bulk mail. Nonprofits account for about 7 percent of all U.S. mail, which totaled almost 203 billion pieces in 2002, according to the postal service.) But this isn't simply a matter of volume. Direct mail fundraising accounts for a major share of the financial support given many of our country's biggest charities, and it has come to loom large on the political landscape as well.

This proliferation of mail has created a challenge for nonprofit organizations to make profits through direct mail. To help meet this challenge, hundreds of consulting firms have come into existence, offering a staggering variety of approaches and levels of skill. Now, more than fifty years into its history, direct mail fundraising has gotten *complicated*. The pages ahead are my attempt to explain some of the complications.

I wrote this book in response to years of seeing desperate and bewildered looks on the faces of clients, employees, and friends. Those looks were often justified. Not only do some in the industry go out of their way to mystify the process but direct mail fundraising can be confusing. In fact, it sometimes seems downright illogical. I hope the following pages help demystify this crazy business and cast a little light on some of its counterintuitive aspects.

Although excellent books have been written about direct mail, and even about direct mail fundraising in particular, all but a few (noted in Resource F) are either highly technical discussions laden with statistical formulas and bearing a disturbing resemblance to college textbooks or are much more superficial treatments chock full of tips about writing good fundraising letters. This book is neither. It presents a point of view that I might as well state clearly at the outset: *Successful direct mail fundraising has little to do with statistics or with letter writing. It's a long-term process that requires intelligent planning and careful, consistent management.*

To succeed in direct mail fundraising over the long term, it's essential to distinguish between *strategy* and *tactics*. As in any other field, you can win the battle and lose the war. In this book, I hope to help illuminate the difference.

In military usage, the distinction between a nation's strategy and its tactics is straightforward:

- *Strategy* is the manner in which a nation seeks to ensure its security in peacetime as well as war, employing large-scale planning and development to make the best possible use of *all* its resources.
- *Tactics* are the choices made concerning the use and deployment of military forces in actual combat.

Because few appreciate this bold distinction, the word *strategy* is often confused with *tactics*. In this discussion, I mean to draw the line just as sharply as do the Joint Chiefs of Staff.

The *strategy* employed by a nonprofit organization includes decisions about its leadership and policy priorities, as well as resource development—not a plan but a vision. To set strategy is not to engage in "long-term planning" to determine how existing resources may be put to the best possible use. Setting strategy means dreaming about what you want your organization to accomplish. How to marshal the resources to reach that goal is an operational question—a matter of *tactics*. Those tactics may include a direct mail fundraising program designed to help get you where you want to go, just as they may also include lobbying, employing public relations tactics, establishing fees for services, or merchandising.

I'm uncomfortable with this bellicose metaphor, however. I'd prefer to describe direct mail fundraising in terms of streams and rivers or seeds that grow into trees, which cluster into groves and then over time become forests. *Strategy* and *tactics* smack of the nasty things I've spent many of my waking hours helping our clients stop. But I know of no other terms that help to draw so clear a distinction between decisions that are really important and those that aren't.

● ● ●

I wrote the original edition of this book in 1989. In the decade and a half that has passed since then, direct mail fundraising has done a lot of growing up. And so have I. Like my colleagues throughout the world, I've learned a great deal about my craft. I've also seen the field grow steadily more complex, sophisticated, and demanding. This new, revised edition of *Revolution in the Mailbox* reflects the more mature perspective that has evolved in the field. The chief elements of that new perspective include the following:

- A deeper understanding of the many specialized ways that direct mail may be used to advance the fundraising process—by promoting monthly giving and legacy giving, for example
- An appreciation of the interdependence of direct mail and other fundraising subspecialties—major gifts and legacy giving, in particular
- Heightened awareness of the value of building strong relationships with donors, as opposed to maximizing short-term revenue
- An emerging perception that the value of direct mail fundraising can be increased through coordination with telephone, on-line, and other communications efforts

That new perspective informed the writing of this largely new book. I have retained (though revised and updated) six chapters from the original edition. But ten of the sixteen chapters included here are entirely new.

In the examples I cite, I refer consistently to *public interest groups*. I mean that term to include nonprofit institutions and charities that provide direct services (including hospitals, colleges, and universities), as well as nonprofit organizations dedicated to social change through lobbying, organizing, or other means.

Much of my professional experience has been with public interest groups or candidates advocating changes in public policy, as many of the illustrations will make abundantly clear. Over the years, my colleagues and I have worked with hundreds of nonprofit organizations, including environmental, civil rights, social justice, women's and consumers' rights, and other advocacy organizations.

However, we've also worked with a great many nonprofits dedicated to cultural, educational, and charitable goals, including universities and colleges, hospitals, and museums. After more than two decades, I feel confident saying that much the same techniques work well for just about any type of nonprofit. In general, obvious differences notwithstanding, what works well for a consumer group is likely to do the trick for a university, museum, or hospital. Moreover, although a political campaign may use the principles of direct mail in ways that are different from those common in the nonprofit world, they're the same principles, too.

Many of the techniques of direct mail fundraising are also broadly transferable across national borders. In recent years, I've been spending a fair amount of time teaching fundraising outside the United States. Judging from what I've learned about direct mail fundraising in Canada, the United Kingdom, Australia, The Netherlands, Germany, France, Spain, Scandinavia, Argentina, and a host of other countries, the same fundamental approach works in a very wide range of circumstances.

●●●

This book won't show you how to write, design, and mail an appeal for funds. Nor will it tell you how to think or plan or manage your organization. It *will* help you understand what direct mail can do for you and how you can best make it work. Its purpose is to explain and illustrate direct mail fundraising *in context,* as the means by which many nonprofit organizations have grown, increased their influence, and ensured their long-term financial stability.

This book consists of four parts. Part One, "Making Direct Mail Work for Your Organization," covers the fundamentals of direct mail fundraising in six chapters. At the outset, in Chapter One, I explain how you can use direct mail to pursue your *strategic* goals. I give you a sense of what you can expect from direct mail and whether it may—or may not—be right for your organization. In the next four chapters, I discuss mailing lists and the preparation of an initial test mailing, detail the anatomy of a direct mail fundraising package, and explain the pros and cons of premiums and other involvement devices. Chapter Six, which closes this section, describes the strategic choices you will face following a successful initial test mailing, giving you a hint of years of hard work to come.

Part Two, "Getting the Most from Your Donors," is an in-depth journey through the challenges and opportunities you'll encounter as you build your direct mail fundraising program. Chapter Seven explains the concept of "Maximizing Donor Value" and lays out the basic principles you'll need to follow to maximize that value. The following five chapters tackle the most broadly useful techniques you might use to build donor value over the years: annual giving or membership programs, monthly giving, high-dollar annual giving clubs, telephone fundraising, and legacy giving programs. Chapter Thirteen wraps up Part Two with an in-depth discussion of donor acknowledgment and cultivation—the stuff of "relationship fundraising."

Part Three, "Direct Mail Fundraising Today and Tomorrow," includes two chapters. Chapter Fourteen deals with the state of the art today, examining multichannel communications and "integrated fundraising." Chapter Fifteen rounds out Part Three with a look at twelve trends that promise to affect the nonprofit sector and the practice of direct mail fundraising for many years to come.

In Part Four, "Four Years in the Life of a Successful Direct Mail Program," I present in some depth the first four years of the work my colleagues and I have done in collaboration with one of our clients—the Union of Concerned Scientists. You'll find statistical reports as well as sample packages there.

A Resources section completes the book. Included are a glossary of the direct mail fundraising terms used in this book, some thoughts on working with a direct mail fundraising consultant, a few ideas about how to respond to the arguments you will inevitably hear used against direct mail, a discussion about the concept of the "fundraising ratio," two early historical examples of direct mail fundraising, and, finally, a list of print and on-line resources to delve further into the strange world of direct mail fundraising.

● ● ●

Chances are, direct mail is one of the most effective tools your organization can use to build your base in the century ahead. But you can do so only by using a creative, no-holds-barred, entrepreneurial approach to direct mail, making use of the newest insights and the latest technologies to gain maximum advantage for your organization.

I look on direct mail fundraising as a *business,* and you should, too; it's an entrepreneurial tool that can be used in a great many ways, for good or ill. Viewed narrowly as letter writing or an occasional fund appeal, direct mail is unlikely to serve you well as the twenty-first century unfolds. But if you can make it serve the needs of your overall fundraising plan, it can help lay the foundation for your organization's continuing success for many decades to come.

Not all the terms used in this book or the methods described are universally accepted among direct mail fundraisers. My colleagues and I in Mal Warwick & Associates, Inc. (Berkeley, California) cherish a view of ourselves as creative, and we've actually won awards and a lot of public attention in support of that view. Even though all of us in the business follow the same basic rules, and it's standard practice to copy successful techniques from one another, the *particular* approach to direct mail fundraising laid out in these pages is based on our own experience.

Much the same goes for my references to telephone fundraising. I'm also involved in that industry, as a cofounder of Share Group, Inc. (Somerville, Massachusetts). The language I use and the examples I cite relating to telephone fundraising are from the experience I've gained through Share.

I am also founder and chairman of Response Management Technologies, Inc. (Berkeley, California), which processes gifts and provides "list maintenance" and data-processing services to many nonprofit organizations. Doubtless, my connection to Response Management not only gives me a deeper understanding of the issues involving "back-end" services (discussed in Chapter Seven) but helps account for my bias favoring specialized service bureaus over in-house donor management programs.

To learn from people with biases different from mine and for a fuller understanding of direct marketing in general and direct mail fundraising in particular, I suggest the books, periodicals, and on-line resources cited in Resource F.

Some of the examples cited here are obviously hypothetical; others are real. Every real-life case study described is derived from the experience of Mal Warwick & Associates, Inc., and so are virtually all of the direct mail packages pictured in the illustrations. Wherever I refer to "us" or "we," that's who I mean.

To avoid distractions and make the subject of direct mail fundraising as accessible as possible, I've chosen not to use footnotes either to note parenthetical points or to cite references for facts or quotes. My graduate school instructors may be very disappointed, but I operate under the assumption that if something's important enough to include in a book, it ought to be in the text, not in a footnote. However, to appease my editor, I've appended a brief References section to cite the sources I've used at key points.

Some of what follows may not be popular in the fundraising community. So be it. My reason for getting into this business in the first place was to change the world. A lot has happened in the twenty-four years since I stopped licking stamps and bought my first computer. As a group, direct mail fundraising consultants have played a major role in many of those events. We've helped nonprofit organizations meet urgent human needs, shape public opinion, and expand the boundaries of our culture. Direct mail has had a profound impact on American politics and society. But I think the world *still* needs changing.

Berkeley, California   Mal Warwick
November 2003

Acknowledgments

It's all Ron Dellums's fault. I got into the direct mail business nearly twenty-five years ago to help Congressman Ron Dellums launch a nationwide fundraising campaign. His 1980 reelection race was expected to be difficult. It wasn't. He won hands down that year, and so did I. Dellums went on to serve a total of fourteen terms, retiring in 1998, having chaired the House Armed Services Committee, the House District of Columbia Committee, and the Congressional Black Caucus. Because he had insisted I personally supervise the direct mail consultants we'd hired, I got a taste of direct mail fundraising at its very best—and I was hooked for life.

Since those exhilarating days in the fall of 1979, when I was often forced to stay up until the early hours of the morning to count all the checks rolling into the Dellums campaign, I've worked with hundreds of nonprofit organizations and political committees. My coworkers and I have mailed uncounted millions of letters and raised hundreds of millions of dollars to promote the public interest. In the process, I've come to know hundreds of supremely talented individuals who have committed years of their lives to make the world a better place—a list of people far too long to reproduce here. They, my clients, ultimately deserve any credit I may get for writing this book. I've learned far more from them than they have from me.

Several of my friends in the public interest community read the manuscript of this book at various stages in its development and offered helpful criticism, sometimes lengthy and detailed. I took all their advice seriously and made many changes they suggested, but not all. In preparing this revised and updated edition, I benefited particularly from timely and helpful comments by the following people:

- Ken Burnett and Harvey McKinnon, two of this planet's most accomplished direct mail fundraisers, read drafts of key chapters and delivered their comments in record time.

- My friend and colleague Joseph H. White Jr., whose knowledge about telephone fundraising is unsurpassed, did the same.
- My friends at the Social Venture Network, coexecutive directors Deborah Nelson and Pamela Chaloult, were particularly helpful in reviewing my draft copy about socially responsible business.
- Alisa Gravitz, executive director of Co-op America, helped steer me through the statistical thicket that surrounds socially responsible investing (SRI).
- I am very deeply indebted to my friends at the Union of Concerned Scientists (UCS), who graciously consented to permit me to include extensive information about their direct mail fundraising program in this book.

Three UCS staff members also contributed extremely helpful comments: Howard ("Bud") Ris, David Whalen, and Emily Ferman.

I'm also in debt to my many friends and colleagues in Mal Warwick & Associates and our affiliated companies. They're an extraordinarily gifted and dedicated bunch of people, and I am privileged to work by their side. For their assistance on this book, they deserve triple credit. Not only did they teach me most of what I know about lists, production, statistical analysis, design, and copywriting, they also stoically covered for me over six months when I stole away from the office to write. Moreover, many individual employees of Mal Warwick & Associates helped me in major ways in writing this book. Some deserve special mention here.

Without the help of Stephen Hitchcock, president of Mal Warwick & Associates, I could not have written *Revolution in the Mailbox*. His continuing encouragement and support, his awesome managerial ability, and critical editorial eye came to the rescue on more occasions than I can possibly recall. Steve's comments on two early drafts of the manuscript and on later drafts of several chapters in particular helped steer me away from dire embarrassment. The wisdom Steve has gained in more than twenty-five years as a professional fundraiser has found its way into nearly every chapter of this book. I've borrowed liberally from him, sometimes consciously, sometimes not.

I also owe a great deal to Gwen Chapman, senior vice president of Mal Warwick & Associates. Gwen's two decades of fundraising experience on three continents and her extraordinary command of the principles of relationship fundraising profoundly influenced what I've written about monthly giving and about the central role of donor care in building strong relationships with donors.

In preparing this revised and updated edition, many others at Mal Warwick & Associates helped in significant ways, particularly in identifying and preparing the entirely new illustrations featured in these pages. Bill Rehm and Mwosi Swenson bore the brunt of my demands, but others also contributed in significant ways—Dan Weeks, Susie Fought, and Patricia Quintana Bidar, in particular.

In the final stages of this project, two people's contributions stood out. My editor at Jossey-Bass, Johanna Vondeling, helped enormously. Her sagacious review of the original text and of my proposed additions and changes helped make sense of what was threatening to become a garbled and unreadable book. Johanna's assistant, Allison Brunner, was also extremely helpful, especially in culling through an unruly mess of proposed illustrations.

For all the many important contributions that others have made to this book, none of them bears any responsibility for its contents. I've borrowed a great many ideas, but the words and images on these pages were all mine except where I've indicated otherwise. Now they're yours, too—and welcome to them!

—M. W.

About the Author

Consultant, author, and public speaker Mal Warwick has been involved in the not-for-profit sector for four decades.

He is the founder and chairman of Mal Warwick & Associates, Inc. (Berkeley, California)—a fundraising and marketing agency that has served nonprofit organizations since 1979, and of its sister company, Response Management Technologies, Inc., a data-processing firm for nonprofit organizations. He is also cofounder (with Nick Allen) of Donordigital.com LLC (San Francisco), which assists nonprofit organizations on-line, and is a cofounder of Share Group, Inc. (Somerville, Massachusetts), the nation's leading telephone fundraising firm.

Warwick has written or edited fifteen books of interest to nonprofit managers, including *The Five Strategies for Fundraising Success* (2000), *Fundraising on the Internet,* coedited with Hart and Allen (2002), and the best-selling text, *How to Write Successful Fundraising Letters* (2001). He is editor of *Mal Warwick's Newsletter: Successful Direct Mail, Telephone & Online Fundraising,* and is a popular speaker and workshop leader throughout the world.

Among the hundreds of nonprofits Warwick and his colleagues have served over the years are many of the nation's largest and most distinguished charities, as well as six Democratic presidential candidates and scores of small local and regional organizations. Collectively, Warwick and his associates are responsible for raising at least half a billion dollars, largely in the form of small gifts from individuals.

Warwick is an active member of the Association of Fundraising Professionals (Alexandria, Virginia), a member of the board of the Resource Alliance (London), organizers of the annual International Fundraising Congress, and its USA Country Representative; he also served for ten years on the board of the Association of Direct Response Fundraising Counsel (Washington, D.C.), two of those years as president.

For more than a decade, the author has been active in promoting social and environmental responsibility in the business community. He was a cofounder of

Business for Social Responsibility (San Francisco) and served on its board during its inaugural year. In 2001, he was elected to the board of the Social Venture Network (San Francisco) and now serves as chair.

Warwick was a Peace Corps volunteer in Ecuador for more than three years. Since 1969, he has lived in Berkeley, California, where he is deeply involved in local community affairs. Early in the 1990s, he cofounded the Community Bank of the Bay (the nation's fifth community development bank) and the Berkeley Community Fund, where he remains active on the board.

Warwick is the grandfather of Dayna, Iain, Matthew, Gwen, Andrew, Kaili, and Benjamin, who all live with their various parents on the East Coast.

How We Got Here
and Where We're Going

Direct mail has already left its imprint on the pages of history. But direct mail fundraising, as it was conducted in its infancy following World War II, bears little resemblance to the intensely competitive and complex industry it has become in recent years. Like other technology-driven industries, direct mail fundraising has experienced accelerating change as one innovation after another multiplied the possibilities in what has often seemed a geometric progression. Yet even so, the changes wrought on American society by our work as direct mail fundraisers dwarf the changes imposed on the practice of our craft.

Beginning four decades ago, a handful of visionary direct mail specialists, largely unknown to the general public, began successfully applying the techniques of direct response marketing to the challenge of creating social change. Like "The Hidden Persuaders" of the advertising world, who were unmasked in a popular book of social commentary at the time, their influence on society far outstripped their reputations. Since the introduction of the ZIP code in the 1960s, their innovations have dramatically changed the American political system.

Writing in the April 1989 issue of *Fund Raising Management*, Roger Craver, one of those pioneers in direct mail fundraising, contends that "the climate of frustration and alienation of the late 1960s and early 1970s was particularly suited for direct mail." Craver writes,

> It all seemed to happen at once, one of those accidents of history when a given technology proves so unusually suited for its times that it goes beyond merely

1

filling a need . . . and begins to effect actual societal change. [In 1969], Richard Viguerie had just launched his pioneering efforts to build the mailing lists and devise the techniques that would give voice to the new conservatives. Morris Dees, a young Alabama lawyer and commercial direct-mail entrepreneur, was plotting the then unconventional use of direct mail to help the anti-war presidential candidate George McGovern. And my partners and I were testing the unheard of concept of recruiting hundreds of thousands of small gift contributors as members of the "citizens lobby" that became Common Cause.

These early experiments in political direct mail fundraising paid off quickly and dramatically. Craver continues:

The political pundits laughed, but they didn't laugh long. Within two years, George McGovern had amassed more than 350,000 donors—giving him enough financial support to bypass the Democratic bosses, go directly to rank-and-file Democrats and secure his party's nomination for the presidency. Common Cause reached the 250,000-member mark and succeeded in its lobbying efforts to end both the outmoded seniority system and the process of secret votes in Congress. And Viguerie stunned conventional politicians with his capacity to raise millions of dollars for conservative candidates.

The revolution led by Craver, Viguerie, Dees, Tom Mathews, Peter Tagger, and others has left an indelible imprint on American society. Popular but unconventional candidates without access to established funding sources have used direct mail to finance some of the most pivotal political campaigns in recent American history. Among them were George Wallace in 1968, George McGovern in 1972, Ronald Reagan in 1976 and 1980, John Anderson in 1980, Gary Hart in 1984, and Jesse Jackson in 1988—the candidates and the campaigns that have changed their parties' politics for many years to come. Against the odds, both conservatives and progressives have gained footholds at all levels of government because of funds raised by mail.

Through direct mail, private citizens by the millions have become personally—sometimes intensely—involved in national politics. Millions have become donors to the Republican and Democratic parties and have helped shape their agendas by the sheer force of their numbers. The contributions of check-writing activists have also sustained campaigns for a great many candidates for the U.S. Senate, House of Representatives, governorships, and other public offices.

Direct mail has accelerated the country's political realignment as a strategic tool in the hands of leaders of the New Politics, especially on the Right. Membership-based, nonparty political committees—both political action committees (PACs) and single-issue advocacy groups—have become fixtures on the political land-scape. Election after election, they selectively direct their resources toward com-patible candidates, helping to shape the future destinies of their parties—and of the country.

But politics is more than candidates and political parties, and the impact of direct mail fundraising extends beyond the boundaries of the formal political process, as Craver points out in his *Fund Raising Management* article:

> Had it done nothing more than contribute to the breaking up of the concen-trated, centralized power of the political parties—enabling more unconven-tional candidates to have their day in the sun—direct mail would have made a significant contribution to American political history. But perhaps even more significant has been its contribution to the building of a massive political force in this country—the citizen action organization.

Direct mail fundraising has given birth to some of this nation's most innovative and effective nongovernmental institutions and given new life to many others. Direct-mail-based public interest organizations have successfully pushed for legal and political reform, protection of the environment and of animal life, safeguards for civil liberties and women's rights, and support for human rights both at home and abroad. Groups on the other end of the political spectrum, similarly spawned by direct mail, have also had great impact by shrinking the reproductive health choices available to women against the tide of public opinion, blocking the gun control desired by a majority of Americans, and ending the political careers of many leading liberals.

In an age of increasing distrust for politics and policymakers and of continu-ally decreasing voter participation, direct mail fundraising has provided many Americans with a simple and effective channel for political expression. Sending a political contribution via direct mail is not a substitute for voting, of course. In fact, the overwhelming majority of political direct mail donors are also voters for whom direct mail affords extra opportunities for political participation. Direct mail has come to play so large a role for a number of reasons, including the following:

• *It's an important source of information.* Unlike much of what passes for politi-cal communication through television, radio, or other media, messages delivered by mail are typically packed with information. Information, in its truest sense, is that which is new and surprising, and direct mail is full of surprises. Only outspoken candidates or nonprofit organizations with clear messages can successfully raise sig-nificant amounts of money by mail. Direct mail doesn't work well unless it's based on *ideas.* Double-talk, compromise, and obfuscation don't sell; only clarity works.

• *It's involving.* Direct mail fundraising targets the best prospects through careful list selection and sophisticated data-processing techniques, so it reaches individuals with messages they're likely to be interested in receiving. And, by definition, direct mail asks for action. In the article I've cited, Craver calls direct mail "the best antidote ever invented for political alienation." In a much more focused way than voting, contributing by mail provides a ready-made means to "do something" about today's headlines. As Craver writes, "Direct mail—with its small checks, its surveys, its angry postcards to the politicians—provides genuine recourse, along with a safety valve for steaming political emotions."

• *It's inexpensive.* Compared to television or newspaper advertising or to most any other form of mass communication, direct mail can be an economical way to get a message across. This is true simply because, properly managed, direct mail can make money, possibly lots of it. At the same time, the price paid by individual donors is small. Nearly everyone with a mailbox can afford an occasional $15 or $25 contribution to make a political statement. Millions take advantage of this bargain. The bargain reached between donor and organization thus results in a great return on investment for both.

Meanwhile, as political direct mail was changing the character of American democracy, similar revolutionary techniques were working their way into the world of fundraising for nonprofit organizations.

New Frontiers in Charitable Fundraising

During the 1960s and 1970s, as Roger Craver, Richard Viguerie, and other direct mail pioneers were launching their early efforts to crash the gates of the political world, others were applying some of their own new direct mail techniques to broaden the base of charitable and religious causes. Large charities that had raised money by mail for two decades were learning from the experience, refining old techniques, and trying new ones. They were joined by a growing number of newcomers. Meanwhile, a boom in commercial direct response marketing was starting, making available to fundraisers a fast-growing body of tested marketing methods. Through the combined influence of all these new players and the accumulated impact of new technology and economic trends, direct mail fundraising has changed profoundly since the 1960s. Among the many changes are these:

• *The advent of the ZIP code.* ZIP codes weren't in widespread use until the early 1970s, although they'd been introduced a decade earlier. The ZIP code made computerization practical. (Just imagine sorting a quarter-million-name statewide list on 3×5 cards into alphabetical order!)

• *Computerization.* These days, we take computers for granted in direct mail fundraising, just as we do in our daily lives. In every aspect of our craft, from maintaining lists and printing names and addresses to managing, analyzing, and even copywriting and designing, our work today would be impossible without computers. Direct mail fundraising is an information-based activity. It's been many years since the 3×5 card and the Addressograph were up to the task of managing the information our business requires.

• *Donor file segmentation.* In the 1970s, with computers becoming more widely available, fundraisers began learning the value of storing and using extensive giving histories for individual donors. Speedy and precise data processing made it possible for direct mail fundraisers to slice and dice their lists of donors and prospects into ever-smaller pieces. Today, mailings may consist of more than one hundred segments or "cells," individually identified so as to measure differences in response and engineer cost savings in future mailings. Just forty years ago, many nonprofits commonly mailed the same resolicitation package to everyone on their donor files. Today, the rule is to classify donors in terms of "recency, frequency, and monetary amount" and to mail many different packages simultaneously to different segments of the same list, as I've described in detail in this book. With this technique, direct mail fundraisers have dramatically increased the net income from nonprofit donor lists.

• *The birth of relationship fundraising.* By recognizing donors' varying levels and types of interest, we've also made vast improvements in communications between donors and the organizations they support. Many nonprofits have derived large, added dividends from their direct mail programs by contributing to the strategically important process of cultivating prospective donors of bequests and other major gifts.

• *Personalization.* Before the advent of the computer and computer-driven printers, direct mail fundraisers almost invariably addressed prospects, even their donors, in the impersonal idiom of the "Dear Friend" letter. Personalization enables fundraisers to include in their appeals not only donors' titles, names, and addresses but anything else a computer may keep on file about them, from facts embedded in a giving history to personal preferences. Once very expensive, personalization has become cost-effective in many applications and is now sometimes used, even in donor acquisition programs. Although it is normally driven by computer formulas that define classes and categories of donors, personalization allows direct mail fundraisers to come surprisingly close to genuinely personal, one-to-one communications, and it's getting better every year.

• *Merge-purge.* This basic tool of direct mail donor acquisition was not introduced until 1968. This sophisticated computer process efficiently reduces duplicate appeals and allows mailers to eliminate previous donors from their prospect mailings. Without merge-purge, the multi-million-piece prospect mailings of the past three decades might easily have provoked much more intense and widespread anger than they have. In addition, merge-purge has helped keep the lid on the rising cost of prospecting. Today, the merge-purge process brings invaluable information to light about the overlap and relationships among mailing lists, so it helps fundraisers target prospective contributors with ever-greater precision. The results are reduced costs, higher response rates, and less frequent donor complaints.

• *Testing.* The conceptual backbone of today's direct mail fundraising was anathema to most fundraisers forty years ago. On those infrequent occasions when it was proposed, testing was typically rejected out of hand as undignified or unnecessarily expensive. The prevailing assumption was that any competent nonprofit manager knew far better than his donors how to promote his own organization. By now, however, most fundraisers have awakened to the reality that donors make their own decisions. Fundraisers' guesses and preconceptions must be tested in the marketplace.

• *Growing competition.* One of the leading charitable fundraising specialists in 1969 was Jerry Huntsinger. Writing in the retrospective twentieth anniversary issue of *Fund Raising Management* (April 1989), Huntsinger contends that increasingly poor response made it unrealistic for most charities to mail ten million or more prospect packages annually. A great many had done so in what he termed the "golden age" of direct mail prospecting in the 1970s and 1980s, but that was becoming less common with every passing year (and has continued to decline). In fact, Huntsinger claims, "Some organizations were shocked to discover they could no longer mail enough pieces to prospective donors to even keep up with the inevitable attrition on their house file!" In other words, some charities were discovering the harsh reality of free market economics: they'd built huge donor files on the cheap in a wide-open market, but increasing competition was preventing them from maintaining their "market share." Huntsinger attributed the problem, in part, to the public's "loss of faith in the integrity of nonprofits." I think that's nonsense. Similar statements surface at fundraising conferences year after year, in the face of unabated generosity by the donor public. But I agree that very few causes and candidates can succeed with the old mass-mailing techniques. I can't recall a time during the past quarter-century that my colleagues ever sent what could reasonably be termed a mass mailing. These days, selective targeting, not mass marketing, is the key to successful direct mail fundraising for most public interest groups.

• *Inflation.* In 1969, the typical cost of mailing one thousand prospect packages was about $85, including list rental, production, and nonprofit postage, which was then $18 per thousand, or less than 2 cents per piece. The returns were usually $125 to $175 per thousand, turning a nice profit. During the past forty-some years, however, production and mailing costs (most notably, postage) have risen 400 to 500 percent, and because of growing competition returns have not kept pace. The average charitable gift has risen, and well-run solicitation programs have continued to yield handsome profits, but donor acquisition efforts are generally far less cost-effective than they were forty years ago.

• *Changes in the postal system.* In the Reagan era, growing postal deficits and pressures for privatization led to big changes in the way the U.S. Postal Service charged for and processed mail. Extensive automation by the postal service forced mailers to conform to new standards of "list hygiene" (ensuring the accuracy and timeliness of information on their lists) and in the design and handling of mailing packages. The procedures imposed by the new national change of address system (NCOA) and certification procedures (permitting mailers to barcode, sort, and bundle mail in the prescribed manner) added new burdens to nonprofits, requiring greater sophistication and professionalism in the design and handling of their mail.

• *The spread of telephone fundraising.* Commercial telemarketing has its roots in telephone sales efforts first undertaken many decades ago, but the systematic use of telephone technology to raise money for public interest organizations is a phenomenon of the 1980s. Few current telephone fundraising firms were in existence before 1980. Their success in obtaining sometimes spectacular results has persuaded most nonprofit organizations to use telephone fundraising techniques in a wide range of applications, despite resistance from many donors (and many of their trustees). Today, telephone fundraising is an integral part of every successful, large-scale direct mail fundraising program.

New Standards of Success

As a result of these factors, the standards of success have changed in direct mail fundraising. Gone are the days when you wouldn't use a mailing list that didn't promise to break even. As Huntsinger notes, "Now, there is a new word on the street: 'Investment.' . . . [Today] many charities are pleased if they can enroll a new donor for an investment of $5 to $10." In fact, now, some fifteen years after Huntsinger wrote, some nonprofits are content to invest $25, $50, or more to recruit a new donor because their donor resolicitation programs are so very profitable, as I explain in this book. The standard of success in direct mail fundraising is no longer a single number expressed in dollars and cents. Like the U.S. private sector, which is waking up to the fact that obsession with short-term profits can undermine a company's long-term financial health, the independent sector today is looking on direct mail fundraising from a longer perspective.

The ultimate standard of success in direct mail is the extent to which it helps an organization achieve its strategic goals. Viewed most broadly today, direct mail fundraising is much more than a source of funds. It can help raise an organization's profile, broaden its public support, provide a means for its donors to involve themselves in its affairs, and furnish an extra measure of stability in a time of change.

You'll note that I didn't include the use of e-mail and the Internet in the list of changes in fundraising since the 1960s. That's not an oversight. As I write this book, the World Wide Web is barely ten years old. In many respects, our lives and our work have changed as a result, but the impact on fundraising has been minimal so far. In spite of occasionally spectacular successes, on-line fundraising has brought generally meager returns, far below those envisioned by its champions in the 1990s. E-mail and Web sites are emerging as useful adjuncts to direct mail and telemarketing in many fundraising programs, but their long-term impact, however promising, has yet to be widely felt.

Long before the advent of the World Wide Web and before the profound changes cited earlier seized hold of the direct mail fundraising field, the world somehow managed to get along without microcomputers, ZIP codes, or laser printers, much less the Internet. The challenge for charitable fundraisers then was to print, address, and mail the largest possible number of letters at the lowest possible cost. Our challenge now is more complex: to make use of a greatly broadened array of fundraising tools to minimize acquisition costs and maximize the long-term value of our donors. Today, we must think of direct mail not as a compartmentalized effort but in the context of a fundraising and communications program that may use many channels.

PART ONE

Making Direct Mail Work
for Your Organization

The first six chapters of this book encompass the fundamentals of direct mail fundraising. Chapter One, "The Strategic Uses of Direct Mail," approaches the topic from a big-picture perspective, discussing what you can expect from direct mail and what you can't. "Selecting Your Audience," Chapter Two, introduces the all-important topic of mailing lists. Chapter Three, "Preparing Your Test Mailing," explains how to design and produce an initial test—your first venture into the world of direct mail donor acquisition. In "Anatomy of a Direct Mail Fundraising Package," which is Chapter Four, you'll get a surgeon's-eye view of a direct mail appeal, component by individual component. Chapter Five delves into "Premiums and Other Involvement Devices," techniques that are widely used to boost response. "Building Your Donor Base," Chapter Six, rounds out Part One with a discussion of the long-term process that characterizes every successful direct mail fundraising program.

1

The Strategic Uses
of Direct Mail

For many nonprofit organizations, direct mail fundraising is a question of life or death. Often it is *strategically* important, simply because so much money is involved.

No one really knows how much American charities raise in a year, but the best available estimate for the year 2002 (from *Giving USA 2003*, AAFRC Trust for Philanthropy, p. ii) is that the figure topped $240 billion. This doesn't include volunteer hours contributed by 83.9 million American adults, representing the equivalent of over 9 million full-time employees at a value of $239 billion, according to *Giving and Volunteering in the United States, 2001*. It's particularly difficult to determine how much of that money was contributed in response to appeals sent by mail. But after studying the figures and the techniques by which they were gathered, the Direct Marketing Association concluded that direct mail yielded more than $44 billion for nonprofit organizations in 2002.

Forty-four *billion* dollars. That's a *big* business by anyone's standards. Direct mail fundraising is a business that very few nonprofit organizations can afford to ignore or misunderstand.

Although direct mail has become increasingly competitive, expensive, and difficult in recent years, other sources of charitable and public interest funding have also become more difficult to tap:

- *Government grants:* Grants from the federal government were sharply curtailed in the 1980s and 1990s, and the return of massive budget deficits in the opening decade of the new century offers little hope that future administrations will be much more generous to nonprofits.

- *Foundations:* At best, foundations have always been reluctant to fund programs in perpetuity. Despite recent efforts to persuade foundation executives to grant funds for general support, most still want only to provide leadership gifts for pilot or demonstration projects. And seed grants for fundraising programs are the exception, not the rule.
- *Corporations:* Corporate giving rises and falls with frequent changes in tax laws and trends in corporate finance. The mergers and acquisitions characteristic of the closing years of the twentieth century and the opening years of the twenty-first have reduced many corporate philanthropic budgets.

In addition, mushrooming sales of products and services by nonprofit enterprises have attracted unwelcome attention by the IRS and Congress, and statutory changes threaten this rich source of financial support for many organizations. By comparison, direct mail may be an extremely attractive option for your organization. It's the most widely employed technique for seeking financial support from large numbers of individuals. Of the estimated $240 billion donated by Americans in 2002, more than $183 billion came from individuals; corporations contributed $12 billion and foundations approximately $27 billion. Even the remaining $18 billion in bequests originated from individuals; they were simply no longer alive. Taken together, contributions from individuals accounted for about 84 cents of every dollar received by charity, and I know of no reason why more skillful use of direct mail fundraising techniques wouldn't allow us to increase that proportion.

Because of its ability to target, reach, and motivate individual people in large numbers, direct mail has come to occupy a significant place in our society and culture. Direct mail helps account for the vigor and broad scope of the so-called third sector or independent sector—that proliferation of seemingly countless voluntary associations in America about which de Tocqueville commented with such wonder nearly two hundred years ago.

There is no other country in which private citizens, working together in voluntary nongovernmental organizations, play such a vital role. U.S. nonprofits meet urgent human needs, train our young, enrich our culture, and help shape our public policy. They are a principal mechanism in the larger system of checks and balances that guarantees the stability of American democracy.

Chances are your organization is already involved in direct mail fundraising. Even if you don't use direct mail to recruit or acquire donors, members, or subscribers, direct mail is probably an essential component of your overall development program. You may just call it something else.

Membership renewal notices, annual appeals, newsletters, special appeals, action alerts, annual reports, house mailings, letters from the executive director, emergency appeals, subscription renewal notices—all these and many more possible forms of communication between you and your supporters play vital roles on the larger stage of your development program. It makes no difference at all whether you *call* these communications direct mail or not.

Direct mail communications can help or hinder not only your fundraising efforts but all the work you do. Too many "emergency appeals" may undermine your credibility. Delays in sending dues renewal notices may cause your membership to shrink. Conflicting messages may confuse your clients or constituents. Failure to keep your supporters up-to-date through a newsletter may mean their response to your annual appeal will be poor. Multiple mailings of the same letter can anger even an ardent supporter. To ensure that all these communications devices play a constructive role, it's important to take a close look at them *as a whole* in the context of your relationship with your constituency and to consider how they all fit into your organization's strategy.

One thing is certain: your supporters will expect something in the mail from you. Mailing brings organizational credibility. Voters often tell campaign volunteers, "I'll just wait till I see something in the mail before I make up my mind." Your donors or members may be waiting, too.

Direct mail fundraising isn't just about money. It's often used to cultivate and recruit volunteers or prospects for fundraising dinners or other events. Direct mail is widely used for grassroots lobbying or other forms of political action by public policy groups and political campaigns. Schools, colleges, hospitals, and cultural institutions make wide use of direct mail to promote their community programs.

Direct mail is a flexible tool that you can use to serve any one of a great number of organizational strategies. If direct mail fundraising works for your organization, it can take you down five divergent paths:

1. *Growth*—by helping you build a bigger membership or list of contributors (called a donor base)
2. *Involvement*—by persuading your supporters to become actively involved
3. *Visibility*—by publicizing your work among a particular constituency or the public in general
4. *Efficiency*—by maximizing the net revenue you derive from your mailings and thus raising funds at the lowest possible cost per dollar raised
5. *Stability*—by reaching and maintaining an optimum level of direct mail fundraising activity

For more information on these concepts, see my book, *Five Strategies for Fund-raising Success* (2000). Later in this chapter, we'll take a look at several hypothetical case studies to explore some of these strategic paths and their tactical implications, that is, the specific forms of activity these contrasting approaches require. I hope that using examples will make the difference between *strategy* and *tactics* clearer. First, however, let's get down to the basics of direct mail fundraising so that we can establish a common basis of understanding the issues.

What You Can Expect from Direct Mail

Direct mail is a difficult and expensive way to raise money. It requires capital investment, marketing skill, patience, and managerial agility.

Still, despite increased costs and an ever-fiercer competition for funds, direct mail fundraising remains the most effective way to build and cultivate a broad financial base. Over time, a properly managed direct mail fundraising program may be able to provide you with predictable, continuing support year after year and yield big dividends for your other fundraising programs as well.

But getting started in direct mail isn't easy. It's even harder if you have exaggerated or otherwise distorted expectations. I suggest the following as the first principle of direct mail fundraising:

> Most of the time, almost no one will respond to your appeals for funds from the public by mail. The only reason direct mail fundraising works is that someone who does send you a first gift is very likely to send another when asked.

Direct mail fundraising is built on slim margins. Many mailings are regarded as very successful if just *one* in one hundred prospects responds with a gift. Of those who do respond, *ten* in one hundred may send their second gifts in response to a subsequent appeal.

The trick, then, is to identify your best prospective donors, to persuade the largest possible number of them to become first-time donors, to educate and motivate those newly acquired donors to give again and again, and to gain the maximum value from your committed donors by providing them with opportunities to support your organization ever more actively and generously.

Nowadays for most nonprofits, acquiring new donors through the mail probably means *losing money*, at least on the initial effort. Nonprofit managers have to expect to lose 15 to 50 percent of their investment in mass-mail "prospecting" or "donor acquisition" programs carried out over time. That loss is sometimes even greater in the initial test mailing, which generally requires an up-front investment in creative and management services.

Despite the initial loss, this investment will help build your list of donors. However, it may be difficult for you to see all the way to the other end of that particular tunnel. I often feel that counseling clients to expand their prospecting efforts in the face of mounting losses is a lot like saying to a child, "Eat your vegetables." Prospecting is sometimes hard to swallow.

If you do, however, you'll see your list grow steadily over time and yield continuing dividends. Your newly acquired donors will, on average, remain donors for about two and one-half years. In that time, they'll typically make two or three additional gifts, averaging up to one and one-quarter times the size of their initial contributions. Many will increase the frequency with which they give; they may also increase the size of their gifts. A very few will stay with you for life, loyally contributing year after year, and even go on giving after they die by remembering you in their wills. With the average charitable bequest estimated by the National Committee on Planned Giving to be $35,000, a few such legacy gifts can make a huge difference in the economics of a direct mail fundraising program.

Equally significant is that among these newly acquired donors will be some individuals willing to contribute—or help raise—major gifts. For some organizations, a major gift can be as little as $100; for others, it may be $1 million or more. But the principle is the same: direct mail can help you identify, recruit, cultivate, and educate that small, vital group of prospective major donors who are capable of making a very big difference for your organization.

There's no way to predict how many legacy and major donors will surface, but for many nonprofit organizations the gifts from these generous and committed donors eventually provide 50 percent—and ultimately perhaps 90 percent or more—of total annual income.

But it takes a lot of hard work to achieve this enormous potential. A successful direct mail fundraising program requires a carefully orchestrated schedule of additional mailings as well as telephone contact. Believe it or not, extensive research and testing have demonstrated that direct mail donors (1) really do like receiving mailings, (2) enjoy giving to lots of organizations, and (3) make repeated gifts to the groups that interest them the most.

That means your most active donors should receive six or more fund appeals per year from your organization. Some groups mail twelve, sixteen, or even twenty solicitations per year while also conducting telephone appeals and staging public events and other fundraising efforts. In the final months before an election, at the end of the calendar year, just before a vote in Congress, or at some arbitrary program deadline, mail and telephone solicitations every seven to twelve *days* are not uncommon.

It's not difficult to understand why we mail so frequently. Most donors, especially direct mail donors, make contributions from *current* discretionary income. At any given time, they're likely to have only small amounts to spare. For all but the very rich or the very frugal, that's life in America today. Even those generous donors whose gifts to you may total more than $100 per year may be more comfortable sending several $50 checks than one much larger donation. They may even *think* of themselves as "$50 donors" and reflexively send checks in that amount to several organizations each month that inspire them to give, perhaps even without regard to whether they've recently given to any of them. Most direct mail donors write checks to charity when they're paying their bills on a weekly or monthly basis. Few people have large, fixed pools of money into which they dip for the funds to make small contributions. Even if they plan and schedule their charitable giving, they're likely to get the funds from their current income stream.

Few donors are aware of how frequently they're solicited by mail. Again and again, surveys and focus groups show that direct mail donors underestimate how many appeals they've received from a given organization. And although you may think that a majority are likely to complain about oversolicitation, most survey respondents say the frequency of appeals from organizations they support is "too little" or "just about right." Complaints much more commonly arise from individuals who *don't* support your organization.

Nonetheless, in a well-run direct mail fundraising program, you'll mail most of your appeals to only *some* of your donors. The key is to pick those who are most likely to respond and to plan the most effective possible sequence and combination of solicitations.

Kind Strangers and Loving Friends

There are distinctly different types of mailings to meet different fundraising needs. In the broadest terms, mailings are intended either to *acquire* new donors, members, or subscribers or to *resolicit* previous donors for additional support. Between them is all the difference in the world. It's the difference between the love of friends and the casual kindness of strangers.

Donor Acquisition

Donor acquisition or prospect mailings—sometimes called cold mail—are designed to persuade each potential donor to take the big step of giving you a first gift. Although there are occasional and notable exceptions, acquisition mailings tend to be relatively inexpensive ($0.30 to $1.00 each) and are often produced in large quantities (fifty thousand to one million letters or more) and mailed relatively infrequently (perhaps two to six times per year). Acceptable response rates—the percentage of those who send gifts—are typically in the range of 0.5 to 2.5 percent.

Acquisition mailings almost always cost more money than the total of contributions received; in other words, they don't often break even. Their success or failure is generally evaluated in terms of *donor acquisition cost*, that is, the difference between the cost of the mailing and the amount it generates in contributions, divided by the number of donors acquired.

For example, if a $50,000 mailing generates proceeds of $40,000 and 2,500 new memberships, the acquisition cost is $4 per member ($50,000 less $40,000 or $10,000 divided by 2,500).

The key is to calculate a donor's *value over time* and keep the acquisition cost as far below it as your organizational strategy may dictate. (We'll go into that arithmetic in Chapter Six.)

The logic of this process is derived from the world of commercial direct mail. Based on the behavior of past subscribers, *Newsweek* knows how likely you are to renew your first-year subscription, and thus they know to the fraction of a cent how much additional revenue they can expect from you. L. L. Bean can guess to the penny how much additional merchandise you'll buy. Both *Newsweek* and L. L. Bean are willing to *pay* to persuade you to purchase a subscription or a woolen shirt. They're counting on the fact that sizable percentages of first-time customers will buy more of their goods. Those percentages are sizable enough that *Newsweek* and L. L. Bean will probably pay a lot *more* in direct mail costs than the revenue they receive from you. But don't shed any tears for them. Neither company is in any danger of going belly-up, because they make their profit in repeat sales that more than compensate them for the loss of money in acquiring new customers. Many large direct-mail-based public interest organizations shrewdly apply similar rules in their donor acquisition programs.

For some organizations (sometimes for valid reasons, sometimes not), *no* net loss in prospecting is acceptable. For others, the acceptable acquisition cost may range anywhere from $1 or $2 per donor to $25 or more.

To achieve maximum economies of scale and help minimize your acquisition cost, you'll usually do best to develop *one* general donor acquisition package and remail it indefinitely in the largest possible quantities, so long as the package continues to produce acceptable results. Although you'll be well advised to test alternative approaches at every opportunity, this standard or control package will become the backbone of your donor acquisition program. Ideally, the control package is an "evergreen" appeal, that is, it is theoretically good for all time. For example, the control package for the *Wall Street Journal's* subscription promotion efforts in 2003 was reportedly first mailed in 1974. Just as examples abound in the world of commercial advertising of familiar, long-running campaigns, there are many other examples of durable direct mail control packages in fundraising for non-profits. Some large programs have several control packages, each targeting a different market, but the principle of standardization is much the same.

See Table 1.1 for a cost comparison of a donor acquisition and a donor resolicitation mailing.

Donor Resolicitation

By contrast, donor resolicitation mailings (also called house appeals or house mailings) have time value and are usually written afresh for each mailing. In an aggressive direct mail fundraising program revolving around a donor list of 250,000 individuals, this might mean designing and writing as many as two or three *dozen* resolicitation packages per year. To achieve optimal impact, you're likely to invest more in these mailings ($0.50 to $5.00 each) and mail them selectively in smaller quantities, depending on the size of your donor list (3,000 to 150,000 letters). Response rates may range from 3 to 20 percent or more but are typically between 6 and 12 percent when sent to active, current donors.

In any given year, you'll mail both donor acquisition and donor resolicitation mailings. To get a sense of the proportions of those mailings in the first year of a program, see Table 1.2.

There are two types of resolicitation mailings: (1) donor or membership renewals and (2) so-called special appeals. Annual membership or donor renewal letters are used both by organizations with formal membership structures and with those that have learned how such devices can boost their renewal rates (the proportion of donors or members who contribute at least once during the year). Such groups mail a *series* of inexpensive renewal letters (as many as ten), with each member or donor receiving as many letters as necessary to force the issue. In a typical renewal series that is spaced out over six to ten months, perhaps 50 percent of the membership will sign up for another year, roughly half of them in response to the very first effort and a quarter in response to the second. The final effort in the series is calculated to recapture reluctant members at a cost at least as low as that of direct

TABLE 1.1. Donor Acquisition Versus Donor Resolicitation Mailings.

Type	Purpose	Cost per Piece	Quantity per Mailing	Response Rate
Donor acquisition	Recruit new donors	$0.35–$0.80	50,000–1,000,000	0.5–2.5%
Donor resolicitation	Generate net revenue	$0.50–$5.00	3,000–150,000	6–15%

TABLE 1.2. **Mailing Quantities in a Typical First-Year Program.**

Month	Donor Acquisition	Donor Resolicitation
January	50,000	
February		
March		1,000
April	100,000	
May		
June		3,000
July		
August	150,000	
September		5,000
October		
November		6,000
December	300,000	
Total	600,000	15,000

mail prospecting (the acquisition cost). To get a sense of how a donor or membership renewal series might be scheduled, see Table 1.3.

But this renewal series is *not* the organization's only source of membership contributions. Well-managed groups also mail special appeals to their members—often no fewer than are mailed by groups without a formal membership structure. Table 1.4 portrays a simplified picture of a one-year mailing schedule for a program that includes three tracks: renewals, special appeals, and acquisition.

Although an aggressive fundraising program may include a donor resolicitation every month, it's unlikely that a large number of the donors on the "file" (computerese for "list") will receive every appeal. Through a process called segmentation, mailers carefully select subgroups of donors for each package and each mailing in order to achieve optimal impact and increase the program's cost-effectiveness. (We'll discuss segmentation in detail in Chapter Four.)

It's normal to evaluate the success of renewal mailings in terms of *net revenue*. Although there are different yardsticks to measure the net, I usually look at the ratio of revenue-to-cost, which tends to range between two-to-one and ten-to-one in all but the very largest programs. (In other words, the cost of a dollar raised will range from $0.10 to $0.50.) The ratio is likely to vary greatly with the segmentation chosen, as some subgroups tend to be far more responsive than others. Accordingly, some donors receive many more mailings than do other donors. See Table 1.5 for a stylized representation of an annual direct mail segmentation plan.

TABLE 1.3. Overall Plan for a Representative Renewal Series.

Effort #	Weeks Before or After Membership Lapses	Theme	Typical Response Rate
1	12 weeks before	"Renew early"	10–20%
2	8 weeks before	"It's time to renew"	6–15%
3	4 weeks before	"A friendly reminder"	4–8%
4	1 week before	"Did you forget?"	3–6%
5	4 weeks after	"Your last newsletter just mailed"	3–5%
6	8 weeks after	"What's the problem?"	10–15%
7	12 weeks after	Telephone reminder	36–69%
Total	24-week cycle		

Note: This plan assumes that renewals are timed to coincide with donor "anniversary dates." In fact, many donor or membership renewal series are mailed on a fixed annual schedule.

TABLE 1.4. Simplified Annual Mailing Schedule for a Three-Track Direct Mail Fundraising Program.

Month	Renewals	Special Appeals	Donor Acquisition
January			100,000
February	10,000		
March			
April	8,000		100,000
May	7,000	2,000	
June	6,300		
July	5,800		
August	5,500		100,000
September	4,900	5,000	
October			100,000
November		10,000	
December		5,000	
Total Quantity	47,500	22,000	400,000

TABLE 1.5. Simplified Annual Direct Mail Segmentation Plan.

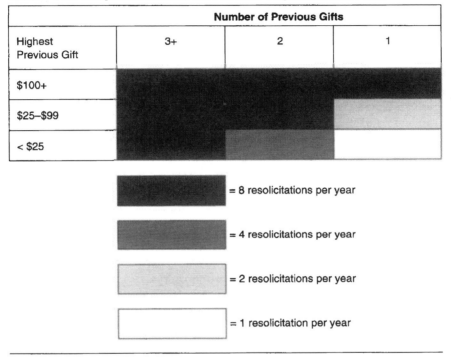

	Number of Previous Gifts		
Highest Previous Gift	3+	2	1
$100+			
$25–$99			
< $25			

■ = 8 resolicitations per year

■ = 4 resolicitations per year

▨ = 2 resolicitations per year

□ = 1 resolicitation per year

In short, then, the challenge you'll face as you set out to launch a direct mail fundraising program is to acquire as many new donors as possible at a donor acquisition cost that is consistent with your strategy and to analyze, cultivate, and resolicit your donor file so you'll derive the maximum benefit for your organization.

The approach you take to direct mail fundraising has to fit *your* organization's needs. Just as a Jaguar isn't the best car for someone whose greatest need is for high fuel mileage, someone's formula-driven approach to direct mail isn't necessarily right for your organization.

Strategy and Tactics in Direct Mail

Now that we share a common vocabulary and framework of understanding about direct mail fundraising, let's take a look at how direct mail may be used as a *strategic* tool.

Through strategic planning, a public interest group can identify its goals and priorities. Ideally, the organization's staff leadership and board will undertake a formal process, producing a written document that spells out its strategy and identifies the tactics to be used over a period of at least three years.

Despite the admonitions of outside consultants and bothersome board members, most nonprofit organizations don't adopt formal strategic plans. Nonetheless, even the most informal and inarticulate group needs to be clear about its long-term goals and know the difference between today and tomorrow. If you don't understand why you're in business and how you'll marshal available resources to serve your organization's ends, you've got much bigger problems than can be solved by starting a direct mail fundraising program.

Once your priorities are clear, however, you can use direct mail fundraising to help you achieve *growth, involvement, visibility, efficiency, stability*—whichever one of these goals your strategy requires. Within the tactical context of your direct mail fundraising program, all five goals may be important and several of them indispensable. But as *strategies,* they're mutually exclusive. To understand the tradeoffs and conflicts among them as you plan your direct mail fundraising program, consider four hypothetical case studies.

Case Study 1: Strategy Dictates Tactics

Your strategic goal as executive director of a newly launched public policy organization is to reverse national policy on one highly controversial issue within five years. The issue isn't so explosive as abortion rights or flag burning; let's say you want to lower the cost of auto insurance. Lacking other means, the *strategy* you've elected to bring this about is to mobilize public opinion and lobby the U.S. Congress for changes in the law.

Your $500,000 budget is met by a few venturesome foundations and fewer than five hundred individual donors. Clearly, you lack the funding you need to mount the massive public relations campaign that might turn the tide in your favor. But you do have enough money to launch an aggressive direct mail donor acquisition program. If initial response is good, you might build a broad grassroots base for change within five years and *ultimately* generate the funds to support a professional media campaign that will change attitudes among the general public and in the Congress.

This strategy dictates a likely set of *tactics:*

- A first-year investment of $150,000 or more in direct mail, with additional investment in the second year
- A grassroots lobbying campaign that asks prospective as well as proven donors to become actively involved by signing petitions, mailing postcards to Congress, and

the like (not to the exclusion of direct organizing and lobbying efforts but to supplement them)

- Distinctive themes, logos, colors, and slogans consistently employed on all materials used in the five-year campaign
- An active outreach effort to involve your donors in educating and recruiting additional supporters

Although mailing millions of letters all across the country will enhance your visibility, it's no substitute for the public exposure that a well-executed advertising and public relations effort might obtain for you on nationwide television. However, without a sizable base and enough of a track record to gain the attention of skeptical reporters, your chances of free media coverage are slim. A massive direct mail-based building program is the fastest way to get there. Moreover, once you're there, the heightened public interest generated by national media coverage will boost your direct mail returns, perhaps dramatically.

To gain the maximum benefit from this approach, you'll reinvest all the proceeds of your direct mail program in additional and larger mailings for at least the first three years. Yes, this means that for three years every nickel of every direct mail contribution to your organization will be spent on mailing additional letters. These letters are the principal tool in service of your strategy, because they educate the public, involve thousands of people in active support of your cause, make you visible all across the country, and generate pressure directly on Congress.

If survey research and initial direct mail testing demonstrate substantial support for your goal of lowering auto insurance rates, this set of tactics will give you a real shot at achieving your strategic goal. But none of these tactics—not even the multi-million-dollar prospecting program that is the centerpiece of the campaign—will be effective in isolation from the others. For example, without strong donor involvement and grassroots lobbying devices, the donor acquisition program will not support your *strategy* of bringing about a change in the law. All these tactics need to be seen in the larger context of organizational strategy and executed as a whole.

To make the strategy work, you'll also have to *plan* the effort with great care. At the outset, numerical projections will be speculative and only marginally useful. But once results are in from successful initial tests, you'll be able to make meaningful projections. You'll be able to see—and plan—your five-year direct mail program as a continuous process, with growth targets established for each quarter-year along the way and a gradually quickening rhythm of activity in the final years that helps you reach your public policy goal.

Strategy often dictates tactics. In this case, a substantial initial investment in direct mail, aggressive donor acquisition, and reinvestment for rapid growth, as well as a multifaceted program of donor involvement, are all simply *tactical* tools to use in support of your strategy.

Case Study 2: Tactics Don't Always Work

You're the executive director of an agency that provides vital human services for a population of one million. The city where your principal office is located takes pride in its progressive tradition of providing for its least fortunate members. Your clients are disadvantaged teenagers. The *strategy* set by your board of trustees is to stabilize the agency's finances by broadening and diversifying your financial base.

Currently, your $1 million budget derives from fees for service, government, and foundation funding, and from the generous support of a handful of major donors, several of whom sit on the board. The agency has good media contacts and has managed to acquire a highly favorable reputation with the general public. Although neither you nor your clients are front-page news, there's lots of drama and human interest in your work. You're convinced that direct mail will work well for you.

However, because some of your larger grants are to be phased out soon, your budget may shrink by as much as $500,000 over the next three years. You hope that a direct mail fundraising program will enable you to make up the loss, thus contributing 10 percent of your annual budget within three years. Over the longer term, you hope it will yield a great deal more through collateral fundraising efforts such as legacy giving and major donor programs. One of your funders has agreed to underwrite the effort to launch a direct mail program.

Among the *tactics* you've chosen to execute this diversification strategy are a public relations campaign to raise your agency's profile and an aggressive donor acquisition program. You hope to build an active direct mail base of some thirty thousand names within three years, because you've been told that a fundraising program on that scale will generate net revenues of $500,000 per year.

That approach won't work. There simply aren't enough people living within the region you serve to sustain a direct mail program of such broad scope. Let's take a look at the numbers:

- Because of donor attrition during the three-year period (through death, illness, address changes, or changing priorities), you'll have to acquire a total of perhaps 40,000 donors altogether.
- To acquire 40,000 donors, you'll probably need to mail 4 million prospect letters. Even with substantial reinforcement from a well-focused public relations campaign, a direct mail response rate of 1 percent would be quite respectable.
- In other words, you'll have to mail as many as 1 million letters in the first year and 1.5 million in each of the following two years. There are only 1 million people living in your region, and relatively few of them can be considered good prospects. (Later, after we've discussed mailing lists in Chapter Four, you'll understand this statement better.)

To carry out this strategy, your agency will need to become a household word locally. In neighborhoods where your best prospects live, you'll need to persuade virtually every household to contribute to your work. This may be practical for a zoo or a museum with a creative community involvement program and lots of tangible membership benefits, but it's not in the cards for a social service agency.

Here, more realistically, are your options:

- Settle for a much smaller donor base and a much more modest contribution to your operating budget. Direct mail probably *will* work for your agency. It just won't live up to unrealistic expectations.
- Forego profits entirely for three years—or even longer—as you reinvest them in donor acquisition and continuing public relations efforts. Even so, you may need to wait a lot longer than three years before the program begins to make a significant contribution to your budget.
- Consider whether the implications of your work warrant mailing outside your region, perhaps even nationally.
- Look for other ways to supplement or substitute for direct mail donor acquisition. A broad-based program of neighborhood fundraising events may be feasible. So might a multimedia campaign to generate "inquiries" about your services from individuals who write or call in response to your offer to tell them "how you can help." Direct mail appeals may succeed with these "qualified prospects" who have demonstrated interest in your work.

However, despite your best efforts, it's possible that direct mail will never generate net revenues of $500,000 per year for you.

Strategy may dictate tactics, but the tactics must be realistic.

Case Study 3: Tactics Affect Strategy

The challenge you face as chief executive officer of a nationwide advocacy group is to maintain your large membership base, which is essential for your ongoing lobbying campaign, while increasing your operating budget by at least 20 percent annually over the next four years. The environmental issues your group addresses are of increasing concern to the general public, and your board is confident that there is lots of room for you to grow. The *strategy* you've successfully pursued for three years already is to publish and promote by direct mail a lush, four-color monthly magazine that is available to members only.

Repeated testing has shown that, by highlighting this attractive membership benefit, you can mail five million prospect letters per year and acquire forty thousand new members at an acquisition cost of just $5 with entry-level dues set at $12. But there's a catch. It costs you another $10 per year to print and mail the magazine to each member, and the typical $12-member doesn't respond well to appeals for additional gifts. The upshot is that your membership program as a whole isn't operating at much better than breakeven. Even including significant revenue from already renewed donors, the program is netting just enough to cover publication, distribution, and overhead costs, with no significant net income to fund that 20 percent budgetary growth that is essential to your strategy.

One *tactical* solution to this dilemma is to raise your membership dues—in effect, your subscription price—to $15, $18, $20, or $25 (with testing to determine the optimal level. (For a full discussion about direct mail tests, please see my book, *Testing, Testing, 1, 2, 3: Raise More Money with Direct Mail Tests.*) Although the cost of fulfilling each individual magazine subscription will rise as circulation falls (because of reduced economies of scale), in all likelihood you'll be able to find a level of prospecting at which you can continue to acquire new members at breakeven while taking those added costs into account.

If you *reduce* your prospecting volume, you'll acquire fewer new members, so your membership base will shrink. But the shrinkage may be limited if you don't encounter great resistance to the higher dues level. And you'll be attracting members who will almost certainly respond better to your requests for more generous gifts. Because repeated testing shows that donors who send larger gifts also contribute more frequently and tend to be more loyal, those who pay dues of $20 or $25 per year are much more likely to be responsive to special appeals. You can then finance the desired budgetary growth from these appeals and from a beefed-up major gifts program. It's also possible that with lower prospecting volume and fewer members, you'll be able to cut costs in your fulfillment and membership departments, achieving the same effect as revenue growth.

But there are flaws in this tactical approach. You'll be operating with a smaller base, which runs the risk of undercutting your lobbying campaign. You may also be forced to lay off staff. Either of these considerations may rule out cutbacks in your prospecting efforts.

Thus the tactics required to execute a sound strategy may dictate other changes in the way you run your organization. Some of these, such as a membership base that shrinks too much or major changes in staffing requirements, may have unintended and unfortunate consequences. Careful planning will help minimize the problems. But only a clear sense of strategic priorities will allow you to make decisions that are right for your organization.

Case Study 4: Time Is a Strategic Tool

You're managing the front-running campaign for governor in a prosperous industrial state with a population of ten million. Your candidate, a popular member of Congress, has everything going for her except money. Though the campaign is solvent and you're unlikely to face significant opposition in the primary, it will be difficult to raise enough money to mount a television advertising campaign in the general election. You'll need at least $4 million to be competitive with the incumbent, whose campaign is awash in funds from PACs.

Your *strategy* to win the general election, now ten months away, is to build a massive donor base that will produce an army of volunteers for an old-fashioned grassroots voter registration and "Get-Out-the-Vote" campaign while funding the overall effort. Your state party organization is weak, and its support for your candidate lukewarm because she represents unpopular policies and unwelcome change. Polls show she can build a majority coalition, but she'll need to do so virtually overnight—and from the ground up.

Direct mail is the principal means you've selected to execute this strategy. You hope to expand five-fold your candidate's existing 20,000-name donor list. With 100,000 donors, a $4 million media budget will be within reach. Such a large list will also enable you to recruit two or three volunteers in every precinct in the state. And the donor acquisition effort itself will carry your candidate's message into millions of households, laying the groundwork for the television and radio advertising campaign planned for the final weeks before the general election. You're prepared to invest as much as you need to make this strategy work.

There seems to be only one problem. The $250,000 your campaign has in the bank must remain there for at least three more weeks, until the next financial disclosure deadline has passed. If you remove the funds before then to launch a direct mail program, your campaign may look weak enough for primary opposition to surface. And you can't find direct mail vendors who are crazy enough to give you credit. In other words, you may lose almost one out of the ten remaining months before the election.

Under the circumstances, even with ten full months ahead, you face a daunting challenge. To acquire 80,000 new donors will mean mailing four million letters (if the response rate is 2 percent—a level that is relatively more common in political fundraising than in the nonprofit world). A populist campaign that sparks widespread enthusiasm and lots of media coverage *might* be able to mail this intensively. The importance of the election and the candidate's broad appeal may make it possible for you to prospect for donors on a modest scale outside the state, thus broadening your direct mail market. But time is a major limiting factor, both in and out of state.

To conduct list and package testing and to read the results, you'll need at least a couple of months at the outset. And unless your results are unrealistically strong, you'll need to wind up your prospecting program a minimum of one or two months before the election. (Irrationally, response in political donor acquisition efforts often drops off as Election Day draws near. And unless you're making a profit from your prospecting program, the value of acquiring new donors will decline sharply as the number of resolicitation opportunities is reduced. In other words, you've got about six months to mail *most* of those four million acquisition packages—about 667,000 *per month*. Cutting one more month from the schedule will increase the monthly prospecting volume to 800,000.

Those numbers aren't impossibly high if your candidate has a national following, but you're unlikely to be able to reach them in the time available. It would be unwise to build your election strategy on such unsteady ground. Direct mail fundraising makes sense for your campaign. It will contribute substantially to your media budget while playing an important role in increasing your visibility, spreading your message, and recruiting volunteers. You just aren't likely to achieve as much as you're hoping.

There is a way to launch your effort more quickly than it might seem. With an urgent overnight appeal to the most generous of your candidate's donors, you can solicit gifts before the financial disclosure deadline. This appeal may generate the seed funds for a large-scale prospecting program while increasing your politically important bank balance. Presumably, you'll be able to negotiate payment terms that allow you to begin work on a large donor acquisition mailing while leaving the money in the bank for the next three weeks. But that still leaves you with overambitious expectations for the direct mail program as a whole.

(A bit of advice for the next campaign: start building your donor base two years earlier, so you'll be facing the active phase of the election campaign with a list of 50,000 donors—and a much more modest tactical challenge.)

As you can see, direct mail fundraising is a flexible tool, adaptable to a wide range of strategic and tactical challenges facing not-for-profit organizations. But if this military terminology throws you off, there's another way you can look at the uses of direct mail fundraising.

Direct Mail as a Problem-Solving Tool

The most productive way I've found to view direct mail fundraising in the strategic planning process is as a method of problem solving. Once you've identified the problem—too few members to give you clout on Capitol Hill, too little money to meet your clients' needs, too much unpredictability in your finances—you can devise a solution using direct mail techniques.

The trick, of course, is to figure out what the problem is.

- In the first of these four case studies (the new public policy organization) is the central problem finding funds for a public relations campaign. Or is it controlling the cost of auto insurance?
- In the hypothetical case of the human service agency, what's more important: broadening the funding base in the long term or supporting the budget in the short run?
- For the environmental advocacy group, is it a higher priority to maintain a large membership base or to maximize net income?

- In the example of the gubernatorial campaign, is direct mail most important for the financial contribution it can make to the campaign or for its broader political value?

The answers to these questions are not obvious. There are sound arguments for either side or for still different points of view. But it's absolutely essential that these questions be resolved. Decisions need to be made one way or another. Muddled priorities are a prescription for failure.

Designing an effective direct mail fundraising program is, first of all, a matter of distinguishing strategy from tactics. And for the program to achieve its goals, that distinction must be clear to everyone involved in its management. The difference between strategy and tactics should never be forgotten.

However, circumstances sometimes conspire against us. In some cases, our strategic needs—the problems we face—can't be addressed using direct mail.

Direct Mail Is Not for Everyone

Not long ago, what passed for conventional wisdom in direct mail fundraising was that your initial acquisition test mailing would be successful if it broke even—in other words, if it yielded enough in direct, immediate contributions to cover the full cost of the mailing. From this conventional point of view, your successful program would then proceed with a series of progressively larger donor acquisition mailings, breaking even all along the way, as you built an ever-bigger list of proven donors *at no net cost.*

We know better nowadays. The recent experience of most small and medium-sized public interest groups—and of a great many large ones, too—has made it clear that direct mail fundraising may be hugely successful for them if they can acquire donors at an acceptable cost and then profitably resolicit them. Even the most modest test results may lay the foundation for a fundraising program of enormous scale.

But before we drift off into never-never land with our eyeballs full of dollar signs, let's make sure we agree on something:

> Every direct mail fundraising program must begin with a test mailing to determine the organization's potential to raise money by mail, and that test mailing really is a test.

Direct mail is a risky business. Maybe, just maybe, your test won't work.

Sometimes a direct mail fundraising program gets off to a slow start. It may take more than one test mailing to identify a successful marketing concept or to find the right market. But for some organizations, the *cost* of direct mail fundraising may be out of proportion to its potential yield.

Remember, a direct mail donor prospecting program must deliver new donors at an advantageous acquisition cost. If it doesn't do that, you'd better head back to the drawing board. Direct mail may not be right for you.

Quite apart from the possibility that your initial test mailing may be poorly conceived or badly executed, public response may be limited for one or more of the following reasons:

- There may not be enough people who agree that your organization fills an important need, or it may be difficult to find mailing lists on which their names and addresses appear.
- People may agree that the work you're doing is important but may not *care* strongly enough to send money.
- The ever-fickle public may feel that the need you're filling has passed or simply isn't urgent enough to require immediate support.

Organizations that operate on a small scale may have an especially difficult time launching the type of large direct mail fundraising programs I'm describing in these pages: those with annual budgets of less than $300,000 or with constituencies of fewer than one million people. Although there are important exceptions, for the most part the market for a local public interest group in all but the largest metropolitan areas may simply be too small to apply these techniques. Professionally managed direct mail fundraising is built on economies of scale.

The limited size of your constituency or market is only one of several sound reasons *not* to embark on a program of direct mail fundraising. Direct mail may not be a good bet for you, and it may not even make sense for you to launch an initial test if any of the following conditions apply:

- You lack the necessary capital to invest in a test mailing.
- Your finances are fragile, and you can't bear the risk of an unsuccessful test.
- The issues involved in your work aren't specific, compelling, and of concern to a broad public.
- You can't effectively distinguish your organization from others serving the same constituency by identifying something dramatic or unique about you or your work.
- Your mission and strategy are unclear, so that it would be difficult to package your programs for a wider public.
- You're just starting out and lack the track record, name recognition, or credentials to establish your credibility.

- You have neither sufficient staff nor an outside firm to ensure that donors will get the *service* they need.
- Your organization isn't committed for the *long haul*.

Can you find your way over those hurdles? Do you already have in place a successful direct mail fundraising program, or have you conducted a successful initial test mailing? Read on, then!

Here are the ten most important things about direct mail fundraising:

1. *Direct mail fundraising is a process, not an event.* Direct mail is a way to communicate with lots of people and to build rewarding relationships with them. Skillfully used (in combination with other direct response techniques), direct mail can lead donors through all the stages of the fundraising lifecycle. Individual mailings are mere building blocks in the relationship-building process; the only way to promote genuine donor development is through a continuing, year-round sequence of communications that includes many mailings in the course of a year.

2. *The true rewards from direct mail come only over the long haul.* The principal virtue of direct mail is that it can generate steady, predictable, undesignated income. Still, the richest rewards from a direct mail fundraising program may come in the form of bequests or other forms of planned gifts, and such a gift may not come until fifteen or twenty years after a donor is recruited by mail. The success of a direct mail fundraising program is often evaluated by comparing the acquisition cost for new donors with the demonstrable long-term value they bring to the organization—benchmarks that cannot even be reliably calculated in fewer than five years.

3. *Cost is less important than cost-effectiveness.* It costs money to raise money. Sometimes net revenue rises when an investment in a mailing is enlarged. In any case, the sheer cost of a mailing is less important than its outcome. It usually pays to invest more in top donors, less in the least responsive and least generous donors. Cheaper is not always better.

4. *The list is paramount.* It's worth emphasizing over and over again: the list is by far the most important factor in a mailing. The difference between mailing to alumni or nonalumni, to old alums or more recent, cash-starved alums, to donors or nondonors, to direct mail responders or nonresponders, or simply to one list that has proven to be responsive instead of another that hasn't, can make or break a mailing.

5. *Next comes the offer.* The offer you make to the recipients of your mailing is next in importance only to the list. If you're mailing to solicit an annual gift or membership renewal, it's important that the offer appear front and center in the package. In fundraising, the offer revolves around the fundamental reason you're mailing, for example, whether to recruit new donors, renew existing donors' annual

support, enlist them in a monthly giving club, secure special gifts, or persuade them to remember your organization in their wills. Each of these "marketing concepts" requires a very distinctive letter.

6. *Segmentation is the key to cost-effectiveness.* Whom you include in a mailing and whom you exclude determines the outcome of a mailing. It rarely makes sense to mail an appeal to everyone on your donor file. Almost always, such an effort will be far more cost-effective if you exclude those who haven't contributed during the last two or three years or who haven't contributed more than token gifts. Equally important, by segmenting your list—dividing it into subgroups based on past performance—you can reserve special treatment for your top donors (first-class postage, personalization, and higher production values). Special treatment like this frequently pays off in bigger returns.

7. *Annual giving provides the structure for direct mail fundraising.* One of the most basic assumptions in direct mail fundraising is that donors must be encouraged to give at least one gift per year; less frequent giving is unlikely to produce enough net revenue to justify the effort. In many organizations, an annual campaign or annual fund serves as the vehicle to inculcate this idea in donors' minds. Other organizations adopt a "membership" structure and often employ a "renewal series" to urge donors to meet their implied obligation to contribute at least once annually. The renewal series, based on the model of magazine subscription renewal notices, entails sending members a series of notices—usually between three and ten—until they respond with gifts. This approach is usually very cost-effective and promotes donor loyalty as well. Even those nonprofits that maintain neither an annual fund nor a membership campaign are likely to mail a year-end holiday appeal to their donors every year.

8. *Testing leads to incremental improvements over time.* The distinguishing characteristic of direct response, which includes direct mail, telemarketing, direct response television, and e-mail marketing, is that its results are precisely measurable. If you want to know which of two offers will produce the better results, you can (normally) construct a test, simultaneously mailing letters containing one offer to Group A and letters containing the other offer to Group B, with the two groups chosen at random from the same list so that they are statistically identical. Testing allows direct mail fundraisers to boost results over time by identifying (and then putting to work) the most successful lists, offers, and messages.

9. *Repetition is essential.* Success in direct mail fundraising, as in any area of marketing or advertising, requires that materials have a consistent "look and feel" over time. This normally means using the same logo, theme, slogan, or tagline long after the organization's board members and executives have concluded that they're boring. Repetition reinforces donors' views of an organization. In modern parlance, it helps a nonprofit establish and sustain its "brand identity."

10. *Without timely and accurate record keeping, direct mail is impossible.* The donor database is the sine qua non of direct mail fundraising. Without an up-to-date database, fundraisers can't measure results, segment, test, or assess the success of their development program. And building relationships with donors requires detailed record keeping; otherwise, how could we know which donors are strong performers and which are weak?

● ● ●

OK, then. Now that we have a handle on the most important factors in direct mail fundraising, let's set out on our journey to get your organization into the mail. It's natural, of course, that we would start that journey by viewing the single most important consideration in any mailing: the list or lists of people to whom we mail. That's the subject of the following chapter.

2

Selecting Your Audience

Stop! Before you plunge into thinking about the lists of people you want to send your appeal to, make sure you're absolutely clear about the purpose of your mailing. Is it intended to acquire (recruit) new donors or members? Or is its purpose, instead, to resolicit (or to cultivate, educate, or upgrade) existing donors? In either case, the choice of lists is critical, but the process for choosing a list is very different. In this chapter, we'll look first at acquisition lists. Then we'll turn to the selection of lists for resolicitation mailings—the process called segmentation.

Choosing Lists for Donor Acquisition Mailings

In the 2002/03 edition of the mailing list catalog used most widely in the direct mail industry, there are entries for nearly nineteen thousand lists. The catalog itself comes in two volumes that together are four and one-half inches thick.

Yes, you got that right: nineteen thousand different mailing lists! It's a *big* business.

Lists are created because organizations save the names of their members or supporters. Publications maintain lists of their subscribers. Government agencies keep records of license-holders and taxpayers. Merchants and catalog merchandisers track their buyers. There are also companies in the business of compiling lists specifically for profit.

Individual lists vary in size from a few hundred names to more than ninety million. All told, there are *tens of billions* of names and addresses appearing in these readily available mailing lists. Most of the more than 280 million living Americans appear dozens of times, and so do quite a few who are dead. Many of us are included as individuals on literally hundreds of lists.

Mailing lists are by no means all alike. There are numerous ways to categorize them, but in the context of direct mail fundraising, it's useful to group them into seven general types:

1. *Donors.* These people have contributed money, most likely in response to direct mail fundraising appeals.
2. *Members.* They've paid membership dues to an organization, probably by mail.
3. *Subscribers.* These folks subscribe to a particular periodical. Many first did so in response to a direct mail subscription promotion.
4. *Buyers.* They've bought books or other goods by mail, in most cases through a catalog they received in the mail.
5. *Inquirers and sweepstakes entrants.* These are individuals who have responded to an ad or a direct mail package with a request for information or a response to a survey or sweepstakes. They sent in little if any money.
6. *Compiled lists.* These are second-generation lists, produced by merging lists from different sources or assembling them from raw data. For example, someone might compile a list of people who have joined or written letters of inquiry to many different organizations, perhaps dissimilar ones. Someone else's idea of a useful compiled list might be those individuals whose lifestyle or demographic characteristics, as revealed by such means as auto registrations or property tax rolls, fit a certain predetermined pattern. With rare exceptions, compiled lists do *not* consist of people whose principal shared characteristic is that they've contributed or spent money by mail.
7. *"Good ideas."* These are the people on your board chair's Rolodex, or a list of your friends or neighbors, or the thousands of individuals to whom you've been sending your newsletter because somebody five years ago was just *sure* they would take any opportunity to support you. (They haven't, and they probably won't.)

There are thousands of available lists in each one of the first six of these categories. In a few cases, they're available directly from the list owner. Hundreds of "list brokerage" firms manage the others, representing the owners to negotiate and manage the arrangements under which outsiders use their lists. The marketplace is extensive, and list brokers tend to specialize, not just in such broad-brush areas as fundraising but in narrowly defined fields such as liberal or conservative political lists, Catholic lists, or New Age lists. I don't hear very often about list brokers going out of business, so I assume they're doing well. (Brokers typically work by commission, charging a percentage of the rental price, so the more you mail, the more money they make.)

Through list brokers, you're able to gain access to the overwhelming majority of those nineteen thousand lists. Most are available on computer tapes in one or another of several standard formats that a direct mail service bureau is able to read. (Some lists are still available only on mailing labels, although that has become rare, as mailers turn increasingly to ink-jet and laser printers to address their mailings.)

> The problem you face isn't getting hold of enough lists. It's figuring out which of them are likely to work for you. Very few will.

Only a handful of lists will be sure bets to work for your initial direct mail fund-raising appeal. These so-called "hot" lists, such as names of people who've written to ask you for information or donors to organizations engaged in very similar work, are sometimes hard to come by. "Warm" lists are a little easier to obtain. These are the files that, based on experience with similar appeals, we feel are likely to be responsive enough to be cost-effective. But most lists are "cold." Only testing can tell whether they'll respond cost-effectively, and in most cases testing is a long shot. The overwhelming majority of cold lists, as far as you're concerned, might as well be printed with invisible ink. They simply won't work for your donor acquisition campaign, and you might as well forget about trying.

A list broker can provide you with a substantial amount of information, free of charge, about each list you want to consider. It's standard practice in the list industry for brokers to supply a "data card" (see Exhibit 2.1) for each list.

Typically, these data cards reveal the total size of the list, the date it was last updated, the circumstances under which it was created, the gender composition, the minimum number of names that must be ordered (or at least paid for), and sometimes a wealth of other data as well. If the list owner will permit you to slice and dice the list, perhaps geographically, by gender, by minimum gift, or purchase amount, for example, the data card will make that clear and state the cost of doing so.

Choosing the right prospect lists is a demanding and sophisticated task, and it's often counterintuitive. For example, as a group, millionaires aren't good donor prospects for a group seeking to aid the homeless; neither are people who are homeless. Just because one group has a lot of money and the other has an intense interest in the issue is no guarantee that either will respond to the appeal. And if you're tempted to send your appeal to doctors or lawyers because both groups are

```
BREAD FOR THE WORLD                                          BREADWORL

   25,907    MEMBERS/DONORS (24 MO)  $75.00/M      -------DATE-------
    3,163    25-36 MONTHS            $55.00/M      AUGUST 2003
             EXCHANGE AVAILABLE
                                                  --AVG UNIT SALE---
                                                  $40.00

                                                  -------SEX--------
                                                  SELECTABLE
DESCRIPTION:
                                                  ----SELECTIONS----
FOUNDED IN 1973, THIS ORGANIZATION ENCOURAGES     STATE      $5.00/M
INDIVIDUALS TO CALL AND WRITE MEMBERS OF CONGRESS SCF        $5.00/M
ON BEHALF OF LEGISLATION THAT WILL BENEFIT HUNGRY ZIP        $5.00/M
PEOPLE IN THE UNITED STATES AND AROUND THE WORLD. SEX        $5.00/M
RECENT PUBLICATIONS AND CAMPAIGNS HAVE FOCUSED ON ZIP+4      $5.00/M
DEBT RELIEF AND DEVELOPMENT ASSISTANCE FOR POOR   ----ADDRESSING----
COUNTRIES IN AFRICA AND ELSEWHERE.                4-UP CHESHIRE  N/C
                                                  P/S LABEL $10.00/M
MAY SELECT @ $5/M:                                MAG TAPE  $25.00/F
                                                  ELECTRONIC$50.00/F
FEMALES 11,290                                    ----KEY CODING----
MALES    8,976                                    $5.00/M

                                                  --MINIMUM ORDER---
SOURCE:  DIRECT MAIL.                             3,000

                                                  ----NET NAME------
                                                  INQUIRE.




                                                  SAMPLE MAILING
                                                  PIECE REQUIRED




         CELCO   carol enters list co., inc.
                 9663C MAIN ST., FAIRFAX, VA 22032
                 (703) 425-0052  FAX: (703) 425-0056
```

EXHIBIT 2.1. List Broker's Data Card for a Direct Mail Fundraising List.

Source: CELCO. Reprinted with permission.

typically well-to-do, think again. Simple ability to give doesn't often translate into willingness to give.

You see, there's an ugly truth that applies even to your organization. Yes, yours is unquestionably the most exciting venture to come down the pike since the founding of the Smithsonian Institution. Even so, *very few people who are approached by mail will agree to support you under the best of circumstances.* That unpleasant fact, together with the limit on the money you're able to invest in direct mail donor acquisition, requires a very selective approach to the tens of thousands of available mailing lists.

To sift through all the possible lists for your initial prospect mailing, we look at each list to evaluate the following elements:

• *Donor history.* The rule of thumb in our business is that *the people who are most likely to give to you by mail are those who have previously given by mail.* I've never heard a credible estimate of the percentage of the population that fits this category, but I suspect it's small—certainly a lot less than half and probably less than a quarter of the American people. The best place to start looking for them is on donor lists.

• *Mail-responsiveness.* Generally, the best prospects are those who've developed the habit of using the postal system. That *doesn't* include everyone. Industry surveys suggest that only a little more than half of the American public will send money by mail for any reason whatsoever other than to pay taxes, rent, or utility bills, and many people still won't even do that. One measure of mail-responsiveness comes from the Direct Marketing Association, which reported to me in response to an inquiry that more than 42 million Americans, or about 21 percent of the adult population, ordered products by mail in the year ending spring 2002.

• *Recency.* One of the problems with most mailing lists is that they're not kept sufficiently up-to-date. In a society where one-fifth of the population moves every year, this can be a real problem. Generally speaking, only a mailing list that has been updated *within the past twelve months* is useful for fundraising purposes. A four- or five-year-old list may be worthless.

• *Accuracy.* A related problem for fundraisers is that the data entry on many publicly available mailing lists is atrocious. Some otherwise attractive lists may be poor prospects for your donor acquisition campaign simply because the list owner or the computer service bureau that maintains the list does such a consistently careless job. Among the most common and problematic errors are failing to record address changes and misspelling names or addresses, both of which lead to high levels of undeliverable mail and to costly duplicate entries.

• *Affinity.* If your organization is building a children's hospital in Africa, donors to Save the Children or UNESCO might be a good bet for you to test in your donor acquisition campaign. The members of the National Rifle Association probably aren't. However, affinity is highly overrated and very limiting. The subscribers to a magazine specializing in international affairs could turn out to be your most responsive list of all. For one thing, that list may be far more accurate and up-to-date than most donor lists. Because it's so difficult to predict which lists will work, we do our best to find out (often through list brokers) which ones worked for similar appeals, thus taking the concept of affinity one step further.

Based on these criteria, you'll select an appropriate "list of lists" for each donor acquisition mailing. In a modest initial test mailing, you might select a dozen lists, ordering samples of five thousand names from each (see Exhibit 2.2).

In a later, larger mailing, you might pick several dozen lists, representing both "continuations" (additional names from lists that yielded good test results) and new, as yet untested lists (see Exhibit 2.3).

The Marketplace of Lists

Most people seem to have the impression that mailing lists are bought and sold. In fact, this is only rarely the case. Lists are typically made available to direct mailers for *one-time use* only and may not be duplicated or re-used without explicit permission (which isn't often granted).

LIST OF LISTS
prepared by Mal Warwick & Associates for
RIVERKEEPER
Mail date: week of May 12, 2003

List Name	Select	Quantity
Adirondack Council	Mbrs (NY)	5,000
American Rivers	Mbrs/Dnrs (NY, NJ, CT)	4,371
Appalachian Mountain Club	Mbrs (NY)	5,000
Common Cause	Mbrs/Dnrs (NY, NJ, CT)	5,000
CoOp America (Green Pages Directory)	Mbrs (NY, NJ, CT)	5,000
Earthjustice	Dnrs (36 Mos/NY)	5,000
Environmental Defense	Dnrs (24 Mos/SCF)	5,000
Friends of Hillary	Dnrs (NY)	5,000
Hightower Lowdown	Newsltr Subs (NY, NJ, CT)	5,000
Pacifica Radio Foundation	Dnrs (NY)	5,000
Public Citizen	Mbrs (36 Mos/$10+/NY)	5,000
Sierra Club	Mbrs (24 Mos/NY)	5,000
Union of Concerned Scientists	Mbrs (NY, NJ, CT)	5,000
Wilderness Society	Mbrs/Dnrs (12 Mos/NY)	5,000
WNET	Mbrs/Dnrs (NY)	5,000
Total		**74,371**

EXHIBIT 2.2. Lists of Lists for an Acquisition Test Mailing.

Source: Riverkeeper. Reprinted with permission of Riverkeeper.

LISTS TO ORDER

Prepared by Mal Warwick & Associates, Inc. for

NATIONAL COUNCIL OF LA RAZA

Acquisition mailing #48–05

400,000 pieces to mail

List Name	Select	Universe	Quantity	Net Qty
Continuations				
America's Magazine	Eng. Edition Actives	13,130	13,130	11,817
Amnesty International	Actives/Hispanic		2,857	2,571
DNC	Active Donors/Hispanic		10,000	9,000
Hispanic Mag	actives	133,000	133,000	119,700
Hispanic Business	Active US Subs	221,961	200,000	180,000
Planned Parenthood	Active Donors/Hispanic	2,910	2,910	2,619
Time Inc. Database	Act. Hispanic/FR Contrib		25,000	22,500
UNICEF	12 mos, 5+, Hisp. Surn.		4,287	3,858
Subtotal			391,184	352,065
Tests				
ACLU	Hispanic Surname		3,000	2,700
Am. Inst. Cancer Research	Hispanic 12 mos. $20+	139,909	5,000	4,500
Amnesty International	Donors TX/NM/AZ	151,479	5,000	4,500
Atlantic Mosaic	Hispanic	45,579	5,000	4,500
American Donor Connect	12 mos/Hispanic/States	182,222	5,000	4,500
Conde Nast	Hispanic	139,345	5,000	4,500
Covenant House	Spanish Speaking	27,857	5,000	4,500
DNC	Donors TX/NM/AZ		5,000	4,500
Handgun Control	Hispanic Surname		3,300	2,970
Latina	Active Subscribers	110,000	5,000	4,500
Planned Parenthood	SCF select		5,000	4,500
SPLC	Hispanic Surname			0
UNICEF	SCF select	198,121	5,000	4,500
United Farmworkers	Active Donors	46,224	5,000	4,500
Subtotal			61,300	55,170
House lists				
Survey Respondents	NCLR House list		5,000	4,750
TOTAL TO MAIL				411,985

EXHIBIT 2.3. List of Lists for an Acquisition Rollout Mailing.

Source: National Council of La Raza. Reproduced with permission.

Sometimes, lists are available on a rental basis. These days, the going rate for most desirable donor and subscriber lists is in the range of 8 to 12 cents per name ($80 to $120 per thousand names). Some lists of buyers are even more costly. If you're forced to rely heavily on rentals, list costs may constitute one-sixth to one-third the entire cost of your donor acquisition mailing.

However, in many cases you'll be able to *exchange* lists and dramatically reduce this expenditure. Normally, exchanges are on a name-per-name basis. In other words, an exchange will obligate you to provide an equal number of equivalent names and addresses from your mailing list, usually weeks or months later. The cost of list exchanges is modest in comparison with list rentals.

The problem is, the owners of some lists that are available only on exchange may not be willing to trade with you. Unless you already have a sizable list of your own to prove your ability to reciprocate, you won't receive permission to use their lists.

If you're like most people I know, however, letting your organization's donor list out of your hands seems about as attractive as contracting a terminal illness. Here, then, is another reality you'll have to face at the outset: in North America, the business of direct mail fundraising is built in large part on (relatively) free commerce in lists, and groups that lack desirable mailing lists or refuse to trade or rent their own are operating at a serious disadvantage. (Circumstances may be different in other parts of the world.)

There are three principal reasons some organizations advance to explain why they won't exchange or rent their lists. All lack substance.

First, it's said that once a list is in the marketplace, it's vulnerable to theft. This idea is simple to combat. Like everyone else in the business, we insert what are termed *seed names* in each list we trade or rent; these are dummy names and addresses known only to us and not to the mailer who's getting our list. When the list is actually used, we receive *seed packages* at these dummy addresses. If packages turn up when they weren't supposed to, we take action. It almost never happens, and practical remedies are available if and when it does.

A second objection often raised to justify withholding a donor list from the market is that it will allow other organizations to "steal" a group's donors by making more powerful and effective appeals. This reflects an unfortunate but common misunderstanding about fundraising realities: no organization "owns" its donors. Almost all donors contribute to a great many organizations, certainly not just one. This is especially true of direct mail donors. In fact, a recent poll of donors in North America cosponsored by my agency and a similar firm in Canada revealed that direct mail donors support an average of fourteen nonprofit organizations per year. Under some circumstances, such as when the timing of an appeal is inconvenient, it might make good sense to deny permission to competitive organizations to use your list. But most of the time it makes no sense at all. The truth is, a directly competitive organization probably has half a dozen other ways to reach *your* donors with its appeal—through the periodicals they're likely to read or the areas where they live or the other groups to which they contribute. You might as well be neighborly about it and get something in return.

Figure 2.1 illustrates the reality that your donors possess many other interests and aren't really "your" donors at all.

The third reason frequently given to deny outside access to an organization's donor list is that the list will be "worn out" by overuse if other groups mail their appeals to it. My intuition tells me that there's some truth to this and, like some of my equally cautious colleagues in the industry, I normally recommend that outside use of a list be limited to a maximum of one mailing per week and avoided altogether during certain critical times on the fundraising calendar. But I honestly can't say I've ever seen any *evidence,* convincing or otherwise, that heavy outside usage of a donor list makes any difference whatsoever. Some people even contend that it's advantageous to allow others to appeal to your list, because it helps cultivate the habit of giving by mail!

What to Do About Duplicate Appeals

At the outset, you may be able to avoid the issue of duplicate appeals. With initial test mailings of fewer than 50,000 names, it's generally not recommended to take steps to reduce duplication. In small mailings, the proportion of duplicates is

FIGURE 2.1. Schematic Representation of Donors' Overlapping Interests.

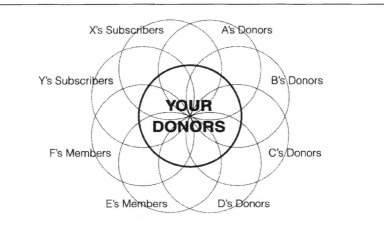

usually tiny. Sooner or later, though, the issue will catch up with you, because your donors (or your trustees) write or call to complain, or because it dawns on you how much money you're losing by printing and mailing duplicates. For some organizations, this becomes an emotional issue of major proportions. It's wise to think through in advance how you'll handle it.

Let's assume you and the chair of your board's fundraising committee have the same visceral reaction to duplicates as I do: you *despise* them. You may also be convinced that enough of your potential supporters will be annoyed by receiving duplicate appeals that in the long run it will even be worthwhile to pay a little extra for the test mailing to cut down the number of duplicates.

Using a computer technique called a merge-purge, it's possible to combine all the names in your mailing into one merged list and then to identify and isolate the duplicates (called multi-buyers, multi-donors, or merge dupes) so you can save money on printing and postage. However, it's not quite that simple.

For one thing, merge-purge is a costly procedure, running nearly 2 cents per name (or $16 to $18 per thousand names). In most situations, a merge-purge will save you money, but not always. In a 50,000-piece test mailing, you're unlikely to pay as much as $1,000 for a merge-purge, but the cost may mount to many thousands of dollars in larger acquisition mailings.

A merge-purge often adds days—perhaps a week or longer—to the time needed to prepare a mailing. Like the added cost, this is a price that needs to be analyzed.

Merge-purge is a broad concept that refers to a range of techniques and approaches. Some merge-purge programs are permissively loose, allowing lots of possible duplicates to get through for fear of cutting down on the number of good names to mail. And some programs are tight; the difference can be considerable. Merge-purge programs sometimes offer many optional features: correcting bad ZIP codes, eliminating incomplete names and addresses, sorting names into order for USPS presort discounts, screening for surnames of particular ethnicity, affixing the congressional district or other geodemographic information, and other possible enhancements. The list is long, and the implications for your direct mail program can be significant.

For an organization with a donor list of significant size, there is one overwhelming reason to conduct a merge-purge for every prospect mailing: it makes it possible to eliminate most (though not all) of your own donors. Not doing so may be very costly. Some of your contributors will become mightily annoyed by receiving duplicate appeals, especially appeals that don't recognize the fact that they've already given you money. More important, however, your prospect letter probably doesn't ask for a big enough gift and will give your donors a way to get off the hook with smaller gifts than they would send in response to a resolicitation. That can make a very big difference indeed in your fundraising results.

If you actually read a merge-purge report, you'll lose forever any remaining illusion that your donors are exclusively your own. The report for your initial test mailing may show 10 or 20 percent overlap among the lists you're testing. In larger rollout or continuation mailings, the duplication rate may be 40 percent or higher. The rate will vary greatly from one list to another, but you're likely to find that the very best lists—those most responsive to your appeals—are the ones that overlap the *most* with your own list (and with each other). Those that overlap the least and are thus most dissimilar tend to be less responsive.

Exhibit 2.4 shows one of several hundred pages in a merge-purge report. It displays forty-eight lists included in a donor acquisition mailing for the San Francisco AIDS Foundation. They're ranked in increasing order of duplication with existing donors to the Foundation. At the low end, 2.08 percent of the names on the J. Crew Active Buyers were duplicates of Foundation donors. At the high end (on the bottom of the page), just under 60 percent of Names Project donors were duplicates. In an ongoing direct mail fundraising program that has yielded a sizable donor list, it's common for the range of duplication rates to be very wide.

In a typical 50,000-piece test mailing, you may find you'll need a total of 56,000 names, or an additional 12 percent, to produce the correct number of mailing labels. Merging 56,000 names derived from, say, 12 different lists, the computer may identify approximately 47,000 as "unique" names. The other 9,000 names duplicate some of the 47,000 unique names and, in some cases, each other as well; 3,000 of the 9,000 merge-dupes match *just one* of the 47,000 names. These 3,000 will be formed into a list of their own; including the 47,000 unique names, this will make a total of 50,000 names "out of merge" on 12 original lists plus a list of merge-dupes. The other 6,000 names are either multiple duplicates (which appear on 3 or more lists) or bad addresses. In the case of this test mailing, we'll ignore all 6,000 of these names (since we're already mailing them at least once), but in a larger, continuation mailing we might mail many of them again. See Table 2.1 for a simplified look at how a merge-purge might work.

Does that sound nuts? It's not. The list of merge-dupes has a special function—one that helps to justify the cost and the time spent on the merge-purge. Since you've already paid for the duplicates at least twice (either in cash or in names to be exchanged), it's perfectly appropriate for you to *mail* to them twice. It's often profitable, since these are the names of those who are most likely to respond to your appeal. Some of these individuals are direct mail junkies who may contribute regularly to scores or even hundreds of organizations (and some are probably consultants like me who are reading everything the competition is sending out).

Chances are, you'll mail the merge-dupes three to six weeks following the main maildate of your test, and the list will likely perform at least as well as the average of the other twelve lists. Occasionally, it proves to be the *best* of them all. In a larger

```
11/05/02  STATSRUS                    TRIPLEX DIRECT MARKETING                    PAGE 2.000
```

| SF AIDS FOUNDATION MP9413A | | | MERGE/PURGE AT A GLANCE |

LIST NAME		ID#	LIST %
SFAF SEEDS		100	0.00
SFAF SAMPLE SEEDS		101	0.00
SFAF LOW	$1–24 .99 0–18	68	0.99
SFAF LAPSED	$25+ 19–36	69	1.17
SFAF FORMER	$25+ 37+	77	1.21
J CREW ACT BUYERS		3	2.08
INSTYLE MAGAZINE		42	2.52
RUN 01	$25+	202	2.84
ENTERTAINMENT WEEKLY		43	3.02
POTTERY BARN		64	3.53
METROPOLITIAN HOME		7	3.74
J. JILL		12	3.79
MARTHA STEWART M		36	4.53
AWSF 01 + 02	$50+	79	4.62
AM INST CANCER RESEARCH	$10+ 6 MO	10	4.69
SUN MAGAZINE		58	5.98
ARCHITECHURAL DIGEST		57	6.45
KQED		14	7.34
NATL FOUND CANCER RESRCH	$15+ 12 MO	50	7.74
ADVOCATE	(0–6 MO)	59	8.17
NEW YORKER	ACTIVE SUBS	44	8.21
SPECIAL OLYMPICS	$10+ 12 MO	45	9.05
OAKLAND SPCA		63	9.96
TARGET MODEL		46	10.07
PUBLIC CITIZEN		47	11.66
CAR 5–8	$25+	201	11.92
ALC 02	$25+	200	12.49
SF CONSERVATORY OF MUSIC		13	13.17
UCS		27	13.85
ORBIS		48	14.62
SAVE THE BAY		24	14.85
ACLU		29	15.25
AMNESTY INTERNATIONAL		25	15.36
OUT MAGAZINE	ACT SUBS	60	15.71
CARE	$10+ 12 MO	22	16.53
CLINTON PRES LIBRARY		18	16.82
LIBERATION PUBLICATION	ACT SUBS	61	18.50
JEWISH FMLY CHDRN SVC SF		21	18.78
SPLC	24 MO	20	18.98
HANDGUN CNTRL	BRADY CAMPAIGN	23	20.37
RAPHAEL HOUSE		53	23.78
LARKIN ST YOUTH SERVICES		54	27.33
GLAAD		28	31.38
TNDC		16	32.38
PROJECT OPEN HAND		8	32.92
GLSEN		26	34.23
AMFAR ACTIVE		62	56.59
NAMES PROJECT		51	59.56

```
          0%    10%   20%   30%   40%   50%   60%
                   % DUPLICATION TO ELIMINATOR(S)
```

EXHIBIT 2.4. Merge-Purge Summary Report.

Source: San Francisco AIDS Foundation. Reproduced with permission.

TABLE 2.1. Simplified Representation of a Small Merge-Purge.

List	Quantity Before Merge-Purge	Quantity After Merge-Purge
1	5,000	3,800
2	5,000	3,900
3	5,000	4,000
4	5,000	4,100
5	5,000	4,200
6	5,000	4,300
7	5,000	4,500
8	5,000	4,600
9	4,000	3,100
10	4,000	3,300
11	4,000	3,500
12	4,000	3,700
Merge-Dupes		3,000
Total	56,000	50,000

mailing, you might mail the names that appeared on three or more lists several weeks after the first wave of merge-dupes.

In this hypothetical example of a 50,000-piece test mailing, the "merge factor" or "dupe rate" (the percentage of names identified as duplicates or bad addresses) is 16 percent (9,000 divided by 56,000). In larger quantities, when you're mailing the full lists and not just small "test panels" of 5,000 names or so, that percentage will go *up*. (Don't ask me why. Blame it on statistics.)

In such cases, with high merge factors the economics of merge-purge will be favorable for you. Your 50,000-piece test mailing will save you the cost of mailing to 6,000 multiple duplicates and bad addresses. If your cost in the mail is $450 per thousand letters, that's a savings of $2,700—far more than you'll pay for the merge-purge. Of course, you might argue that you never had any intention of mailing to more than 50,000 individuals, but the truth is, you're getting the *benefit* of mailing to 56,000. In much larger quantities, if the merge factor is still high, the advantage might be even greater, since merge-purge costs fall more rapidly than most other mailing costs as quantities increase.

The merge-purge is just one of those many details that can make or break a donor acquisition mailing. As you suspect, no doubt, there are comparable factors that determine the outcome of a resolicitation mailing. By far the most significant of those factors is segmentation.

Segmenting Your Donor File for Resolicitation Mailings

To appreciate why segmentation is so very important, print out a portion of your donor file that will show, name by name, the amounts and dates of the gifts you've received from your donors over, say, the past five years. A glance will make it very clear to you (if it isn't already) that some donors are more equal than others. You'll see a few who've given unusually large gifts, others who've given many small ones, and yet others who used to give but haven't done so during the past year or two.

This wide variation in donor behavior, which is inevitable in any sizable population, is the underlying reality of segmentation—the process whereby we slice and dice a donor list into subgroups or segments. The purpose is to boost fundraising results by treating each segment in a manner consistent with its behavior—investing more time, effort, and money in resoliciting the most responsive donors and much less in appealing to those who have proven least responsive.

In fundraising, four principal criteria are used to define these segments:

1. *Recency:* Based on the last date on which a donor has contributed to your organization and usually measured in chunks. Donors whose last gift was received during the past six months, say, form one segment. Those whose last gift was received between seven and twelve months ago form another, and so forth.
2. *Frequency:* The number of gifts received from a donor during a particular period of time (sometimes one year, sometimes two or three). Measuring frequency, we usually distinguish between one-time donors (1x), two-time donors (2x), three-time donors (3x), and donors of four or more gifts (4x+).
3. *Monetary amount:* Often defined as either the highest previous contribution (HPC) received during the donor's entire history (or sometimes during a limited number of years) or as the last or most recent contribution (MRC). Some nonprofits may instead measure donors' cumulative giving, either in the course of the current year or over a lifetime of giving.
4. *Source or channel:* The means by which a donor's first gift (or most frequent gifts) has come to the organization. This criterion permits us to distinguish among direct-mail-acquired, telephone-acquired, and event-acquired donors, and donors from other sources. The distinction can be extremely significant, because donors who are accustomed to one such channel may be quite unresponsive to appeals they receive through other channels.

Combining these four criteria, we are able to identify those among an organization's donors who are the most responsive and those who are least so. A moment's thought will make clear that donors whose gifts are generous and who have contributed both frequently and recently are likely to be the most responsive to subsequent appeals. By contrast, those who have contributed only tiny amounts and on only rare occasions, the last of which was more than two years ago, are least likely to respond to renewed appeals. By applying a fourth criterion—the source or channel of giving—we might further narrow down the target population to include in a direct mail resolicitation appeal, eliminating event donors, for example, as they haven't established a history of responding to appeals through the mail.

For a stylized representation of this approach to segmentation, see Figure 2.2. As you can see, the very best donors cluster in the top near corner: they have frequently given generous gifts, and at least one of those gifts has been received in the last three months. The quality of the list diminishes as you move outward from that corner in any direction.

To see just how dramatically different the results can be from one segment to another, see Exhibit 2.5, which depicts the results from a resolicitation mailing. Most of the differences you see (in the rate of response to the mailing and in the amount of the average gift) are the result of the innate behavioral differences of the donor segments themselves. But those differences are exaggerated, because the

FIGURE 2.2. Three-Dimensional Representation of a Simple List Segmentation Plan.

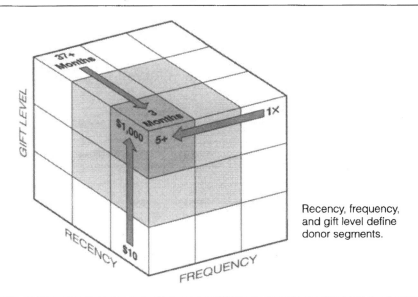

Recency, frequency, and gift level define donor segments.

Bread for the World—Project 60–83
Year-End Thank You—Ornament   **May 22, 2003**

Project type:	Special Appeal	Quantity:	15,417		
Mail date:	November 29, 2002	Budgeted cost:	$40,660	Projected revenue:	$75,000
Returns thru:	May 12, 2003 (114 days)	Final cost:	$35,805	Revenue to date:	$191,598

Segment	Quantity	Cost per piece	Total gifts	Pct resp	Total revenue	Avg gift	Rev per piece
Highest Previous Gift							
$1,000+	497	2.48	51	10.26%	100,710	1,974.70	202.64
$500–999	546	2.42	52	9.52%	11,416	219.53	20.91
$250–499	969	2.38	68	7.01%	11,615	170.80	11.99
$100–249	6,085	2.35	415	6.82%	34,172	82.34	5.62
$50–99	7,320	2.26	344	44.69%	14,048	40.83	1.92
Most Recent Gift							
13–18 months	576	2.36	24	4.16%	57,935	2,413.95	100.58
7–12 months	7,507	2.32	484	6.44%	73,689	152.25	9.82
0–6 months	6,806	2.32	411	6.03%	39,782	96.79	5.85
19–24 months	528	2.29	11	2.08%	555	50.45	1.05
Giving Frequency							
3+	13,902	2.32	859	6.17%	166,115	193.38	11.95
2x	719	2.33	40	5.56%	3,380	84.50	4.70
1x	796	2.35	31	3.89%	2,466	79.54	3.10
Miscellaneous							
Misc	0		83		19,637	236.58	
Project Totals	15,417	2.32	1,013	6.57%	191,598	189.13	12.42
Core Donor Analysis							
Hi-$ Core	15,414	2.32	930	6.03%	171,961	184.90	11.16
Lo-$ Core	3	2.26	0		0		

EXHIBIT 2.5. Flashcount for a Special Appeal Mailing (page 1 of 10 pages).

Source: Bread for the World. Reproduced with permission.

appeals sent to the most responsive segment were "personalized" (that is, they contained the donors' individual names and addresses), and they were mailed via first-class postage. Appeals mailed to the less responsive segments went via bulk mail.

● ● ●

OK. Now that you've got a sense of how your donor file may be segmented to maximize your fundraising results and how you can choose lists for donor or member acquisition mailings, it's time to turn to the process of preparing your initial test mailing. That's the subject of the following chapter.

3

Preparing Your Test Mailing

Let's be optimistic. We'll assume that the chair of your board's finance committee hasn't vetoed your plan to explore direct mail fundraising. In fact, she's helped you persuade other board members and your senior staff that the great potential in direct mail is worth the risk and the investment, even if you have to wait for several years to enjoy the payoff. You've budgeted the funds for a test mailing, obtained promises from board members of substantial additional capital if the test is successful, and contracted with a consultant who will work with you to develop the test package, acquire mailing lists, and manage the testing effort on your behalf.

Now, let's make sure we see eye-to-eye on some of the basic terms and premises of direct mail fundraising.

What Makes Direct Mail Work—or Fail

You, as the leader of your organization, are the most important ingredient in your direct mail program, not so much because of your management or marketing skills but because of the quality of your leadership. Over time, the perception people have of you and your work will account for at least half the credit (or blame) for the success or failure of your direct mail fundraising efforts.

Your organization's record and the credibility and power of your message, the ties of your work to issues of broad public concern, how much publicity you get, and how good it is—all these factors will help determine how well you do in the mails. But they're only half the story.

Several other factors—ingredients you and your consultants can control—will greatly influence the results of your efforts to raise money through direct mail. Together, these controllable factors are about equal in impact to the leadership, reputation, and programmatic assets that you bring to the program. If the half that's controllable is viewed as a pie, the pieces or segments of the pie would be (1) list selection, (2) the offer, (3) format, (4) copywriting, (5) design, and (6) timing. Each topic is discussed in turn.

1. *List selection.* As I note in Chapter One, this is far and away the most important controllable ingredient of a successful direct mail fundraising program; call it half the pie or about as much as all the other controllable elements combined. The most brilliant appeal for the most dynamic and well-managed organization in the world won't work at all if mailed to the wrong people. The lists selected for your initial donor acquisition test mailing must accurately reflect a cross-section of your potential constituency or "market." They should be lists that have been proven responsive to similar appeals. To make the right list choices for your mailing, someone will have to put in a great deal of time and effort. It's difficult to spend too much time selecting the lists.

2. *The offer.* How we structure the "pitch"—what we ask for and what we tell people they're going to get in return for their support—is the most important creative element in our work. Like list selection, I included the offer in my list of the ten most important things about direct mail fundraising. Call it 25 percent of the pie. Every package needs to be built around a marketing concept—a simple, straightforward connection between the offer and the market, or intended audience. Before we write a single word of copy, we spend as much time as necessary to find the right marketing concept and frame it with the right offer. The right decisions at this stage of development can make copywriting easy and stack the odds in favor of a successful outcome.

3. *Format.* The size, shape, and color of the envelope, the character of the inserts, the quality of the paper and printing, the appearance and accuracy of the recipient's name and address, and the extent (or lack) of personalization may all have significant bearing on the results. (*Personalization* is a regrettably inelegant term that signifies that the addressee's own name, address, or other known individual facts are printed somewhere in the package.) Making the right format choices, especially the size and shape of the package and whether or not to personalize (and if so to what extent), accounts for about 10 percent of the total. All the components of a direct mail package must fit together smoothly into an effective, working whole. Above all, a direct mail package must be not only cost-effective but also *credible*; the form of the package needs to match its purpose. We use a

very wide variety of formats because every fundraising campaign is unique and requires a unique competitive edge (see Table 3.1).

4. *Copywriting.* The actual wording of a fundraising appeal is less important than it's cracked up to be. Typically, the copywriter is responsible for researching the project and the letter-signer, devising the marketing concept, framing the offer, and in many cases for making major design and format suggestions as well; if all this is what is meant by copywriting, the job is absolutely crucial. But the copywriter's words themselves may not account for more than 5 percent of an appeal's success or failure. Many people insist that the letter is the single most important element in a direct mail package, and we put a great deal of effort into creating compelling fundraising letters. But there's more to writing a fundraising package than just creating the letter. We devote great care to the creation of the outer envelope, response device, and all other package elements. Good direct mail copywriting ties together all these pieces with the marketing concept.

5. *Design.* Once the format is set, the designer's skill can have influence on the outcome equal to that of the copywriter, or 5 percent of the total. Bad design can obscure or undercut the best of offers. There are a great many specialized techniques in the direct mail design trade. After years of trial, error, and heartache, typically including brochures too big and envelopes too small, direct mail designers become superbly skilled at putting these techniques to work for their clients.

6. *Timing.* It would be foolhardy to pretend that timing doesn't influence the outcome of a mailing. But timing comes into play in direct mail in two ways, only one of which is controllable. If you have the ill fortune to mail 300,000 donor acquisition letters to the San Francisco Bay Area the day before a major earthquake (as I did), you'll suffer the consequences of bad timing. (You needn't take the rap,

TABLE 3.1. **Factors That Make Mailings Work—or Fail.**

Factor	Contribution
Your organization's record, message, and leadership	50%
List selection (or segmentation)	25%
The "offer"	10%
Format	5%
Design	5%
Copywriting	5%

though. I certainly didn't!) However, if you fail to mail an appeal to your donors sometime during the final two months of the year, you'll surely be leaving money on the table, and it *will* be your fault. The jury is out on the impact of seasonality on direct mail fundraising results (although it's difficult to find a fundraising mailer who believes it's advantageous to mail during the depths of summer), but the advantage of mailing resolicitations at year-end is universally recognized, and there's general agreement that the first two months of the calendar year are relatively favorable as well. Taken as a whole, however, timing is a wildcard in the hand you're dealt when you launch a direct mail appeal. There's no point in assigning a percentage to it; it can be all-important or not at all important.

Now that all that's straight, you're ready to start. What's the first thing to do now? Think. Because you're going to need a Big Idea.

Your Marketing Concept

The marketing concept is the idea that pulls all the elements together—lists, offer, and signer—and ties them up with a bow. Direct mail fundraising is a form of marketing, and obtaining each individual contribution is a matter of closing a sale. Your "sales"—the monetary lifeblood of your organization—may sharply rise or fall as you succeed or fail in conceptualizing a marketing proposition that motivates your members, donors, or prospects. Keep this fundamental principle in mind:

> Each of your mailings requires a unique marketing concept. Every mailing and every marketing concept must fit into an overall marketing strategy.

If it makes you uncomfortable to use the language of marketing, you might think in terms of creative concepts or try an altogether different way of looking at the matter. Think about meeting donors' needs and solving their problems. Then your marketing concept might be thought of as the short form of a contract between you and your donors.

Your donors have to get something in return from you. Although their motives for contributing to your work may seem to be uncomplicated altruism, the act of giving money reflects deeply held values and beliefs and responds to inner drives for acceptance, for belonging, for feeling useful and effective, and for propagating their values and beliefs. (See my book, *How to Write Successful Fundraising Letters* [2001], for an analysis of these and other factors that motivate donors to give.) These powerful impulses create expectations that are dangerous to ignore. Your marketing concept needs to address some of these deep-seated needs in an explicit and meaningful way.

Ask yourself what satisfaction a donor will receive from making a contribution to your organization. It might derive from any—or many—of the following:

- "Doing something" about a critical problem, if only to protest or to take a stand
- Associating with a famous and noteworthy person
- Getting back at the corrupt or the unjust
- Belonging—as a member, friend, or supporter
- Speaking one's mind or offering an opinion
- Gaining access to inside information
- Learning about a complex problem or issue
- Being protected from the destruction of cherished values and beliefs
- Preserving one's worldview
- Gaining a personal connection to another individual who possesses an emotional, passionate involvement in some meaningful dimension of life
- Releasing emotional tension caused by a life-threatening situation, a critical emergency, or an ethical dilemma

A marketing concept won't work unless it can be expressed in a single sentence (although that sentence may be godawful complicated). To give you a sense of what I mean, here are four examples:

1. As one who appreciates the finer things in life, you will cherish for many years to come each magnificent issue of our bimonthly magazine on the visual arts, which you'll receive free of charge as a Charter Member of the Museum with a contribution of $45, $75, $150, or more, and you'll have the satisfaction of knowing that your gift will help us to showcase the exciting new work of emerging artists in our region.
2. By displaying the free stickers I'm sending you, signing the enclosed Protest Petition, and sending a tax-deductible gift of $25, $50, $100 or more to the Coalition, you will join thousands of other animal lovers in America who are committed to stopping once and for all the shameful and short-sighted murder of sea mammals.
3. As a former U.S. diplomat with firsthand experience in Third World hotspots, I am writing you and a few other distinguished Americans who have demonstrated a commitment to world peace, to ask you to join me as a Sponsor of the Institute's innovative new conflict-resolution program with a tax-deductible gift of $1,000.

4. Your renewal gift of as little as $25 to help house America's homeless children will buy $50 or more worth of lumber and tools, because it will be matched dollar for dollar by an anonymous donor through the Center's highly successful Matching Gift Program—so you'll get double the satisfaction from your act of generosity.

Note that each of these marketing concepts makes clear *whom* you're writing, *what* you want from them, *why* you need money, and what you're *offering* in return. A fully developed marketing concept must include all four of these elements. (Please note that I don't mean to suggest the overcooked prose in any of the examples would actually appear as-is in any fundraising package; they're simply summaries of marketing concepts.)

In each of the examples, the organization has clarified precisely what it wants from the donor—a particular sum of money and possibly other things as well—and what the donor will receive in return (although that may be implied or intangible). The marketing concept makes the connection between the signer of the appeal and the recipient, in recognition of the reality that the relationship will satisfy not only your organization's needs but the donor's needs as well.

Decide at the outset what you've got to "sell" and who you think will "buy" it. What you offer may be largely, or even exclusively, intangible, but even intangible benefits must be made explicit.

This task is akin to the fundamental challenge faced by any dynamic enterprise, whether nonprofit or commercial: figuring out what business you're really in. That may not be at all obvious. It may take considerable research and careful thought. But it's important you get it right.

Consider the four organizations cited in the foregoing examples:

1. In the eyes of the general public and in budgetary terms, the Museum's principal activity—the business it's in—may actually be to publish a bimonthly magazine on the visual arts, despite the fact that the Museum's board may consider its mission to be showcasing young local artists. The marketing concept rightfully focuses on the magazine.
2. The Coalition's lobbying campaign about the murder of sea mammals may require more funds and more staff time than the public education program that its strategic plan identifies as its primary mission. It may make more sense to say that the Coalition is in the business of influencing policymakers, not educating the general public. The Protest Petition highlighted in the marketing concept reflects this reality.
3. The Institute's "innovative new conflict-resolution program," envisioned as the centerpiece of its long-term strategy, may be less significant than its effort

to recruit hundreds of prominent American citizens as sponsors. The Institute may actually be in the business of organizing, lobbying, or doing public relations, not conflict resolution. It's appropriate that the marketing concept emphasize the many nonmonetary contributions sponsors make to the Institute.

4. Because of its focus on the needs of homeless families, the housing construction program instituted by the Center may be less important than the social services provided by Center staff. Thus the Center's marketing concept legitimately focuses on children and on donors' satisfaction at helping other people.

Unlike some other forms of advertising, *direct mail fundraising is rarely subtle.* When it is, its subtlety is simply and economically expressed. You have about four seconds for the recipient to decide whether to open your appeal. Once she's opened it, you may have another minute or two to involve her in reading the letter and to begin answering her many skeptical questions. Unless you want to lose her from the outset, you'd better be prepared to hit her over the head with a simple, straightforward proposition that's clear from beginning to end. Your principal task is to *motivate* the recipients of your appeals to *act* in a particular way—to reach for their checkbooks right away. In such circumstances, subtlety rarely works.

The very best direct mail packages reflect the marketing concept on every sheet of paper, from the outer envelope through the letter and supplementary enclosures to the response device (often called a coupon or reply device). Even the reply envelope won't escape unscathed if you think your concept all the way through from beginning to end. (In an emergency appeal, for example, you might print the name of the campaign or the word "Emergency" in the upper-left-hand corner of the reply envelope.) Effective outer-envelope teaser copy will draw the recipient directly into the package in a straight line to the heart of the marketing concept.

For example, a teaser might consist of brief copy along any of the following lines:

- Special Report to Members
- Here's something you can do RIGHT NOW about [fill-in-the-blank]
- Annual Renewal Enclosed
- [fill-in-the-blank] endangered! Please help us protect them!
- You have been nominated for a leadership role.
- National [fill-in-the-blank] Survey Enclosed. Please return within 10 days.

An effective teaser helps guide the reader along the way to the end of the process: sending a gift. But if the "end" is a check that arrives in the mail, the "beginning" is the market itself: that group of individuals to whom you're mailing your letter. No direct mail marketing concept will work unless it's firmly grounded in an understanding of the list or lists you use.

The Initial Test Mailing

As the very first step in a planned campaign to establish a broad financial base for your organization, my colleagues and I normally conduct a donor acquisition or prospect *test* mailing. Although the scope of initial tests varies from as few as 2,000 letters to as many as 500,000, we typically begin with a mailing of between 30,000 and 100,000 packages. Usually, a test mailing will involve from one to three different fundraising letters, each with its own marketing concept.

The character and contents of the packages we mail may vary considerably, but they all share at least one common feature: some mechanism to identify each resulting gift by its *source*. To study the results of the mailing, we have to distinguish among the returns from different lists and from different package versions (if more than one is mailed). Normally, this mechanism is a "keycode"—an alphanumeric symbol identifying the package and the list that correspond to each response we receive.

For example, the keycode 620218 might signify a response to the 18th list and the second of two packages in mailing number 62. Coding mechanisms of this sort allow us to *test* in what the more presumptuous direct mail specialists call a "rigorous, scientific manner."

The *goal* of the initial test mailing is to determine your organization's potential to sustain a cost-effective, broad-based, direct mail prospecting program through which you can build a substantial list of responsive donors. The specific *objectives* are typically as follows:

- To test at least six and perhaps as many as thirty lists from several different "markets" or constituencies for their potential to yield acceptable returns
- To produce donations over the first few months that recover a substantial portion of the cost of the test
- To generate hundreds of new donors, members, or subscribers
- To produce at least one marketing concept and package design that will be the basis for subsequent resolicitation and prospecting mailings—which is *most important of all for the future of your direct mail fundraising program*

A typical initial test mailing at 2003 prices costs from $35,000 to $80,000 (including all production and mailing costs as well as the consultant's fees). The average cost of a 50,000-piece test of one package was $30,000 to $45,000. Major cost variables include the number of different "packages" employed, the number of letters mailed, the consultant's fees, the quality of printing, the postage rate, and the technology used to print, address, and process the mailing. Receiving and processing responses, banking the money, and updating the donor list entail a modest additional cost. See Exhibit 3.1, which illustrates a budget for a typical 50,000-piece initial test mailing.

It's always difficult, at best, to estimate the returns from an initial test mailing, but it's rarely prudent to assume it will recover more than two-thirds of its cost, and successful tests sometimes return only one-third. We've occasionally conducted *profitable* test mailings, but I'm always loath to predict that outcome from an initial test. When starting a direct mail fundraising program from scratch, the management and creative fees can constitute a substantial overhead and raise the unit cost of the initial mailing. What you spend on the test mailing constitutes an *investment* in the possibility of a long-term development program.

ACQUISITION TEST MAILING

Prepared by Mal Warwick & Associates, Inc. for

GOODWORKS

Acquisition mailing #66-01

Letters to mail, budget: 50,000

Letters mailed, actual: 50,000

FINAL BUDGET

	Budgeted Cost per 1,000	Budgeted Cost	Percentage of Total
List rentals and exchanges	$100.00	$5,000.00	15.6
Merge-purge	17.00	850.00	2.7
Printing	138.00	6,900.00	21.6
Personalization and letter	30.00	1,500.00	4.7
Postage	150.00	7,500.00	23.4
Copywriting		6,500.00	20.3
Design and typesetting		1,250.00	3.9
Production management		1,000.00	3.1
Mailing fee	25.00	1,250.00	3.9
Shipping and miscellaneous		250.00	0.8
TOTAL COSTS		$32,000.00	100.0

EXHIBIT 3.1. Budget for a Typical 50,000-Piece Initial Test Mailing.

Ten to sixteen weeks normally elapse from the time you and your consultant agree to conduct an initial test mailing until the day it's in the mail. When bulk rate postage is used, the first returns are likely to arrive no sooner than ten days after the mail date, and it may be a total of three weeks before you receive *significant* returns. However, we usually prefer to wait for an additional three or four weeks of significant returns before drawing even preliminary conclusions about the effectiveness of the mailing. And to get a clear picture of the project—to draw conclusions about which lists might be included in a second, "continuation" mailing—we like to have a full eight to sixteen weeks of returns. In other words, a total of about five to eight months will elapse from the formal commitment to conduct a test mailing until the results are analyzed. In Table 3.2, you'll see a model timeline for an initial direct mail fundraising test.

In some cases, the timetable for the initial test can be accelerated and results made available much sooner, but that's not always advisable. Both creative development and list acquisition are complicated and time-consuming processes, often surprisingly so. Devising an effective marketing concept normally takes concentration and time. List brokers and computer service bureaus have timetables, procedures, and priorities of their own; so do printers and "lettershops" (where the individual components of your mailing will be collated, inserted, and packaged for the post office). It's risky to speed up the people who perform these vital services. Another of the ways corners can be cut (with uncertain effect) is to eliminate the merge-purge—the step in the process that reduces the number of duplicate appeals.

Choose the Right Signer

For reasons that are not entirely clear to me, at least one-third of the initial test mailings we've helped to launch over the years have been delayed—sometimes for more than *a year*—while the executive director or the board chair chased after the supposedly perfect signatory. It's not worth the wait.

In fact, you should immediately rule out the following three persons as prospective signers for your direct mail donor acquisition letter:

1. That Hollywood star you cornered at somebody else's fundraiser, who told you then he'd really love to help you out
2. The famous novelist who went to college with the chair of your board and who could probably help punch up the letter a little bit, too (and maybe even write it herself)
3. That college professor who's a world-renowned expert in the issue your group is addressing and is well known to all forty-five people in his field

That famous novelist, actor, or expert *may* have the name recognition to get an envelope opened, but will anyone be convinced she knows what she's talking

TABLE 3.2. **Timeline for an Acquisition Test Mailing.**

Time	Action	Notes
7 weeks before maildate	Let list broker know that a mailing is scheduled.	Send a sample of mailing, prior results if available, lists to begin clearing. You'll need to have at least one of the packages written and approved at this stage so that the prospective lists can see what you're sending out. The broker will have some suggestions for tests. Give two weeks for lists to clear.
5 weeks before maildate	Order lists after sending a list plan to client for approval.	Allow two weeks for lists to be delivered to merge-purge house.
3 weeks before maildate	All copy should be finalized and sent to designer for art.	
19 days before maildate	List should be "cut" (merge instructions to data management house completed).	Merge takes 7 days, 9 with a national change of address (COA).
2 weeks before maildate	Art should be finalized and approved and sent to printer.	
13 days before maildate	Client sends house file to data management house for suppression.	
10 days before maildate	Merged list should be shipped to printer on a Friday for Monday arrival.	
7 days before maildate	List arrives for personalization and package preparation.	
Maildate	All packages "drop." Remember, with bulk-rate nonprofit postage, the USPS has eleven days to process your mailing and deliver it to your prospective donors.	
3 weeks after maildate	Multi-buyers (names that appear on two or more of the lists you rented) drop.	

about? Is she genuinely involved in your issue, preferably in *your* organization as a long-time board member or volunteer? Is her image such that she'll be taken seriously? What will she say if someone asks her a question about you on a TV talk show? And is she really widely known among the general public and not just to a narrow audience? Name recognition is easily overestimated, and it may not last.

For a successful direct mail fundraising program, the person who signs your appeal needs to be prepared for the long haul, too. Does she understand that if the letter works well, you need to mail it again and again to achieve economies of scale? Or will she inform you after you've printed her name on 250,000 envelopes for the next mailing that she's decided not to allow you to use her name anymore? (Yes, you guessed it: this actually happened to me.)

Now, how about copy approval? Is that Hollywood star of yours available to review the draft of the letter, or is he on location in Tashkent for the next four months and reachable only by camel train? Will his agent, manager, or assistant actually show him your letter? Once the copy reaches him, will he declare dogmatically that he won't sign anything longer than one page? Will he insist on rewriting the letter because it doesn't fit his image to ask directly for money? Will he refuse to allow you to include any references to his own, relevant experiences because "that's too personal"? Will he sit indecisively on the text without responding to your phone calls, while the maildate for your test slips ever farther into the dim recesses of the future?

Lest these problems sound farfetched, I hereby affirm that I have encountered every single one of them at least once, and in some cases five or six times, within the past two decades. This experience has helped lead me to the conclusion that the chief executive of your organization is probably the very best signatory for your donor acquisition letter.

After all, who can more *credibly* tell your story than you? A famous name alone is no guarantee of good response for a direct mail appeal. Time and again, I've seen appeals signed by Hollywood stars or celebrated authors outclassed by comparable letters mailed over the signatures of unknown, unsung staff or board members.

Staff signatures don't seem to work as well in politics as they do for nonprofit groups. Generally, it's essential that the *candidate* sign fundraising appeals. However, sometimes the campaign manager or fundraising chair may be a stronger signatory than even the most famous political candidate. In all cases, the key is *credibility.*

If someone else can tell your story more credibly than you—someone with good name recognition to boot—you may be well advised to take a back seat. If you do, just be sure the signatory you've selected has really bought into the process and won't cause more trouble than he's worth.

And lest you're tempted, out of insecurity, a need to compromise, or other motives to *cosign* your letter with a second person who will lend authority to the appeal, keep this in mind:

A direct mail fundraising appeal is not a manifesto. It's a one-to-one communication—a letter from one person to another, written in the first person singular and addressed in the second person singular. Its success requires an emotional bond between the two. Only one person can sign a fundraising letter.

Whatever *individual* can write most convincingly and emotionally about your work is the best person to sign your appeal.

Mastering Design and Production

It's all too easy to get carried away with the fun of crafting a marketing concept, writing copy, and selecting lists and forget that somebody's actually got to get your appeal printed and in the mail. This is not as easy as it may sound. There may be as many as two or three *dozen* organizations that participate in one way or another in the production process, and someone needs to monitor their work. Here are the players in the production of a typical direct mail donor acquisition mailing:

- The *U.S. Postal Service,* which lays down stringent rules and regulations for direct mail format and design and requires a significant amount of paperwork from every nonprofit mailer—all of which must be in good order before the mailing may be printed. Naturally, the postal service plays the central role in distributing the mailing as well, and its schedules need to be taken into account when planning a mailing. (For example, the production manager must build extra slack into the schedule during the final weeks of the year, when the volume of mail is at its peak.)
- The *list broker,* who coaches you on list selection, "clears" the lists (that is, secures permission from list owners for you to mail), and then "orders" the lists you ultimately decide to mail (that is, sends instructions to the list owners' service bureaus or data processing departments to supply copies of the appropriate portion of each list).
- The *list owners or their service bureaus*—perhaps several dozen of them in a large mailing—each of which must "fulfill" the list broker's orders and deliver the correct number and selection of names to be merge-purged.
- The *merge-purge house* or service bureau, which must assemble and merge the lists, converting them to its standard format if necessary, and run the merge-purge operation, forwarding the "output" to be used to address and keycode the mailing.
- The *designer,* who must find the most effective way to lay out the copy and prepare artwork for the printers, following both the project budget and any

design specifications laid down either by the copywriter or by the production manager.

- The *printers,* often including at least two companies (one to print the flat components of the package, the other a specialist in printing envelopes), which are responsible for delivering finished material to be collated and assembled at the same time as the merge-purge output arrives. (From time to time, when special operations such as die-cuts or binding are involved, there may be a third or fourth company involved as well.)
- The *lettershop,* where the package elements are stuffed and addressed and postage affixed, if necessary. (Occasionally, this involves two steps using different vendors, one to print the names, addresses, and other personalized data on the printed material, the other to collate and assemble the package.)

As you might imagine, all this scattered activity can present a daunting management challenge. The production manager, whether on your in-house staff, employed by your consulting firm, or working freelance by contract, must be an extremely competent manager. To get a mailing out on time requires careful advance planning and an almost obsessive effort to stick to the schedule.

The Best Time to Mail Your Appeal

"The best time to mail your appeal is when you've got it printed and there's enough postage in your account." When my direct mail mentor gave that answer to an earnest question I'd asked about seasonal influences on direct mail fundraising, I didn't know whether to be puzzled or annoyed. Then came five or six years during which I watched appeals be delayed by red tape, procrastination, reluctant funders, screwups in the postal system, and computer crashes, as well as arguments about seasonality. Finally, several dozen clients later, I understood at last:

> If you're waiting for the perfect time to mail, your letters may never make it to the mailbox. And if there's any key to success in direct mail fundraising, it's this: you have to mail, and mail, and mail some more.

Yes, there *are* seasonal influences on direct mail fundraising, just as there are on most other forms of marketing. A seasonality study conducted by a leading list brokerage firm showed that in one twelve-month period an estimated 20 percent of all fundraising appeals went into the mails in November, whereas 14 percent were mailed in August and nearly 12 percent in February. But those figures change greatly over time, according to the same study. My agency's own testing has shown January and August to be the most favorable months for prospecting, increasingly so in recent years. Chances are, though, the patterns of seasonality will be different for *your* organization than they are for others. And unless you've got a huge budget for testing, you may never be able to afford the research needed to determine the seasonal patterns that bear on your particular direct mail program.

And besides, you can't possibly mail *only* during what you think is the "best time."

Some groups limit their prospecting to one or two large mailings per year, presumably in the most favorable months. With sufficient capital, that may well be a defensible donor acquisition strategy. (However, sticking to a single donor acquisition mailing each year virtually eliminates the possibilities of testing package variations or mailing the very best lists more than once annually, and a single, large prospect mailing puts substantial strain on an organization's cash flow.)

Resolicitations are another matter altogether: donor resolicitation is a year-round process. As much as 40 percent of all the funds contributed by mail are donated within the final two months of the calendar year and the first month of the following year. For most—not all—nonprofit organizations, November and December are the best times to seek renewal gifts. But the most successful year-end appeal won't come close to making up the revenue lost by failing to resolicit your donors during the other ten months of the year.

Keep in mind, too, that a month that's dead time for one group's fundraising program may be fruitful for another's. We've often found that mailing during months that are generally avoided by large, established charities produces better results for organizations that are less well known. Not everyone can compete with the Sierra Club or the Salvation Army, and you might be unwise to try.

● ● ●

Now, please join me in Chapter Four. There, we'll take a look at the typical contents of a direct mail fundraising package and at some of the issues commonly raised about them.

4

Anatomy of a Direct Mail Fundraising Package

n this chapter, I'll show you in pictures and words the individual components of a typical direct mail fundraising package.

Keep in mind as you examine each of the elements portrayed in this chapter that there is no best or perfect example of any one of them. Every element in a successful direct mail fundraising package is a part of a *whole,* unified by a marketing concept.

In Part Three, we'll take an inside look at four years in a particular nonprofit direct mail program. There you'll have an opportunity to examine, page by page, the entire contents of several fundraising packages that were written for one organization in the course of four years of work.

Right now, though, let's take a quick look at what many fundraisers consider the most important element in a direct mail package: the outer envelope.

The Outer Envelope

Outer envelopes, otherwise called carrier envelopes or simply carriers or outers, come in a bewildering profusion of shapes, sizes, and colors. Occasionally, direct mail fundraising appeals are packaged without envelopes, in the form of self-mailing brochures or magazines or in such nontraditional formats as "card decks" (which are just about what they sound like they are). But most fundraisers keep coming back to the boring old technique of inserting letters in envelopes because, most of the time, it *works* better than other formats.

Direct mail designers, copywriters, and envelope manufacturers wrack their brains for ever newer and more unusual wrappings, in relentless pursuit of the envelope to end all envelopes: one that *everyone* will open (see Exhibit 4.1). But reality intrudes; through our research, we've learned that, despite all these clever machinations to capture their attention, what people really look at first is how their names and addresses are spelled!

Postage

In its inscrutable wisdom, Congress requires the U.S. Postal Service to offer a wide variety of postal rates and delivery options. Although runaway inflation has reduced the advantage (and federal budget cutting has almost entirely eliminated it), slightly lower rates are still available to most nonprofit organizations. The very cheapest rate applies to huge mailings that are presorted into bundles for individual letter-carriers, but discounts are also available on first-class postage if you presort. There are also several format options: stamps, metered postage, and preprinted postal "indicia." Choosing among them is not a trivial matter, because any one may significantly affect a mailing's results.

It's tempting to use the least expensive postage, but here's another one of those counterintuitive aspects of direct mail: the opposite is often true. We make extensive use of first-class postage because it gets there faster and more reliably, because it's forwardable, because it gets more envelopes opened, and, most of all, because research sometimes shows that first-class postage is more *cost-effective* than cheaper postal rates. Ultimately, you usually get just what you pay for (see Exhibit 4.2).

The Letter

If I've heard it once, I've heard it ten thousand times: "Why do you insist on sending out these godawful four-page letters? *I* never write such long letters, and I'm sure I'd never *read* them!"

Well, let's review the facts: (1) By testing this proposition again and again, we know that, most of the time, longer letters generate more donations than shorter ones, and (2) studies show that lots of people actually do read four-page fundraising letters; in fact, many people even *like* getting them. This continues to be true even now, after years of overflowing mailboxes and even though *you* may automatically throw them into the trash. Ultimately, direct mail fundraising doesn't work on theory or intuition but on empirical fact.

Fundraising letters are almost as varied as the envelopes they're mailed in. But they're not much like business or personal letters, or even like advertising copy. Direct mail fundraising follows rules and rhythms of its own.

EXHIBIT 4.1. Outer Envelopes from Direct Mail Fundraising Packages.

Sources: Save-the-Redwoods League, reproduced with permission; National Council of La Raza, reproduced with permission; Feingold Senate Committee, reproduced with permission.

EXHIBIT 4.2. Postage Options Used in Direct Mail Fundraising.

Sources: National Council of La Raza. Reproduced with permission.

Keep in mind, too, that the typical direct mail donor is a well-educated, church-going woman in her sixties. She may be one or even two generations older than the nonprofit staff members who raise objections to long letters—and she just might have different reading habits! A successful appeal letter is likely to include five essential ingredients:

1. It establishes a one-on-one *linkage* or identification between the letter-signer and the person to whom the letter is addressed.
2. It presents an *offer* of an opportunity to participate in your organization (as a subscriber or member, for example, or by supporting some particular program).

    3. It makes a compelling *case* for the offer.
    4. It establishes *urgency.*
    5. It *asks* for a specific sum of money.

The reason most direct mail letters include these five ingredients is that testing proves fundraising appeals usually work better if they do. And that, in turn, is why they're typically long; it's often hard to tell enough of the story in just one or two pages to motivate a donor to act. To work well, a letter needs to make every reasonable argument for the donor to send money now and to anticipate—and satisfy—every reasonable objection.

The Reply Device

A detached, stand-alone reply device or response device or form (occasionally called a donation coupon, though I don't favor the term) has repeatedly proven to be an indispensable element in fundraising packages, with only rare exceptions. For one thing, using a reply device is the most efficient way for you to obtain the donor's name and address, which normally appears on a label or direct imprint on the reply device. But there's an even more important reason we include these devices. Studies show that donors are more likely to respond if they're given something to *do* other than just write and return a check. If nothing else, they give donors a chance to correct the spelling of their names and addresses. The reply device is the first thing most donors see when they open a fundraising package. Many donors set appeals aside, promising themselves they'll write checks later; they often keep reply devices but toss out the letters.

Many reply devices offer special opportunities for extra *involvement:* checking boxes, filling out surveys, signing petitions, or the like. Response rates tend to rise the more such opportunities a package offers, but the average gift often falls at the same time, since many of those who return petitions or surveys will send a dollar or two, presumably to help with "processing," instead of the larger sums the letter suggests. Involvement devices such as petitions usually aren't effective in fundraising, however, when they're added gratuitously such as in a magazine sweepstakes offer; they work best when there's a credible link with the organization's strategy. (See Exhibit 4.3.)

The Reply Envelope

Direct mail fundraising appeals work best when it's easy for a donor to respond. This almost always means they'll include a reply envelope, and most of the time it will be a business reply envelope (BRE) that the donor can mail postage-free without hunting for a stamp. (It will cost your organization $150 to open a business

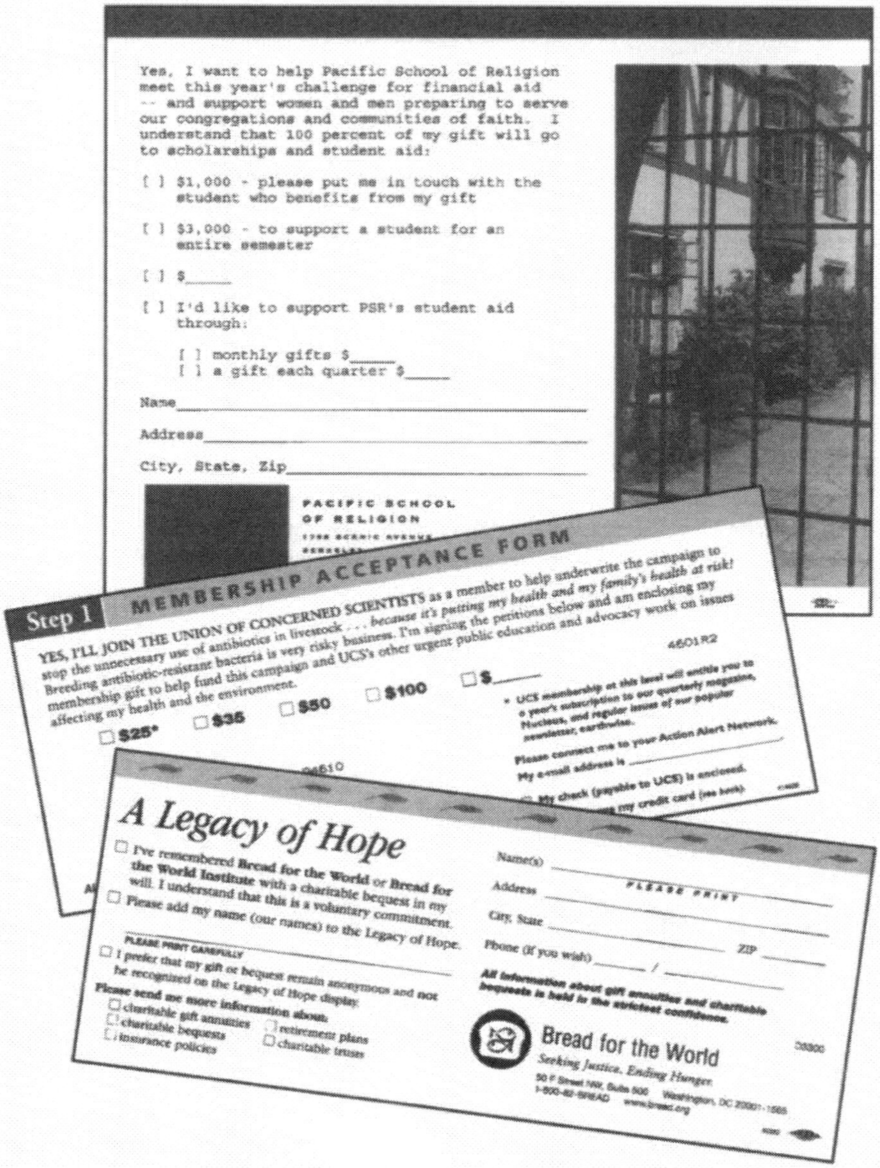

EXHIBIT 4.3. Response Devices from Direct Mail Fundraising Packages.

Sources: Pacific School of Religion, reproduced with permission; Union of Concerned Scientists, reproduced with permission; Bread for the World, reproduced with permission.

reply account and another $0.47 to $0.97 per item to process your return mail. To qualify for the lower rate, you must pay another $475 and deposit additional funds to cover the return postage in advance.) But in many circumstances it makes sense to ask donors to affix their own stamps; some organizations obtain higher response when they do. Other times, it's wise to put a "live stamp"—a real, live first-class stamp—on the reply envelope. Only experience and testing can establish the appropriate approach for each mailing.

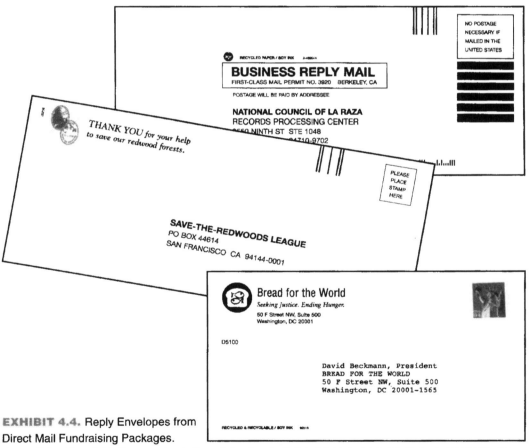

EXHIBIT 4.4. Reply Envelopes from Direct Mail Fundraising Packages.

Sources: National Council of La Raza, reproduced with permission; Save-the-Redwoods League, reproduced with permission; Bread for the World, reproduced with permission.

The Brochure

For some reason (which has always escaped me), many organizations want to include their general brochure in an initial direct mail fundraising test. This is rarely a good idea. The marketing concept at the heart of a fundraising appeal needs to be tightly focused; everything in the package should address that same focus. Even a brochure specifically designed and written for your direct mail package—one built on the same marketing concept—may not be much better than your general brochure. More often than not, testing shows that informational brochures *depress* rather than enhance response. They seem to distract donors from the essential task we want them to undertake: writing a check.

However, there are exceptions. From time to time, I have had exceptionally good luck with brochures specially written and designed to be included in a special appeal or renewal mailing *when those brochures strongly reiterated the ask*, effectively reinforcing the message in the letter, not supplementing it. (See Exhibit 4.5, which includes examples plucked more or less at random from my mailbox.)

Front-End Premiums

Ask anyone in the advertising business to identify the most powerful word in the English language, and you're likely to be told the word is *free*. Wonder no more, then, why so many direct mail fundraising packages come with free stickers, decals, stamps, key chains, address labels, letter-openers, bumper stickers, and other such items. These are so-called front-end premiums, as opposed to back-end premiums, which are sent only in response to gifts from donors. The psychology established by these unsolicited free gifts is not subtle: the operative mechanism is *guilt,* and it's no accident that many donors send in a dollar or two in response. But there may be better reasons for you to use front-end premiums; at their best, decals, stamps, and such can also be effective involvement devices that give donors something to do, reinforce the marketing concept, heighten your organization's visibility, and even play a role in your public education program. (See Exhibit 4.6.)

Other Enclosures

Some direct mail packages are fattened up with additional enclosures. There are "lift letters" signed by celebrities or experts, which are normally brief and to the point. There are "buckslips"—usually small slips of paper that dramatically illustrate some attractive feature of the offer, such as a free calendar or book in return for gifts above a certain level, or highlight some up-to-the-minute information about the organization's work. There are news clippings, internal memoranda, budgets,

EXHIBIT 4.5. Brochures from Direct Mail Fundraising Packages.

Sources: Democrat-Republican brochure, from the New Majority Education Fund, reproduced with permission; Bush brochure, composed and designed by Friends of the Earth and Lewis Direct, reproduced with permission.

and other supporting documents meant to strengthen the letter's case for supporting your organization. Only methodical testing can establish when these items will improve the results. Often they don't.

The possibilities for enclosures are virtually endless. (See Exhibit 4.7.)

Putting It All Together

As you can see, putting a direct mail fundraising package together is not simply a matter of writing a letter and wrapping it up. In fact, the letter is often the *last* element I write. Rather, the entire package must reflect a clearly thought out marketing concept. Once that is fixed in your mind and on paper, you can start with any

EXHIBIT 4.6. Front-End Premiums from Direct Mail Fundraising Packages.

Sources: DSD Management and Fundraising Services created the pets premium for the East Bay SPCA, reproduced with permission; AIDS Project labels from AIDS Project Los Angeles, reproduced with permission; Amnesty International sticker from Amnesty International, reproduced with permission.

element of the package. In most cases, I begin with the reply device, which encapsulates the marketing concept.

The outer envelope, which gives donors or prospects their first look at your package, bears special consideration and may take a lot of work. Some writers claim they spend a third or more of the time allotted to copywriting and design on the copy for the outer envelope, especially in the case of acquisition packages. An especially clever or provocative teaser, calculated to entice prospects to open the envelope, may be the hardest thing of all to write. But the very biggest challenge is to write outer envelope copy that is fully consistent with everything *inside* the envelope and leads recipients directly into the marketing concept.

All the pieces in a direct mail package must fit together neatly or they'll confuse rather than motivate. They'll prompt a response only if you've carefully thought through your marketing concept before you start to write.

In this chapter, I focused on the contents of donor acquisition packages. In theory, there's little difference in the contents of acquisition and resolicitation mailings. But in reality, for most nonprofits special appeals and renewal packages are

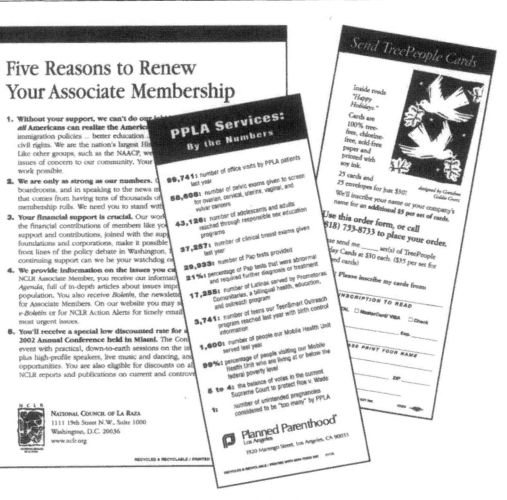

EXHIBIT 4.7. Other Enclosures from Direct Mail Fundraising Packages.

Sources: National Council of La Raza, reproduced with permission; Planned Parenthood Los Angeles, reproduced with permission; TreePeople, reproduced with permission.

slimmer than those used in most acquisition mailings. Budgetary limitations dictate that in most cases. A typical special appeal for a fair-to-middling-size nonprofit organization is likely to consist only of a letter, a response device, and both outer and reply envelopes.

● ● ●

Now let's turn our attention to a few of the enclosures that require a closer look: premiums and involvement devices. That's the topic we'll take up in Chapter Five.

Premiums and Other Involvement Devices

If you think for one minute that you can ever know why a donor chooses to open one of your fundraising letters—even if you *ask* him—then you're on the wrong track and have a lot to learn about donor motivation. Chances are, there are both rational and irrational factors at work in every case, and the range of possible explanations is bewilderingly broad. Consider, for example, the following possible reasons:

- He feels a deep connection with your organization and will open any envelope you send him, regardless of what you've printed on the outside.
- He's bored and hopes to find something interesting inside.
- Your organization represents a cause in which he has considerable interest.
- He thinks your letter comes from another, similar organization he has supported in the past.
- The teaser copy you've printed on the outer envelope intrigues him.
- You mangled the spelling of his name, and he wants to find out what jerks could screw it up so badly.
- He's gotten letters from you in the past that he's never opened, and he figures it's about time to find out what you've got to say.

The list is probably limitless. But even such a short list as this should include at least one other possible explanation:

> He opened your letter because he knows it contains something of value—and it's free.

Those things of value—the front-end premiums I introduced in the preceding chapter—undoubtedly cause tens of millions of direct mail fundraising letters to be opened every year. Many of the nonprofit world's biggest and most successful direct mail programs have been built on the back of front-end premiums such as name-stickers, calendars, greeting cards, key chains, pencils, pennies, and even books.

The Pros and Cons of Front-End Premiums

The simple fact that front-end premiums induce (or help induce) people to open fundraising letters is the key to their widespread use. In a word, they usually *increase response.* More people open letters containing free gifts, and more people respond. We know that front-end premiums increase the number of responses because we mail packages with and without them and almost invariably see the response rise when they're included.

However, we also know that adding a front-end premium to a direct mail fundraising package typically lowers the average gift mailed in response, sometimes dramatically so. It's common to find lots of small contributions—many as little as a dollar or two, frequently in cash—among the responses to a front-end premium package. Anecdotal evidence strongly suggests that these tiny donations result from the belief of many donors that they're obligated to pay for what they get (even if the copy clearly states that they're not). And they mistakenly believe a dollar or two will cover the cost of the premium, no doubt unaware of the reality that processing a single small gift might cost a charity more than the amount they've been sent.

These two phenomena illustrate the strongest arguments raised both for and against the use of front-end premiums. "They boost response," say the advocates. "They attract contributions that don't represent philanthropic motives," respond the critics. "And you have to send them more premiums to get them to respond again." The advocates' argument is self-evident. The critics' is harder to demonstrate.

Some long-term studies have, indeed, shown that donors acquired through premium-based direct mail programs are less loyal and less responsive to subsequent solicitations. Others have shown that there is no discernible difference in performance between donors acquired with premiums and those recruited without them.

In practice, this becomes tantamount to a theological discussion. What it boils down to is this: some fundraisers just don't *like* premiums. Others say, "Whatever works."

If you're like most fundraisers and undecided about which way to turn, here are a few questions to ask yourself and your colleagues when you consider whether to test front-end premiums in your donor acquisition mailings:

- Are you planning to test a premium that's appropriate for your organization—one that relates, at least in some indirect way, to your mission, one that helps educate the public about your cause, or that helps increase your organization's visibility?
- Do you have the staff and systems in place to cope with a larger than normal number of responses, including many very small gifts, some of them in cash?
- Do you have—or are you planning to build—a very large donor file, so that it will be cost-effective for you to resolicit donors of very small sums? (Production and mailing costs may be too high for you to send appeals to $5 or $10 donors unless you can realize substantial economies of scale, as those donors are unlikely to send you more than another $5 or $10.)
- Is the look and feel of the premium-based package you're considering consistent with the public image of your organization? Many—by no means all—premium-based packages are decidedly downscale in appearance. For some nonprofits, this may pose a disadvantage.

While you stew on these troublesome questions, consider for a moment another potential application of premiums in direct mail fundraising: the back-end premium.

Back-End Premiums

You've probably encountered back-end premiums dozens of times as you sort through your mail. The give-away usually reads something like this: "FREE with your membership gift of $25 or more." The offer of a back-end premium might be made in any one or several of the following ways:

- In a teaser on the outer envelope
- On the response device
- In the text of the letter
- In a postscript
- On a buckslip (see Chapter Four)

A back-end premium may be a book, a backpack, a bauble, or any one of thousands of other possible rewards for sending a gift. Although it's important that a front-end premium be appropriate to the organization that sends it, it's even more vital that a back-end premium resonate with the nonprofit's mission or character. Front-end premiums are, necessarily, inexpensive items obviously calculated to encourage readers to respond. Back-end premiums, which are often significantly more expensive, more clearly reflect on the organization.

An environmental organization can appropriately send new members a fanny-pack, because environmental donors are presumably more interested in the outdoors than the general public is. A cancer research organization would probably raise eyebrows if it sent a fanny-pack. There's no reason to believe that donors to a cancer research organization would have any special love for the outdoors. More important, one of its donors might well think it's curious (or objectionable) if a medical research group spent money on fanny-packs. However, prospective donors to either organization might not think twice if they received a front-end set of name-labels in a membership invitation package.

Cost is always a consideration with premiums. A premium must make a package more cost-effective. The added cost it represents needs to be returned—ideally, many times over—in additional revenue from the mailing. It's simple to determine whether a front-end premium works: all you need to do is to compare the acquisition cost with and without it. Back-end premiums sometimes present a bigger challenge.

Consider, for example, a direct mail campaign in which a group we'll call The Coalition offers a free book, written by its executive director, as an incentive for donors to contribute $50 or more. The book costs The Coalition $5 to produce and ship, and repeated testing makes it clear that the offer increases the average gift per donor by $4. Obviously, a straightforward reading of the numbers suggests that the book offer is *not* cost-effective. Any time I have to pay $5 for a $4 value, I'll question the purchase, as will you. But think about the following facts before you reach a conclusion:

- Overall, the book offer raised the average gift from $29 to $33. But it *doubled* the number of $50 donors. And experience shows that donors whose first gift is $50 or higher are substantially more responsive and loyal than donors who first contribute $25 or $30.
- Those $50 donors who received (and may have read) the executive director's book have been positively reinforced in their support for The Coalition. Even if the book just sits on a shelf, it's an enduring reminder of the donor's connection with the organization. And there's no way to gauge the value of *that!*

How, then, do you evaluate the effectiveness of the back-end premium? In this hypothetical case, it's a judgment call. As a fundraiser focused on building long-term relationships with donors, my judgment would err on the side of the premium.

Donor Involvement Devices

There is something "involving" about almost every premium. When I pick up a set of name-labels and turn them over in my hands, I'm involved, just as I would be when I finger a key chain, a bookmark, a calendar, or almost any other front-end premium that presents me with an opportunity for a tactile experience. When I look forward with anticipation to receiving The Coalition's free book, I'm involved. In either case, there's a new dimension added to my relationship with the organization that goes beyond the level, because I have transcended the role of passive reader and become actively involved.

However, there are many other ways to involve donors in a direct mail fundraising package. These include surveys, petitions, quizzes, postcards, and other devices that require the reader to take some action in support of the organization or its mission beyond sending a contribution.

As with front-end premiums, the result is typically to raise the rate of response and to lower the average gift. However, there's an added benefit that comes from the use of such involvement devices: the respondents are usually good prospects for donor acquisition the second—or even the third—time around. It's not unusual for such lists of "warm prospects" to respond at a rate two or three times that of the average donor on a prospect list. Given the continuing challenge of finding responsive donor acquisition lists, this can be a decided advantage.

Under the right circumstances, premiums and other involvement devices can enhance a direct mail fundraising program. But the circumstances aren't always right. Sometimes the organization's strategy doesn't lend itself to such an approach.

Stick to Your Strategy

Ponder these two contrasting hypothetical cases.

Case 1

Because the mission of End Injustice Now! is to seek changes in public policy, it's engaged in extensive grassroots lobbying efforts. The organization must recruit tens or hundreds of thousands of supporters to build pressure on Congress to oppose critical legislation. Its direct mail fundraising program can directly support its mission by including opportunities for donors to act within both acquisition and resolicitation packages.

Case 2

By contrast, the Metropolitan Symphony Orchestra is intent on involving its supporters in quite a different way: by persuading them to attend its concerts as well as to contribute cash contributions. The Symphony's donor acquisition mail could conceivably include complimentary concert tickets (or discount coupons), but other sorts of involvement devices might distract readers from its core message. In addition, marketing research has clearly demonstrated to the Symphony that both its audience and its donors are upscale. Inexpensive premiums (such as name-stickers, for example) might well detract from the Symphony's appeal to its prime market.

There is, then, something inherent in the appeal of certain nonprofit organizations (or of particular fundraising campaigns) that either lends itself to the use of premiums or does not. But there is another crucial reason premiums or involvement devices may not be suitable for your organization: your fundraising strategy simply may not require them.

Let's say, for example, that your principal goal is to lower your cost of fundraising (that is, to pursue a strategy centered on efficiency). Or, to take an even simpler case, there could be a ceiling on fundraising expenses in your budget. Both premiums and involvement devices cost money, of course, and in either of these circumstances it may be important simply to spend less money on fundraising, even at the cost of sacrificing the additional net revenue you might gain from premium-based mailings.

However, if premiums or involvement devices seem to lend themselves well to your fundraising strategy, be careful: you can't dabble in premiums. The character of your direct mail program (and of your fundraising program as a whole) is likely to be changed by extensive use of premiums. Usually, the most effective way to renew donors acquired through premium-centered direct mail is to offer—you guessed it—more premiums. And if donors become used to participating in your work through involvement devices such as petitions or postcards, they may respond less well if you suddenly decide to eliminate such devices. The use of premiums and involvement devices is not a trivial matter. Use them thoughtfully.

● ● ●

Now we're ready to move on. We'll assume that you've conducted your test mailing and are pondering what to do next. Will you plunge deeper into the world of direct mail fundraising or write off the initial experience as an unfortunate diversion? In the opening section of Chapter Six, which follows, we'll examine how you may determine the success or failure of your initial test mailing.

Building Your Donor Base

've described the ideal direct mail prospecting program as one that attracts new donors at an acceptable acquisition cost. But what does *acceptable* mean to you?

Take my word for it: the breakeven prospecting that may seem acceptable in the abstract could be impossible for you to attain. You could be making a big mistake to hold yourself to that standard simply because it seems right somehow. Building your donor base will mean a great deal to your organization. It may be worth paying a lot of money to keep your list growing. Your challenge is to figure out how *much* it's worth.

In Chapter Seven, we'll examine several different methods for evaluating the worth of the donors you recruit through prospecting. You may then be able to apply specific numbers to your donor acquisition program, establishing criteria that relate uniquely to your organization's strategy and the role you've assigned to the direct mail program. In this chapter, we'll look at the possibilities and the pitfalls of sustaining a direct mail fundraising program over the long term. First, let's figure out whether it's worth trying.

The Difference Between Success and Failure

You've finally gotten enough results from your initial test mailing to tell the story, and what they say is absolutely clear and unequivocal: *maybe* it's going to work. Here, briefly, is what's happened.

You've tested two slightly different versions of one package using samples from ten lists, splitting each of them down the middle. The total cost of this 50,000-piece test was $35,000. Your projections show that you'll receive a total of $22,500, and despite cautionary warnings, your board of directors had been expecting at least $30,000. From this initial test, you'll gain about 500 donors at an acquisition cost of $25 per donor—a level that is too high for your organization to sustain. (That's calculated as $35,000 − 22,500 = 12,500 ÷ 500 = $25.)

Judging from the latest "flashcounts"—periodic list-by-list reports—one of the two package versions appears to be performing slightly better than the other; a statistical analyst who isn't too much of a purist would agree that it's a better bet for the future. It might even produce results as much as 20 percent higher than the other ones, and you're all convinced, in hindsight, that you could substantially boost the returns even more with several simple changes in the copy.

Even with the better of the two existing packages, your mailing broke even on only three of the ten lists. Notably, however, two of those three are very large lists, with substantial potential for further mailing.

You project that you'll be able to recover three-quarters of the costs and fees you might invest in a second, continuation, or rollout mailing of 75,000 pieces. Your more favorable projections are based on using the more successful of the two packages, mailing to substantial numbers of new, yet unmailed names from the three most responsive lists, and making what you believe are improvements in the copy. Also the increased quantity and diminished start-up costs will lower the mailing's unit cost. As a result, you expect you'll recover about $22,500 out of $35,000, gaining 1,000 new donors at a cost of $12.50 each. Your capital is limited, and you're just now beginning to put into place the fundraising programs that will enable you to maximize the value of these donors. Even so, you might reasonably expect to derive at least $20 in net revenue per donor per year on average, so an acquisition cost of $12.50 seems sustainable.

However, in a second mailing, you hope to learn enough from further list and package testing to lower that acquisition cost on subsequent mailings to the range of $5 to $8, although there's no guarantee you can do so.

To proceed with a second mailing means either a fight with your board right now or, possibly, a bigger conflict further down the line. What do you do?

The only way I know to deal with a problem of this sort, which is maddeningly common, is to decide *in advance* how to define a "successful" outcome for your direct mail test. There's no such thing as a workable universal definition, but here's a principle to start from:

> The criteria that distinguish success from failure must be directly based on your organization's resources and strategic goals.

For some organizations, the scenario I've sketched is very attractive. A well-capitalized group with an appealing action program and a handful of wealthy major donors might be nuts not to go ahead under these circumstances. So would one that's seeking to change prevailing attitudes on a matter of broad policy and requires significant grassroots participation to do so. In both cases, the circumstances place a premium on building a large donor base.

Similarly, an organization committed to a long-range membership growth *strategy*, with sufficient capital on tap to make it work, might well decide it's worth paying even $25 per donor. A $25 new-member acquisition cost, corresponding, in the hypothetical case, to returns of only slightly more than 50 cents on the dollar in prospecting, might be well worthwhile for such an organization. They'll recover their investment within less than a year, given the generous returns they receive from membership dues, special donor appeals, and collateral fundraising efforts that feed off the membership list.

By contrast, a narrowly based and underfunded effort to launch a new organization through the mails might wisely decide to leave the field with results like those described. The same goes for a well-established charity with a fully staffed development department. For a large organization, the case *against* direct mail in this scenario is even stronger if this, its first foray into direct mail donor acquisition, was a wistful effort to diversify its funding base. (More than once, I've seen half-hearted, compromised efforts at direct mail undertaken by cautious organizations that quickly ended because they never were convinced their work lent itself particularly well to the emotional rough-and-tumble of direct mail. Some groups might be better off not trying.)

Every organization is unique. Your challenge is to make direct mail work uniquely for *you*.

How to Choose Lists for the Next Mailing

As you set out to select prospect lists for the second mailing in your donor acquisition campaign, you'll be forced once again to address those strategic considerations that determine the levels of investment and risk acceptable to your organization. To view the sort of projections my colleagues and I use when selecting lists for a rollout mailing, please take a look at Table 6.1.

In Table 6.1, I've listed the fifteen possible lists you've identified to be used in your continuation mailing: List A through List O. They range in size ("universe") from 3,000 names to 250,000, with a total universe of one million names. Four months ago, you mailed to ten of them—A through J—so you can project the response rate and average contribution you anticipate from each of them. If you use all ten in your rollout, you'll be "remailing" four small lists, remailing portions

TABLE 6.1. List Selection Model for a Hypothetical 150,000-Piece Rollout Mailing.

List	Universe	Quantity	Percent Response	Average Gift	Gross Income	Cost	Number New Donors	Net Income	Cumulative Income	Acquisition Cost
A	5,000	5,000	4.0%	$20	$4,000	$2,000	200	$2,000	$2,000	($10)
B	10,000	10,000	3.5%	18	6,300	4,500	350	1,800	3,800	(5)
C	3,000	3,000	3.0%	18	1,620	1,200	90	420	4,220	(5)
D	15,000	15,000	2.5%	16	6,000	6,750	375	(750)	3,470	2
E	5,000	5,000	2.0%	18	1,800	2,000	100	(200)	3,270	2
F	75,000	25,000	1.8%	20	8,750	11,250	438	(2,500)	770	6
G	150,000	25,000	1.5%	18	6,750	11,250	375	(4,500)	(3,730)	12
H	25,000	12,000	1.3%	16	2,400	4,800	150	(2,400)	(6,130)	16
I	5,000	5,000	1.0%	14	700	2,000	50	(1,300)	(7,430)	26
J	200,000	20,000	0.8%	18	2,700	9,000	150	(6,300)	(13,730)	42
K	150,000	5,000	0.8%	16	600	2,000	38	(1,400)	(15,130)	37
L	25,000	5,000	0.8%	16	600	2,000	38	(1,400)	(16,350)	37
M	52,000	5,000	0.8%	16	600	2,000	38	(1,400)	(17,930)	37
N	30,000	5,000	0.8%	16	600	2,000	38	(1,400)	(19,330)	37
O	250,000	5,000	0.8%	16	600	2,250	38	(1,650)	(20,980)	44
	1,000,000	150,000	1.6%	$18	$44,020	$65,000	2,468	($20,980)	($20,980)	$9

of two others, and mailing to additional, yet untouched names on six lists. The other five lists—K through O—are to be newly tested, and it's anybody's guess what will happen when you mail to them; to be conservative, I've assumed poor results.

In Table 6.1, I've ranked the fifteen lists from best-performing to worst in terms of response rate. I've calculated the probable results of mailing to what appears from the test results to be the optimum quantity on each list. In practice, my colleagues and I would discount the projected results by up to 20 percent for the sake of caution, but I've omitted that step here. To further simplify the picture, I've also arbitrarily assumed that you won't run a merge-purge.

For each list, Table 6.1 presents the mailing cost and anticipated gross and net returns, the projected number of new donors, and the acquisition cost for that list. (Costs vary from one list to another because some are available to you only as rentals and others only on exchange.) Under the "Cumulative Income" column, the table shows on each row the *cumulative* profit or loss of mailing to all the lists down to and including the one on that row.

For the top five lists—List A through List E—I anticipate that you would mail to every available name. For most of the others, you'd select only a percentage of the names available. (To "roll out" to all the available names on a large list without repeated testing is a risky proposition.) This points to a total mailing quantity of up to 150,000 packages—only 15 percent of the total number of names available on the fifteen lists. With lists that perform only moderately well at best, it's often unwise to roll out to the full universe.

In the long run, mailing to Lists K through O—the five test lists—may be the most significant aspect of this second mailing. Together they constitute half of the universe for the mailing as a whole. Each consists of at least 25,000 names. List N alone contains 250,000. To succeed with any of the five will make a meaningful contribution to the success of your direct mail program. Every prospect mailing should include list tests of this sort to explore new markets. You can and should mail more than once to those lists that constitute the core of your donor acquisition program because they work so very well, but there's a limit to remailing. List testing is never-ending.

On the final row of the chart, you can see the total and cumulative impact of mailing all fifteen lists in the quantities indicated: a response rate of 1.6 percent and an average gift of $18. With a budget of $65,000 and projected gross revenue of $44,020, the mailing is projected to lose $20,980, acquiring 2,465 new donors at an acquisition cost of $9 per donor.

Now here's where your strategy takes specific tactical shape. If your strategy requires you to *build your donor list as quickly as possible,* and you've got the money to do so, your best tactical move is to mail all 150,000 names and perhaps more besides. At an acquisition cost of $9, you may feel you're getting a bargain on nearly 2,500 new donors. Capital permitting, you might opt to mail 50,000 names or more on List G and all 25,000 names on List H. If you're feeling really lucky, you might also test larger quantities on some of the new test lists.

If, however, your strategy requires that you *conserve capital* or if your cash flow is simply inadequate to the task, you might mail only the top six or seven lists. Using Lists A through F will yield an estimated 1,553 new donors and a net profit of $770. Mailing to 10,000 or 20,000 names on List G will eat up that profit, and more. But you'll still cut the projected loss in half, and the resulting acquisition cost for the mailing as a whole will be only about $5—a level you might well find acceptable.

Nearly one-third, or $6,300, of the projected loss for the mailing as a whole will come from List J, and more than one-half from Lists J and G combined. Those two lists, however, represent 350,000 prospective donors—more than one-third of the total universe for this mailing. If you're following a growth strategy—and particularly if workable large lists are few and far between for your program—you have to mail to these and other large lists despite painful losses.

Note that you're projecting a profit on only *three* of the fifteen lists individually. If you limit your prospect mailing to those three alone, you'll have a total of only 18,000 names available—a quantity too small to mail cost-effectively. The profits you project on Lists A, B, and C are significant only in that you expect them to cancel out the losses on Lists D, E, and F. Even if your strategy is particularly cautious, you'll be well advised to mail the largest possible quantity that will produce breakeven results for the mailing *as a whole*.

You'll play out this process of prospect list selection again and again over the years, and at every stage your strategic goals will guide you in this selection. From time to time, cash flow considerations—or headline-grabbing events—may arbitrarily limit your freedom of action, but if they do so consistently, you'll need to reexamine your strategy and look for a way to capitalize your direct mail program.

The First Three Years

Let's assume you've chosen to take the plunge and proceed with a donor acquisition program, despite the equivocal results of your initial test. I'll assume further that your organization is new and underfunded and that this is your first foray into the mails: you don't have either a large pool of capital or a significant existing donor list to underwrite an aggressive growth strategy.

If the response to your second mailing improves, here's a schedule of the mailings you might conduct in the first three years. For the sake of simplicity, I'll assume you received test results in the fall and your first-year program will get under way in January. Table 6.2 depicts your first year's mailing schedule and the increasing size of your donor list as the year unfolds.

In the first year, you've mailed a little over half a million letters. The lion's share of the effort consisted of progressively larger donor acquisition mailings, conducted about once every three months.

Through quarterly donor resolicitation mailings, you've netted enough to underwrite your investment in prospecting. (Note that in none of the resolicitation efforts have you remailed *all* of the donors you've acquired; some gave gifts so small that they're unlikely to be cost-effective to mail again. There are other, profitable uses for such names.)

If yours is a typical experience, you'll end the year at breakeven after all of this activity, despite its unexciting beginning. Table 6.3 shows what the second year's program might look like.

By stepping up your donor acquisition program from 500,000 to 700,000 letters, you've added nearly 10,000 donors to your file. Meanwhile, you've increased

TABLE 6.2. Growth of a Hypothetical Donor File in Year 1.

Year 1	Prospecting Volume	Resolicitation Volume	List Size
January	75,000		500
February			1,500
March		1,350	1,500
April	125,000		1,500
May			3,250
June		3,000	3,250
July	150,000		3,250
August			5,350
September		4,750	5,350
October	150,000		5,350
November			7,350
December		6,500	7,350
Year 1 Total	500,000	15,600	7,350

TABLE 6.3. Growth of a Hypothetical Donor File in Year 2.

Year 2	Prospecting Volume	Resolicitation Volume	List Size
January	200,000		7,000
February		6,500	10,000
March			10,000
April	150,000	9,000	10,000
May			12,000
June		10,500	12,000
July	150,000		12,000
August		10,500	14,000
September			14,000
October	200,000	12,000	14,000
November			17,000
December		15,000	17,000
Year 2 Total	700,000	63,500	17,000

the frequency of donor resolicitation efforts from four in the first year to six in the second. Chances are, you've posted a *significant net profit* from direct mail this year because your donor list has now reached a size at which resolicitation mailings are typically very cost-effective. (In mailings of 10,000 names or more, economies of scale are comparatively significant, and a list of that size will permit you to exercise greater selectivity when you decide *which* donors to mail to.)

In the third year, your direct mail fundraising program may unfold as shown in Table 6.4.

By sustaining the same 700,000-piece-per-year rate of donor acquisition efforts, you've added another 10,000 names to your file in this third year.

However, the size of your donor base has grown only half that much, because you've been weeding out dead wood all along the way. You've dropped many of those first-year contributors who haven't sent checks since then, and you've taken extra pains to improve the accuracy of the file through address correction procedures.

Even so, you haven't mailed all the available active donor names in *any* of the eight resolicitation mailings. In six resolicitations, you've increased your net profits through careful segmentation based on individual donor histories. In addition, both early and late in the year you've added small mailings that target only your most generous and responsive donors. (In Chapter Seven, we'll discuss the targeting issues that arise in resolicitation programs.)

TABLE 6.4. Growth of a Hypothetical Donor File in Year 3.

Year 3	Prospecting Volume	Resolicitation Volume	List Size
January	200,000		16,000
February		14,000	18,500
March		3,500	18,000
April	150,000	15,500	18,000
May			19,500
June		16,000	19,500
July	150,000		19,000
August		17,000	21,000
September			20,500
October	200,000	16,000	20,500
November		5,000	22,500
December		20,000	22,500
Year 3 Total	700,000	107,000	22,500

In this third year, you've seen your investment—and your patience—really start paying off in a big way. The continuing cost of acquiring new donors represents only a fraction of the net proceeds of your increasingly frequent and selective donor resolicitation efforts. And the donor base you've already built will continue paying off in a big way for many years to come.

Investment Strategies from a Banker's-Eye View

As you've already learned, direct mail fundraising runs on two tracks: donor acquisition and donor resolicitation. If you're starting from scratch, *acquiring* donors will dominate your attention for the first year (or two years, or even three, depending upon how much capital you have and how many risks you can take). As your list grows, however, *resoliciting* your donors will come to mean more and more to you. The profits from a single donor resolicitation mailing—just one of seven or ten you may conduct in your program's third year—could easily dwarf the net revenue from even a wildly successful initial test mailing, no matter how substantial it seemed at the time.

By the same token, those profits from resolicitation may make your initial losses from prospecting look downright puny.

To get a sense of how these factors play themselves out over time, let's take a look at two hypothetical examples: CITIZENS FOR and PEOPLE AGAINST.

CITIZENS FOR and PEOPLE AGAINST: A Comparison

CITIZENS FOR is not well funded. The group started on a shoestring two years ago and only recently managed to beg, borrow, and steal $35,000 for an initial direct mail test. Fortunately, CITIZENS FOR's 50,000-piece test was a big success. It yielded 800 members whose average contribution was $22.50. The group grossed only $18,000 from this initial effort but was encouraged to proceed because six of the ten lists tested were at breakeven or better and one of two package variations substantially outperformed the other. The successful package variation and six of the ten lists accounted for the lion's share of the $18,000 in revenue, strongly suggesting that in a second, continuation or rollout mailing that eliminated poorly performing lists, response to the winning package will be much higher overall.

Following a contrasting strategy, PEOPLE AGAINST is also on the road to a successful long-term direct mail fundraising program. With an identical 1.6 percent response and $22.50 average gift, the well-funded group shrugged off its $17,000 loss and is ready to pull out the stops to launch a major nationwide campaign.

Because of their sharply different financial circumstances, CITIZENS FOR and PEOPLE AGAINST follow different strategies, even though the results of their initial test mailings were statistically identical. CITIZENS FOR sets out to tap the profit potential of its direct mail fundraising program at the earliest possible opportunity, while well-heeled PEOPLE AGAINST has its sights set on a more distant future. Neither strategy is better than the other; each serves the group's strategic requirements.

In Table 6.5, you can see what these two groups' contrasting experiences look like, year by year, in the five-year period following their initial tests.

As you can see in the table, PEOPLE AGAINST, with the resources and the grit to push the limits of the market in its donor acquisition program, has built a file that is *five times* as large and netted more than *four times* as much as CITIZENS FOR.

This doesn't mean that the more aggressive strategy is better than the other. I confess that the entrepreneur in me finds PEOPLE AGAINST a more interesting organization. Its "high-risk–high-gain" philosophy is the way to make the most of what direct mail has to offer. But such a hard-hitting approach may be inappropriate and even impossible for CITIZENS FOR, no matter what its inclinations might be.

However, the capital (and the level of risk) actually involved in even the larger of these two programs was quite small compared to the ultimate returns from the program. CITIZENS FOR and PEOPLE AGAINST advanced $35,000 each for their test mailings. CITIZENS FOR needed no more than another $15,000 to launch its first 75,000-piece continuation or rollout mailing, and nothing more thereafter. Its total investment was $40,000; measured against a five-year net of nearly $650,000, that seems puny. It's a return on investment of *1,625 percent!* I don't know about *your* banker, but mine thinks that's not a bad deal for CITIZENS FOR.

By contrast, though, PEOPLE AGAINST made out like a bandit. For its first 250,000-piece rollout, the group had to add about $40,000 to the $18,000 contributed in response to the initial test mailing. Its banker was a *little* worried, but from that point on, the program was self-sustaining. Profits from resolicitations funded the larger and more costly acquisition mailings in Years 3, 4, and 5 and left a *lot* to spare. A total cash investment of $65,000 yielded more than $2,700,000 in net revenue available to finance PEOPLE AGAINST's programs—a return on investment of *4,154 percent.*

Admittedly, that's one of the more advantageous ways to view the return on an investment in a direct mail fundraising program. A more conservative method is to examine the amount of capital tied up in the program at any one time, that is, the funds needed to pay the bills for those large, repeated donor acquisition mailings, and compare it with the net returns for that year only.

For CITIZENS FOR, this amount never exceeded $40,000—the approximate total cost of one of its 75,000-piece prospecting efforts plus one of its larger donor

TABLE 6.5. **Five Years, Two Contrasting Direct Mail Strategies.**

Year 1

CITIZENS FOR conducts four 75,000-piece donor acquisition mailings, for a total of 300,000 prospect letters, building its list from 800 at the outset to 5,300 by year's end. The proceeds from quarterly donor renewal mailings, combined with modest profits from prospecting, yield a net profit of over $45,000.

PEOPLE AGAINST aggressively pursues a growth strategy, mailing 1 million donor acquisition packages in the first year. While the list grows to more than 12,000 by the end of this period, profits from an intensive donor renewal program aren't enough to erase the loss. PEOPLE AGAINST ends the first year another $7,000 in the red.

Year 2

CITIZENS FOR continues to pursue its cautious, cash-flow-conscious approach, mailing just 300,000 acquisition appeals (as it will each year throughout the 5-year period). The donor list passes the 9,000-mark by year-end; aggregate net profits for the full year top $81,000.

Having built an active donor list of over 12,000 names at a net cost of a little more than $1 per name, PEOPLE AGAINST calculates it's not being sufficiently aggressive. It steps up its prospecting effort to 1.5 million letters in the second year. Despite this increased investment, the program nets $217,000 because donor renewal efforts yield large profits.

Year 3

The CITIZENS FOR list passes the 12,500 mark, and the organization tops $139,000 in net direct mail revenue after paying all program costs and fees.

PEOPLE AGAINST's file nears 50,000 names by year's end after another 2 million acquisition letters. Net profits for the year are $492,000.

Year 4

CITIZENS FOR's 300,000-piece prospecting program pushes the donor list to over 15,500. With stepped-up resolicitation efforts, net cash yield from the program is $177,000.

Dropping 2.5 million prospect letters, PEOPLE AGAINST's file tops 73,500. Net program revenue is $825,000 for the year.

Year 5

CITIZENS FOR has over 18,000 donors by the end of the year. Net profits for the year are $211,000.

PEOPLE AGAINST drops 3 million acquisition letters, and its file passes the 100,000 mark. Its net for the year is $1,200,000.

The 5-Year Period

CITIZENS FOR has mailed 1,550,000 donor acquisition letters and netted $648,000 from direct mail after paying all costs and fees. Its file includes 18,000 active donors.

PEOPLE AGAINST has dropped more than 10 million prospect letters and built an active donor list of 100,000 names. Its 5-year net profit was $2,728,000.

resolicitation mailings that might have been conducted at about the same time. In its first year, then, CITIZENS FOR's return on investment calculated in this manner was 113 percent. In Year 5, it was 528 percent.

For PEOPLE AGAINST, the capital required to finance continuing direct mail operations rose perceptibly as the scale of prospecting grew. In Years 1 and 2, PEOPLE AGAINST needed up to $130,000, and even in the second year net profits of $217,000 represented a return of only 167 percent. By Year 5, the group needed to devote nearly twice as much cash to cover ongoing program costs; current capital investment of about $250,000 yielded net profits of over $1,200,000—a return of 480 percent.

Of course, there's another thing about bankers (as well as the trustees and executives of most charities): they don't like risk.

Without question, CITIZENS FOR's strategy entailed lower risks than that of PEOPLE AGAINST. While my colleagues and I tell our clients—and ourselves—that the risks are very limited in a carefully managed direct mail fundraising program, they're nonetheless real.

I've never yet lost a mailing because a mail truck caught fire, but such things have happened to others (on *rare* occasions). And from time to time, we've seen mailing results dip, sometimes very sharply, because of headline-snatching catastrophes such as a stock market crash or a massive earthquake. It makes no sense to deny these problems and even less sense to let them stop you.

The only way I know to address the problem of risk is to *manage* it, expecting occasional setbacks and maintaining the program's momentum in spite of them. As the leader of almost any successful new enterprise, whether a business, a nonprofit organization, or a political campaign, will tell you, the only reliable way to achieve success is to keep plugging away, day after day, week after week. The rewards don't often come quickly. But, ultimately, the profits from a well-conceived and well-managed direct mail fundraising program may justify not just a little risk but a whole lot of hard work as well.

Alternative Approaches

The approaches followed by CITIZENS FOR and PEOPLE AGAINST represent just two of many possible alternative strategies. Others include:

- Seeking huge numbers of donors at gift levels under $10 on the average and resoliciting them as frequently as every week; programs of this type may entail tens of millions of prospect letters annually and donor files consisting of hundreds of thousands of names.
- Investing large sums in costly prospect packages in order to acquire new donors at a high entry level ($50 and up for single gifts and $10 to $25 per month in

pledge or sustainer programs), and investing more in upgrading them to even more generous levels of support

- Establishing an arbitrarily low initial membership fee of $5 or $10 to build the largest possible membership with attractive (and expensive) benefits that cost you a lot more than the entry-level dues, and then identifying and upgrading those members willing and able to provide significant gifts
- Acquiring "qualified" (proven) prospective donors at little or no cost through some form of sweepstakes offer, thus allowing more cost-efficient donor acquisition, and building large lists that will generate substantial rental revenue

Although the possibilities aren't genuinely endless, they might as well be. After all, there are more than one hundred million households in the United States, and there's probably somebody in the industry who thinks that just about every one of them is a good candidate for someone's direct mail fundraising program.

Evaluating the Tradeoffs

I'm sure it's becoming clear by now: if you've turned to direct mail as a way to grow, to diversify your sources of funding, and to broaden your financial base, direct mail is likely to be a waiting game for you.

In the hypothetical cases of CITIZENS FOR and PEOPLE AGAINST sketched earlier, you can detect some of the tradeoffs you're likely to confront—often a matter of time versus money. To cast a little more light on these issues, here are two concrete, real-life examples.

The Campaign

Two years and seven months have gone by, and *finally* The Campaign's direct mail fundraising program has gone into the black. You've mailed 800,000 prospect letters, yielding 12,400 new donors at a net cost of $49,000, or $3.95 per name. Donor resolicitation profits of $130,000 have barely covered this loss plus other costs and fees totaling $81,000. After raising a grand total of $557,000, The Campaign has netted the munificent sum of $1,500 through its direct mail fundraising program.

What could possibly make this program a good deal for The Campaign? Here are three of the reasons it is:

1. *Major donor revenue.* From the outset, The Campaign has been systematically approaching the most generous donors acquired in your direct mail program, treating them as *prospects* for larger gifts. In this aggressive effort, your development department has netted more than $300,000 in just the first two years and

seven months. They'll derive hundreds of thousands, perhaps eventually millions more, from these same donors in the years ahead.

2. *Public relations value.* The Campaign's message has already reached over a million people through direct mail, including a great many national opinion leaders. The Campaign's public profile has risen perceptibly in these first few years, in part due to the added exposure afforded by direct mail. As a public advocacy organization with a continuing need for publicity, this has great value for The Campaign, estimated to be worth $250,000 at the very least.

3. *Future direct mail revenue.* Starting virtually from scratch, you've already built an active donor list of 13,000 names. Although profits from The Campaign's donor resolicitations were limited in the first two years, averaging about $6,000 per mailing, they've been running two or three times that much in the third year (in part because of the greater economies of mailing to a larger list). In the next twelve months, that list will *net* The Campaign more than $200,000 in direct mail revenue alone, *after* deducting all consulting and program management fees and the continuing costs of acquiring new donors at the rate of $4 to $6 per name.

4. *List rental revenue.* The Campaign may now choose to increase its current revenue by offering its list of 13,000 donors for rental to approved nonprofit mailers. If it pursues this option aggressively, it can net upwards of $25,000 per year for the next year or two.

In other words, even this seemingly lackluster program hasn't just broken even. The Campaign has directly received costly services or cash from collateral fundraising to the tune of more than $550,000 (adding $300,000 in net revenue from major donor fundraising to $250,000 in public relations value but *not* counting potential list rental revenue). This has *doubled* the immediate returns from the program. Because of the contribution made by direct mail to The Campaign's major donor fundraising program, which is properly seen as a long-term development effort, the real net value of the thirty-one-month campaign was probably nearer $1 million.

In this case, a $38,000 investment in an initial direct mail fundraising test accomplished exactly what it was supposed to do. Direct mail has planted a tree that will go on bearing fruit for The Campaign for many years to come.

The Institute

With another organization, The Institute, your experience has been much closer to a case study custom-made for a textbook on fundraising:

- In six years, The Institute's direct mail fundraising program has netted $3.4 million from gross receipts of $6.5 million.

- Beginning with just 200 donors, The Institute has acquired a total of more than 50,000 contributors. The average contribution of their resolicitation gifts was an unusually high $64.
- A grand total of 4.6 million letters has yielded 114,000 contributions averaging $50—gross revenue of $5.7 million. (Telephone fundraising and other collateral efforts produced another $800,000.)
- The Institute posted a net profit from direct mail operations of $119,000 in its very first year. In Year 2, net revenue topped $290,000. By Year 5—the high point of the program—the net approached $900,000.
- The dramatic growth of The Institute's direct mail fundraising program paralleled the growth of its operating budget from $300,000 in Year 1 to $2.5 million in Year 5. Many of the new funds raised in large gifts came from donors originally acquired through direct mail.

In this apparently idyllic picture, however, there are hidden and massive problems. They're best highlighted by the fact that The Institute's net from direct mail dropped precipitously, from almost $900,000 in the fifth year to barely more than $500,000 in the sixth—and the seventh year promised to be far worse.

How could such a thing happen, with a donor list of 50,000 names? It occurred for one simple reason: *The Institute decided to stop prospecting.*

After a massive prospecting binge, The Institute virtually ended its donor acquisition efforts. Because response rates were dropping—and The Institute's management was preoccupied with internal management issues—the organization cut its prospecting volume from 1.7 million letters in the fifth year to fewer than 300,000 in the sixth. Not only did this short-sighted decision curtail The Institute's future growth, it also cut off the rich supply of fresh, responsive new donors that made it possible for the group to have netted almost $1 million in a single year.

Some people speak of direct mail fundraising as a treadmill: if you're among the minority of nonprofit organizations able to get up to speed, you can climb on the belt, but getting off is a lot more difficult. The Institute's experience illustrates one aspect of this problem. The principal lesson its program illustrates is this:

> You can't expect to build a list of loyal and responsive donors through direct mail and then simply leave the game, expecting them to sustain your continuing operations at the same level indefinitely.

Direct mail fundraising requires *continuous* prospecting because of attrition. People die or move without leaving forwarding addresses, their financial circumstances change, and so do their interests and loyalties.

Remember that direct mail is a *process,* not a passing event. And there's no point at which the process ends or achieves perfection. It's a continual search for new marketing concepts that serve *your* strategic needs because they work a little better than the old ones. The way we identify those new concepts is through testing. This complex topic lies beyond the scope of this book. For an introduction and overview of testing, though, see *Testing, Testing, 1, 2, 3: Raise More Money with Direct Mail Tests* (2003).

● ● ●

Meanwhile, it's time to gain a broader view of the many proven techniques you can employ to get the most from your donors. We'll take that up in the next section, beginning with Chapter Seven, "Maximizing Donor Value."

Getting the Most from Your Donors

The seven chapters of Part Two explore the nuts-and-bolts techniques that allow fundraisers to secure the greatest possible benefits from their direct mail programs. Chapter Seven, "Maximizing Donor Value," provides an overview of the donor development process, placing these techniques in a larger context. In Chapter Eight, you'll learn about "Annual Giving and Membership Programs." Chapter Nine covers "Monthly Giving." "High-Dollar Annual Giving Clubs" is the subject of Chapter Ten, and telephone fundraising is spotlighted in Chapter Eleven. "Legacy Giving" is covered in Chapter Twelve. Chapter Thirteen treats the underrated topic of "Thank-Yous, Welcome Packages, and Cultivation Mailings."

7

Maximizing Donor Value

Most donors acquired by direct mail will support your organization in an active way for only a short time. A smaller number will remain with you for many years, completing the full cycle of donor life. That cycle has the following four stages: (1) interest, (2) support, (3) commitment, and (4) legacy.

1. *Interest.* Among those relatively few recipients of your donor acquisition package who spend more than the four seconds it takes to decide to throw it away will be some for whom you'll have created some level of awareness about your organization and its work. A minority of those people will, in turn, demonstrate their interest by mailing you a first-time gift. You can't count on these people as committed donors; they're simply declaring that they've gotten a good first impression of you. Now you've got to convince them that you're really worthy of their support.

2. *Support.* Through the conversion process that your donor acknowledgment and donor resolicitation program is designed to promote, you'll convince a majority of your one-time donors that you're worth more active support. The second, often more generous gift you elicit from a new donor is a more meaningful statement of conviction. She may well be a candidate now for an ever more substantial role in your organization.

3. *Commitment.* In response to your efforts to upgrade your donors, many will enter onto a level of financial commitment meaningful to you as well as to them. But to take this big step toward a major gift may require substantial personal contact as well as months or years of donor education through such means

as newsletters and in-depth reports on your activities. It's important, too, that you do everything possible to make the donor's experience rewarding for her, as well as for you, by publicly recognizing her contribution, if she wishes, and by thanking her not just with an impersonal note but warmly and often.

4. *Legacy.* A continuing process of cultivation, education, and appreciation will induce some of your major donors to regard their participation in the work of your organization as one of their major contributions in life. These are the people who will serve as volunteers, perhaps even on your board of trustees; they will talk about your work among friends and family, make sizable annual gifts or establish planned giving programs, and remember you in their wills. Ultimately, the bequests and other major gifts you receive from these exceptionally strong supporters may dwarf the contributions from all your other donors combined. They're a living reminder that fundraising is a long, long process.

You'll derive the *full* value from your direct mail fundraising program only if you're able to work with your donors at every one of these four stages. Direct mail can start—even, in some cases, jump-start—the development process. But fundraising is a flesh-and-blood relationship that ultimately requires personal contact to realize its true potential.

What's a Donor Worth?

Sentimental or political considerations aside, it's entirely possible for an organization with at least a four-year track record in direct mail to calculate with meaningful precision the value it derives from the average new donor, which is termed the *long-term value* (sometimes *lifetime value*). It's rarely *easy* to do so. But there are at least three methods that may help you get a handle on this fundamental question.

Method 1

By studying your donor renewal rates, you may be able to determine the average "life" of your donors. In direct mail fundraising, that averages out to about 2.6 years, or 31 months. During that time, the typical donor's two or three renewal gifts will average about 20 to 25 percent higher than her first gift. If she joined you with a contribution of $25, you'll likely receive another $90 (three times $30).

If the *average* gift in your acquisition program is as high as $25, this arithmetic is realistic. If the average is much lower, it may not be true; donors of less than $15 are less likely to renew.

After deducting applicable renewal costs and fees, your net from this source should be about $60. Add to that figure another $10 in net list rental revenue (five years at $2 per year), and the total value of that donor is $70, or about $27 per year during the donor's "lifetime" of giving to your organization.

If you have a sophisticated development department, with an aggressive major donor program and other opportunities to elicit more frequent and larger-than-average gifts, that number may be twice as high or even higher. Some well-established national public interest groups, for example, expect to net an average of more than $70 *per year* from newly acquired members.

Method 2

By listing all the fundraising efforts you expect to undertake in the coming three years to elicit additional support from newly acquired donors or members and by projecting the returns you might reasonably expect to receive, you can calculate the total expected revenue per donor. (It's easier if you do so for 1,000 or 10,000 donors and then divide accordingly, as shown in Table 7.1.)

Judging from the first method, it seems that each new donor is worth a total of $70 to you. Using the second method, it's $71. Either way, an acquisition cost of $5 to $10 per name seems eminently reasonable, and two or three times that much, or even more, would make perfectly good sense if fast growth is essential to your strategy.

Setting that level, however, is a matter of tactics. The strategic problem is to determine how quickly you want your donor base to grow and how much you can afford to invest in growth.

Method 3

This task becomes easier if you bring a truly long-term perspective to bear in your strategic planning. View direct mail fundraising over a *ten-year* period, and the picture will look genuinely rosy. Just take a look at Table 7.2, which deals with a hypothetical organization different from the one depicted in Table 7.1.

In this third method of calculating the long-term value of a donor or member, we take into account not only dues income but profits from special appeals, a lucrative monthly sustainer program, and other fundraising efforts such as merchandising, planning events and travel, or offering other products and services to members. The upshot is that one thousand donors, acquired in Year 1 at an acquisition cost of $5 per donor, yield a total of $203,904 over ten years, or $204 per donor. That's net revenue averaging more than $20 per year for a decade. Doesn't $5 seem downright paltry by comparison?

However, the donor's long-term value and the donor acquisition cost are statistical concepts. The truth is, all your donors are not worth the same amount.

TABLE 7.1. Calculating Long-Term Value, Method 2.

	Quantity Mailed	Cost per 1,000	Response Rate	Contributions	Average Gift Amount	Gross Revenue	*Net Revenue
Year 1							
Acquisition Mailing	100,000	300	1.00%	1,000	$25	$25,000	($5,000)
Special Appeal 1	1,000	500	9.00%	90	43	3,870	3,370
Special Appeal 2	1,000	600	6.00%	60	36	2,160	1,560
Special Appeal 3	1,000	700	8.00%	80	38	3,040	2,340
Special Appeal 4	1,000	450	5.00%	50	34	1,700	1,250
Special Appeal 5	1,000	500	8.00%	80	38	3,040	2,540
Renewal 1**	950	500	19.00%	181	25	4,513	4,038
Renewal 2	770	500	16.00%	123	23	2,832	2,447
Renewal 3	646	500	11.00%	71	22	1,564	1,241
Renewal 4	575	500	9.00%	52	22	1,139	851
Renewal 5	524	500	6.00%	31	21	660	398
Renewal 6 (phone)	492	2,000	14.00%	69	35	2,411	1,427
Pledge Commitments	1,000	1,000	3.00%	30	240	7,200	6,200
Totals/Year 1	109,957					$59,129	$22,662
Renewal Rate			52.68%				
Net Revenue Per New Member							$22.66
Year 2							
Special Appeal 1*	750	500	10.40%	78	49	3,857	3,482
Special Appeal 2	750	600	6.90%	52	41	2,142	1,692
Special Appeal 3	750	700	9.20%	69	44	3,015	2,490
Special Appeal 4	750	450	5.80%	44	39	1,701	1,363
Special Appeal 5	750	500	9.20%	69	44	3,015	2,640
Renewal 1*	750	500	21.90%	164	29	4,722	4,347
Renewal 2	586	500	18.40%	108	26	2,851	2,558
Renewal 3	478	500	12.70%	61	25	1,536	1,297
Renewal 4	417	500	10.40%	43	25	1,098	889
Renewal 5	374	500	6.90%	26	24	623	436
Renewal 6 (phone)	348	2,000	16.10%	56	40	2,256	1,559
Additional Pledges	750	1,000	2.00%	15	180	2,700	1,950
Totals/Year 2						$29,516	$24,703
Renewal Rate			61.06%				
Net Revenue Per New Member							$24.71

TABLE 7.1. Calculating Long-Term Value, Method 2, Cont'd.

	Quantity Mailed	Cost per 1,000	Response Rate	Contributions	Average Gift Amount	Gross Revenue	*Net Revenue
Year 3							
Special Appeal 1*	563	500	12.00%	68	57	3,839	3,557
Special Appeal 2	563	600	7.90%	44	48	2,116	1,778
Special Appeal 3	563	700	10.60%	60	50	2,996	2,603
Special Appeal 4	563	450	6.70%	38	45	1,695	1,441
Special Appeal 5	563	500	10.60%	60	50	2,996	2,715
Renewal 1*	563	500	25.20%	142	33	4,687	4,405
Renewal 2	421	500	21.20%	89	30	2,713	2,503
Renewal 3	332	500	14.60%	48	29	1,408	1,243
Renewal 4	283	500	12.00%	34	29	989	847
Renewal 5	249	500	7.90%	20	28	547	422
Renewal 6 (phone)	229	2,000	18.50%	42	46	1,965	1,506
Additional Pledges	563	1,200	1.50%	8	170	1,434	759
Totals/Year 3						$27,385	$23,779
Renewal Rate			66.75%				
Net Revenue Per New Member							$23.78
Total/3 Years						$116,030	$71,144
Net Revenue Per New Member Over 3 Years							71.15

*Assumes a 25 percent shrinkage of list over previous year and a 15 percent increase in response rate and in average gift amount.

**Assumes 95 percent of members will receive renewal notices.

Long-term value varies by the year in which a donor joins an organization, the list source, and giving characteristics.

Gift level may be the most significant of these variables. Of every one thousand new donors you acquire through direct mail prospecting, fifty may give initial gifts of $50 or more, while one hundred each contribute less than $15. Those at the bottom of the scale may, in effect, be worth nothing at all to your organization, because testing repeatedly shows that donors of less than $15 are difficult to upgrade. By contrast, your new $50 donors may be worth a great deal indeed. They're by far the most likely of your new donors to remit additional gifts and are more likely to increase the level of their support.

TABLE 7.2. Calculating Long-Term Value, Method 3.

Year	1	2	3	4	5	6	7	8	9	10	Total
Number of members retained	1,000	600	420	328	278	242	218	198	181	164	
Average gift including dues	$25.00	$27.50	$30.25	$33.28	$36.60	$40.26	$44.29	$48.72	$53.59	$58.95	
Average number of gifts per member	1.3	1.3	1.3	1.3	1.3	1.3	1.3	1.3	1.3	1.3	13
Other income from same members	$1,000	$660	$462	$360	$306	$266	$240	$218	$199	$181	$3,892
Number of monthly sustainers	20	44	57	63	66	63	60	57	54	51	
Average annual income per sustainer	$163	$171	$180	$189	$198	$208	$219	$230	$241	$253	
Gross Income	$36,764	$29,650	$27,162	$26,462	$26,636	$26,056	$25,902	$25,859	$25,782	$25,668	$275,941
Acquisition cost per member	$5.00										
Membership renewal cost per member	$0.00	$1.95	$1.76	$1.58	$1.42	$1.28	$1.15	$1.04	$0.93	$0.84	
Special appeal cost per member	$4.80	$5.28	$5.81	$6.39	$7.03	$7.73	$8.50	$9.35	$10.29	$11.32	
Fundraising cost per sustainer	$8.40	$8.40	$8.40	$8.40	$8.40	$8.40	$8.40	$8.40	$8.40	$8.40	
Other fundraising costs per member	$2.00	$2.20	$2.42	$2.66	$2.93	$3.22	$3.54	$3.90	$4.29	$4.72	
Total Fundraising Cost	$36,968	$6,028	$4,668	$4,013	$3,722	$3,492	$3,381	$3,313	$3,253	$3,200	$72,038
Net Income	($204)	$23,622	$22,494	$22,450	$22,914	$22,564	$22,521	$22,546	$22,529	$22,468	$203,904
Cost Per Dollar Raised	$1.01	$0.20	$0.17	$0.15	$0.14	$0.13	$0.13	$0.13	$0.13	$0.12	$0.26

> There is a very high correlation between the level of the donor's original gift and the likelihood that that donor will still actively support you more than a year later.

A rigorous long-term-value analysis of a fundraising program should break out the value of an organization's donors in categories determined by the size of their initial gifts. Among other things, an analysis of this sort might point the way toward a new approach to prospecting that emphasizes lists yielding above-average gifts.

Will Your Donors Remember You?

If you're paying good money to recruit new donors, you'd better get your money's worth. That's what donor resolicitation efforts are all about.

The fundamental principle of all professionally managed donor resolicitation programs is to *mail early and often.* Many people, especially, it seems, those who serve on nonprofit boards, find this maddeningly counterintuitive. Chances are you eat, sleep, and breathe your work. It may be difficult for you to accept the fact that for someone who sent you a $25 check two or three months ago, your organization might not be the most important thing in her life this week. She *may* recall sending you a check, but the odds that she'll remember what you told her in your acquisition letter are very slim.

Something important is lurking in the background here:

> Direct mail fundraising is a form of advertising, which is based on repetition.

Unless you get back in touch with that new donor very quickly and repeat the same themes and symbols in your resolicitation, she may no longer be a good prospect for additional support. And the chances are you'll have to ask her *several times* before you get a second gift.

You needn't take my word for this. Just try calling at random a few dozen of your new donors acquired by direct mail two or three months after you receive their first gifts (and before you mail them anything else). I predict that you'll emerge the humbler from the experience.

It's conventional in the direct mail fundraising business to define everyone who's given you a single gift as a *donor.* But in a real sense, a first-time contributor is really just a *qualified prospect;* she may now be aware of your work, but she probably knows little about it, and she's clearly not a committed supporter. To tap the financial potential she represents, you'll have to educate and motivate her.

Psychologically, it's a big step for most people to send a *second* contribution; that implies a level of commitment many people are never willing to demonstrate. In fact, it's likely that anywhere from one-third to one-half of your first-time contributors will *never* give you a second gift. But once people have given *two* gifts, they're much more likely to contribute yet again, perhaps much more generously.

In general, it's prudent to expect that no more than half your new donors will renew their support within the twelve-month period following their first gift. Of those who do so, a much larger proportion is likely to give again within the subsequent year. The progression is likely to look something like this:

Of your new donors, 30–40 percent renew in Year 1
Of donors renewed in Year 1, 50–60 percent renew in Year 2
Of donors renewed in Year 2, 60–70 percent renew in Year 3
Of donors renewed in Year 3, 70–75 percent renew in Year 4
Of donors renewed in Year 4, 75–80 percent renew in Year 5
Of donors renewed in Year 5, 80–85 percent renew in Year 6
Of donors renewed in Year 6, 85–90 percent renew in Year 7
Of donors renewed in Year 7, 87–91 percent renew in Year 8
Of donors renewed in Year 8, 88–92 percent renew in Year 9
Of donors renewed in Year 9, 89–93 percent renew in Year 10

The upper limit is imposed by death, illness, changing fortunes, shifting interests, and addresses lost when donors move.

In an organization that's been in operation for many years, it's common for more than 65 percent of *all* donors to renew their support in any given year. That may represent a renewal rate of less than 50 percent for first-year donors and an average renewal rate for multiyear donors of 75 percent or more.

The most urgent task of a donor resolicitation program is to convert the largest possible percentage of your recent first-time contributors into *donors*. Increasing their renewal rate from 40 to 50 percent or from 50 to 60 percent can have profound financial implications for your fundraising program in later years. Just as you've invested in acquiring new donors, it's worth spending money to persuade them to become active supporters. This process, sometimes called donor conversion, typically entails a quick thank-you in response to the first gift and then a series of donor resolicitation letters about once every two or three months for the next year or year and a half.

For many nonprofit organizations, an annual renewal system modeled on the magazine subscription renewal process is the backbone of the direct mail fundraising program. Whether applied to organizations that offer formal membership opportunities or to those who simply wish to inculcate the habit of annual giving in their donors, an annual renewal system is often the most effective tool available to maintain a high "renewal rate" (the proportion of an organization's donors who renew their support in a given year). Once they've renewed their support through the annual renewal system, many members or donors are good prospects for special appeals—resolicitation mailings that seek support for particular projects, address especially urgent issues, or commemorate special occasions. One-third or more of your active members will send gifts over and above their dues or annual gift. They'll feel more involved in your work and may more readily respond to invitations to become more active, perhaps as volunteers. But they'll expect you to deliver on your promises. If your membership acquisition letter says members receive a quarterly newsletter, you'd better be sure you send one every three months. If you've promised a premium for gifts above a certain level, you're in trouble if you don't have a system in place to send it out quickly. Membership systems have many advantages, but they demand discipline and efficiency; each carries a price tag of its own. In the following chapter, we'll explore the linked concepts of annual giving and membership programs.

Nearly equal in priority to renewing your donors is to *upgrade* them—convince them to give bigger gifts. Donor upgrading techniques favored by many public interest organizations include gift clubs and monthly sustainer programs. Both are devices to involve donors more intimately in the organization's work and to provide them with special rewards or recognition.

Monthly Sustainer Programs

Monthly sustainer or pledge programs offer new giving opportunities to small donors, whose gifts can add up very fast. At $10 per month, a donor's annual contribution is $120—far more than she's likely to give through dues notices and special appeals if her initial gift was a typical $15 or $20. Thoughtfully designed and managed with skill and persistence, a sustainer program can attract as many as 10 percent of your donors and become the financial backbone of your direct mail fundraising program. In one organization with which I'm familiar, 4,500 of 45,000 donors contribute monthly gifts; in the aggregate, those monthly sustainers account for nearly one-third of the organization's $4.5 million operating budget. However, a monthly pledge program requires patience, considerable staff time, and special attention. In Chapter Nine, we'll explore sustainer programs.

Giving Clubs

Giving clubs provide a sense of belonging and special purpose to those donors who contribute large amounts of money. For example, you might offer special status through The President's Circle for $1,000 per year (paid in one sum or installments), conferring attractive privileges, benefits, and recognition not available to your other donors. Or you might choose to confer special status on those donors whose cumulative lifetime giving has exceeded that amount. A fully developed giving club can raise substantial sums from a large donor base, but it requires careful attention by staff. Many giving clubs are assigned full-time staff to deliver the promised benefits, privileges, and recognition and to attend to donors' correspondence and special requests. We'll explore giving clubs in some detail in Chapter Ten.

Donor Cultivation

Ultimately, however, your success in cultivating donors may have the greatest impact on your organization's long-term financial health. A handful of your direct mail donors may eventually become major donors, whose individual gifts could possibly equal all the support you receive from the rest of your contributors combined.

But bequests and other forms of planned giving represent the pinnacle in upgrading donors. Such legacy gifts frequently dwarf individual donors' lifetime giving. It's not unusual, for example, for a donor who's sent a handful of $5 or $10 checks to bequeath to a charity a gift of $35,000 or more. In Chapter Eleven, we'll probe this high-potential area of fundraising and the ways in which direct mail techniques can be used to promote it.

Because your donors will become more and more valuable over time, your donor resolicitation program should seek to retain them as long as possible once you've converted them from one-time contributors into committed donors. "Donor retention" is a function of the impact and attractiveness of your programmatic work at least as much as it is of your fundraising efforts, but an effective donor resolicitation program can easily lift donor retention by 10 percent or more each year. Over the long haul, that 10 percent lift will have a profound impact on your budget: a 10 percent annual improvement over typical donor renewal rates will *more than triple* the number of donors remaining active on your file after ten years (see Figure 7.1).

Grassroots organizations often use "emergency" appeals to boost their fundraising revenue. Threatening to close the doors if there's poor response to an emergency letter may be an effective short-term fundraising technique, but it's unlikely to work as well the second time around. More important, it's short-sighted to cry wolf. Few donors will invest sizable sums in an organization that's on the brink of bankruptcy. A public interest group's long-term self-interest lies in enhancing, not undermining, the public's confidence in its integrity and stability.

Your approach to donor resolicitation must relate to your organization's strategy. For example, if your organization has a strong development department with a well-established fundraising program that includes major donor giving clubs,

FIGURE 7.1. Donor Attrition over Ten Years in a Hypothetical Direct Mail Fundraising Program.

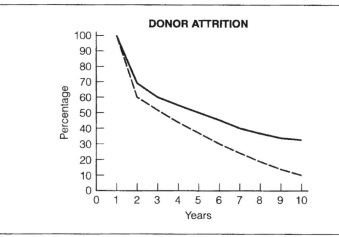

Note: The figure illustrates how a relatively subtle difference—just 10 percent—in the performance of a donor development program can dramatically affect the rate of donor attrition. The solid line indicates the percentage of new donors remaining at any given point in time with a relatively effective donor retention program. The dotted line shows the percentage left under a relatively ineffective donor retention regime. As you can see, the more effective program results in a donor file that is approximately four times as large after ten years.

planned giving, bequests, and other special donor opportunities, your direct mail donor resolicitation program should probably emphasize donor education and *cultivation*. By using such tactics as highly personalized thank-you packages and phone calls, donor newsletters and other free publications, and "high-dollar" direct mail packages designed to elicit much larger gifts, your direct mail donor resolicitation program may prove to be a rich source of prospects for your major donor fundraising efforts. The large contributions that ultimately result will represent a handsome return on a relatively modest investment in donor cultivation.

By contrast, if your organization has had neither the time nor the opportunity to build a strong overall development effort, your direct mail program may constitute a large share of your "major donor" fundraising efforts. If this is the case, your direct mail program needs to be as profitable as possible, while providing sufficient opportunities for donor *upgrading*, so you can get the most from your donors. This may mean mailing very selectively to your donors and treating the most generous of them to particularly strong, personalized packages and friendly phone calls. In effect, this approach mimics the personal attention major donors would get from a professionally run development department.

How Often Should You Mail?

Although you need to plan the frequency of your resolicitation mailings in the context of your organizational strategy, the rule of thumb my colleagues and I follow is to mail *more* often rather than less. This is true because most gifts from individuals and the overwhelming proportion of gifts solicited by mail come from what I call available income—that modest balance left in donors' checking accounts after the bills are paid each month. The amount of available income varies with life's circumstances, but it's rarely large. To maximize your share of that income when it becomes available, you can't rely on soliciting your donors just once or twice a year. Your net profits from direct mail are likely to rise as you increase the frequency of appeals to your donors—up to a point.

However, that logic can all too easily be carried too far. Many factors enter into the decision about how frequently to resolicit donors by mail, and it is *by no means* always advisable to mail more rather than less. Here are some of the reasons.

First, for some nonprofit organizations, it's simply not practical to solicit donors more than two or three times per year. Sometimes staff is stretched too far with other responsibilities and incapable of running more than a couple of fundraising campaigns during the year. Sometimes, no matter how good the prospects of success from adding another appeal to the schedule, the necessary funds to produce a mailing can't be found.

Second, certain donors *should not* be solicited more than once or twice per year. These include donors who have specified that they do not wish to be asked for funds more than once a year, as well as donors who have amply demonstrated over the years that they never give more than one gift per year.

And third, in high-dollar and major donor fundraising programs, it's important to stay in regular touch with all donors (unless they have specifically asked that you not do so). However, the balance in such programs typically shifts from solicitation to cultivation mailings. High-dollar donors give gifts that are sufficiently large that (1) they tend to remember having given them and (2) they're likely to contribute much smaller sums if asked for money more frequently.

With all that said, I believe that the rock-bottom minimum number of solicitations per year is two (except with donors who have insisted on only one). In practice, that would typically mean mounting a holiday campaign at year-end in the nature of a renewal request, plus a special appeal sometime earlier in the year, usually in the spring. I don't recommend that any nonprofit organization with a sizable base of direct mail donors limit itself to such a schedule. Those with fewer donors and more limited resources may have no choice.

Such exceptions aside, however, frequency of solicitation is the key to maximizing returns from most of your direct-mail-acquired donors, usually four to eight times per year (counting the renewal series as one solicitation). And the key to making that approach work is to stick to the schedule.

If your mailing schedule calls for eight appeals this year—roughly six weeks apart from one another—a slippage of ten days to two weeks for each of the first three mailings will mean that you're likely to mail seven times, not eight. Another month's delay could cut your program down to six appeals. In that case, you won't be getting full value from your donors. The financial impact can be sizable.

Should You Raise More Money or Lower Costs?

An intelligent donor resolicitation system can easily be undermined by undue attention to the fundraiser's nemesis—the fundraising ratio, that is, the cost of a dollar raised (see Resource E for a fuller explanation). Let's say your board's fundraising chair tells you it's unacceptable to continue paying 38 cents to raise every dollar in your direct mail donor resolicitation program. She says you have to drive the ratio below 30 cents (see Table 7.3).

That may be easy to accomplish, as you can see in Table 7.3. Simply reduce the frequency of your resolicitations, which will improve the response rate on each mailing. Stop mailing to less recent and less generous donors, which will raise both the average gift and the response rate. And mail cheaper packages, which might lower the average gift and the response rate but is likely to raise proportionally more money for every dollar expended. In the example illustrated here, this combination of choices will succeed in raising the response rate from 6 percent to 8 percent

TABLE 7.3. Cutting Costs Can Be a Losing Proposition.

	Current Resolicitation Schedule	Proposed Resolicitation Schedule	Difference
Number of resolicitations	8	4	(4)
Average number of donors resolicited per mailing	20,000	15,000	(5,000)
Year's total resolicitation quantity	160,000	60,000	(100,000)
Number of gifts received	9,600	4,800	(4,800)
Average percent response per resolicitation	6%	8%	33%
Year's gross resolicitation revenue	$336,000	$192,000	($144,000)
Year's total cost of resolicitations	$128,000	$50,000	($78,000)
Net resolicitation revenue	$208,000	$142,000	($66,000)
Cost per dollar raised	$0.38	$0.26	(32%)

and the average gift from $35 to $40. The cost of the direct mail donor resolicitation program accordingly will drop from $128,000 to just $50,000. The fundraising ratio thus will plunge from 38 cents on the dollar to 26 cents, an improvement that will please your fundraising chair—until you explain the disadvantages.

In this case, overemphasis on efficiency in your donor resolicitation program would be counterproductive because (1) your net revenue will drop by $66,000, or nearly 32 percent, and (2) your donor list will shrink by several thousand individuals. By mailing 100,000 fewer resolicitation letters, you won't just be cutting costs, you'll also be missing opportunities to convert new donors into active supporters and to persuade lapsed donors to come back into the fold. Your organization would continue paying the price of this short-sightedness for many years to come.

Remember, your donors are your friends, and they *want* to hear from you.

Which Donors Are Key?

At first, nearly all the donors you acquire from direct mail acquisition will be, for all intents and purposes, of equal importance. Initially, you'll have just a few thousand on file. Your biggest challenge then will be to find cost-effective ways to stay in touch with them and build their understanding of your work. If you're lucky, you'll net at least modest amounts, which will help subsidize your prospecting program.

Once you're beyond the four- to six-thousand donor level, you can begin segmenting your file (as described in Chapter Two). Segmentation is the key to a profitable donor resolicitation program over the long term.

> Remember, segmentation is based on one simple truth: some people give more money than others.

As you'll recall, those who've contributed most generously, most frequently, and most recently are your best prospects for additional gifts. They're the people to whom you should be paying the most attention and in whom you should be investing the most in your donor resolicitation efforts. Depending on the precise criteria applied, these core donors may include anywhere from 15 to 30 percent of your file, but the chances are they contribute three-quarters or more of the *net* income from your fundraising program.

You may be tempted to refrain from resoliciting anyone who's just given you a gift or even to methodically eliminate from later appeals those who respond to the first or second letter you've sent this year. In most cases, this is a very big mistake, for three reasons:

1. The appeals you write are—or should be—one of your donors' primary sources of information about your work. Not to inform the donors who have shown the *most* interest in your organization reflects misguided priorities. Resolicitation is part of the process of "bonding" and cultivating your donors, some of them potential major contributors.
2. Your donors contribute to you from their *current* income. Most write checks that are small by their own standards, and many are willing to do so several times a year. By failing to solicit them regularly, you'll lose a great deal of money.
3. Recent contributors are *most* likely to give again. They're the most interested, the most responsive, and the best prospects for special opportunities such as monthly sustainer programs or gift clubs.

An intelligent approach to segmentation requires that you establish the most cost-effective frequency of contact with each segment of your donor file. You might choose to group the individuals on your list into four broad categories:

1. Core donors, including your most generous, most frequent, and most recent contributors
2. Active donors, who aren't quite so generous, frequent, or recent as core donors
3. Lapsed donors, whose last gift arrived at least a year or eighteen months ago but not longer than two or three years ago
4. Former donors, who haven't contributed for two or three years or more

It's simply not worth treating all four of these groups in the same way. The only segment that's really worth your full attention at all times is your group of *core donors*. You should be in touch with them no less frequently than once every two months (six times per year) and perhaps more often than once per month.

Your *active donors* may not respond well to such frequent contact. Four to six times per year should suffice.

You may recapture a significant proportion of your *lapsed donors* with two, three, or four mailings this year.

The more recent of your *former donors* may be worth one or two last direct mail efforts this year but probably not more.

The biggest cliché in fundraising is the Pareto Principle, the so-called 80–20 Rule: 20 percent of your donors will contribute 80 percent of your fundraising revenue, even though they may require only 20 percent of your fundraising budget. The other 80 percent—soaking up four-fifths of the budget—will yield only 20 percent of your revenue. Identifying and cultivating your core donors and treating other significant segments of your donor file in different but appropriate ways, is an effort to turn the 80–20 Rule on its head. In fact, in most well-managed fundraising programs today, a handful of top donors account for a substantial proportion of the revenue, sometimes 50 percent or more. The top 20 percent, then, may collectively account for more than 90 percent of total revenue.

Through segmentation, you can invest greater resources to maximize the returns from your most productive segments and minimize the cost of working with those that are less productive. This will help ensure that you get the highest possible net profit from your direct mail fundraising program.

In the long run, however, your direct mail program may pay off even more handsomely with *major* gifts from a few individuals. As your donor list grows, you should put into place a system of "donor research" to determine whether new donors are good prospects for large gifts. These are the individuals you'll want to cultivate carefully. You'll write and call them personally and arrange face-to-face visits, if possible. Their contributions, amounting to many thousands of dollars, may represent the *real* payoff for all the hard work that's gone into your direct mail fundraising program.

You may wish to conduct donor research in-house, checking the local library's *Who's Who,* the *Foundation Directory,* Standard & Poor's *Register of Corporations, Directors and Executives,* and other likely sources of information about wealthy individuals. Chances are, though, you'll find that donor research is as taxing and distracting as other labor-intensive aspects of your fundraising program.

Some large nonprofit institutions, especially colleges and universities, support substantial donor research departments. If you have little or no development staff, you may conclude it's worth paying someone else to do the job of donor research. A variety of professional services are available in this important field. The directories of vendors published by fundraising trade periodicals contain the names of firms that provide such services.

Who's Counting and Keeping Track of the Money?

As your donor base grows, you'll probably begin paying more and more attention to two of the most nettlesome questions about direct mail fundraising: (1) Who's going to count the money? and (2) Who will keep track of all the people who give it to you?

It's important to think through your answers to these questions *before* you mail your initial test. The decisions you make in this area of so-called back-end services are fateful. And they may not be obvious.

Here's the fundamental principle on which an intelligent back-end system for direct mail fundraising is based:

Donors are people, and they deserve to be treated as individuals. They also tend to give more money when they're treated well.

In practice, this means you'll need:

- A quick-turnaround donor acknowledgment program
- An extensive database maintenance system that includes almost every scrap of useful information your fundraising results can provide about each individual donor
- A meticulous system of data entry, with built-in quality control procedures to maintain a file of the highest possible accuracy
- A working system for your staff to respond to individual donor questions and complaints in a timely and polite manner

A system to deliver all these services may cost you $2 to $3 per donor per year. Admittedly, such a costly back-end system may not work well for a direct mail fundraising program involving hundreds of thousands of $5 or $10 donors. Three dollars per year per donor will probably eat up too much of the profits. But a program in which the average gift is $15 or higher, thus allowing for upgrading, may not live up to its potential *without* the sort of labor-intensive back-end system necessary to ensure that your list will lend itself to credible, personalized appeals.

About every six months, almost like clockwork, one of our long-standing clients asks me, "How big a computer do I need to hold my list? How much will a computer like that cost?" The question may appear disingenuous—obviously, there's more involved than computer hardware—but it highlights one of the enduring sources of confusion in direct mail fundraising: whether to hire additional staff or train volunteers to provide back-end services in-house instead of retaining a service bureau or subscribing to an on-line donor base management system.

The best answer to that question—like most other things about direct mail—has its roots in your organizational strategy. With a multi-million-dollar direct mail fundraising program involving many tens or hundreds of thousands of donors in an intensive program of communications and resolicitation, an in-house service bureau might make sense. It might also be cost-effective at the other end of the scale, with a small, inactive direct mail program if your staff or an exceptionally well- trained, disciplined, *long-term* volunteer can handle the job in a timely and consistent manner.

But most of the time, for direct mail fundraising programs of the type and the scale described in this book, keeping the work in-house makes no sense at all. An in-house system for back-end processing will burden your organization with specialized staff and computer hardware and software, and it will subject you to all the headaches entailed by running what is, after all, a business. Very few nonprofits or political campaigns can run such a business in a consistently efficient and cost-effective manner.

Once again, it's worth taking a leaf from the annals of the business world and asking yourself the single most critical question you can pose about your organization: *What business are you in?* With an aggressive direct mail fundraising program and a growing donor file to match, you could easily discover that you're really in the data-processing business if you try to build an in-house service bureau, no matter what your mission statement might say. Willy-nilly, the tail wags the dog. To avoid this problem, some organizations find it worthwhile to pay professionals to do the job, *even if* they're convinced they can do it just as well and perhaps even more cheaply.

Back-end services require a respect for complex procedures and a compulsive attention to detail. The job looks deceptively easy, but it may require an investment of tens or hundreds of thousands of dollars in systems analysis, programming, training, and maintenance for you to do it right. The cost of the computer hardware is a minor consideration by comparison.

One alternative favored by many organizations is to buy or lease a specialized fundraising software program. There are many on the market, some offered in conjunction with dedicated hardware systems, others sold "in the can," with or without continuing technical assistance. If it works well (which, in my experience, is all too rare an occurrence), a system of this sort might lower your investment in an in-house service bureau. But it begs the question of where the job should be done. I believe that, unless you're at a big-budget charity that can afford high-priced data processing staff, your wisest course is to retain a specialized service bureau to manage all your back-end operations and be held accountable for doing the job right.

Alternatively, you might consider a Web-based donor management system, which would allow you to outsource the technical aspects of the back-end operation (but not such things as processing gifts and updating your donor file). Several application service providers (ASPs) offer such services. (But if you choose to go that route, be sure you choose a firm that is financially stable and well enough managed to give you confidence that it will still be in business next year or the following.)

There are at least four separate (though not necessarily separable) tasks in a back-end system:

1. *Cashiering:* processing and depositing contributions to your bank account
2. *Caging:* processing and recording the list-by-list and package-by-package information encoded on the response devices in your mailing and outputting it in the form of flashcounts (progress reports on your mailing that break down the results by list or segment)
3. *Acknowledging donors:* thanking your donors and perhaps asking for another gift at the same time
4. *Maintaining lists:* updating your donor file, recording both new information and corrections to the old, and providing periodic analytical reports that depict the cumulative impact of all your fundraising programs, segment by segment

In the earliest stages of your direct mail fundraising program, it may be most efficient for your staff to tend to cashiering, caging, and acknowledging donors. If you have an effective list maintenance system in place, it may also be worthwhile to fold in the early test results. But once your direct mail program is under way, I believe it usually makes sense to transfer your list maintenance to professionals. Ideally, you'll find a service bureau that caters to direct mail fundraisers and offers an integrated system of caging, maintaining lists, and acknowledging donors.

It may be advisable for you to continue cashiering your direct mail returns in-house, especially if they're just one of several active sources of income and you're already equipped to process large numbers of checks. In such circumstances, however, you'll need to transfer the raw data from your direct mail program to the service bureau (or the ASP) on a timely basis.

As your direct mail fundraising program grows in scope and complexity, the demands on your back-end systems will increase geometrically.

● ● ●

Now that we've gained some perspective on how to maximize donor value, let's turn to what I regard as the most fundamental tool in the realm of resolicitation: the annual giving or membership renewal process, which is the subject of Chapter Eight.

Annual Giving and Membership Programs

Scrape away all the jargon and fantasy that adhere to the concepts of fundraising and philanthropy, and what's the core idea you find at the center? It's this:

> Nonprofits want repeat gifts from donors. And most donors give repeatedly.

I know of no law or graven tablet that establishes this principle. But it's clearly the basis of almost all contemporary fundraising programs. And no wonder. As we've seen, it's difficult and often costly to recruit new donors—so much so that new donors' first gifts rarely represent a net financial gain for a nonprofit organization.

This reality underlies what so many of us old hands in fundraising regard as a universal principle: our first professional duty is to *build relationships with our donors*. Because only by building strong relationships with donors can we hope to secure the repeat gifts that make the whole process worthwhile.

In direct mail, four methods are commonly employed to give donors opportunities to make repeat gifts:

1. *Frequent resolicitation mailings* (special appeals), anywhere from a minimum of three or four per year to two or more *per month*. Sometimes these appeals are labeled renewal mailings, but they are not often related to the calendar.

2. *The annual fund or annual campaign,* which employs a series of resolicitations calculated to secure at least one gift per donor per year. These are usually done on a calendar year basis.

3. *Membership or donor programs* that seek annual membership renewals. These are frequently combined with appeals for additional gifts as well.

4. *Monthly giving* (often called sustainer or pledge in the United States, elsewhere regular or committed giving) programs. These programs usually secure scheduled monthly gifts from selected donors through credit cards or preauthorized checking using electronic funds transfer (EFT). Monthly giving by check is little known outside the United States, though it's still a significant factor here.

Those who choose the first option—relying on frequent appeals—usually treat each mailing as a campaign in its own right. They argue that they secure a higher number of gifts per donor per year by not focusing donors' attention on an annual giving calendar. Too many donors, they say, feel that their obligation to a nonprofit organization is complete once they've sent one gift per year.

The annual fund or annual campaign—the predominant model in fundraising for higher education as well as many other nonprofits—is based on the hope that, by committing to *annual* gifts, donors will see their support as a long-term (even life-long) proposition. Frequently, nonprofits that employ this fundraising model want to limit their fundraising appeals to a particular time of year. An annual campaign lends itself well to a schedule that is limited to, say, three or four months of the year. Besides, annual campaign advocates argue, donors who are repeatedly asked for special gifts without reference to a long-term commitment to an organization are likely to lose interest over time and simply stop giving.

Like annual funds, membership programs base their appeal on a yearly calendar, but they offer a deeper sort of relationship to their donors. Members' responsibilities, benefits, and privileges are clearly spelled out (at least in theory). Members are therefore more likely to show loyalty and to renew their support year after year, at least so long as they continue to perceive the benefits of membership to be worth the price. Without the inducement of valuable benefits, membership advocates say, donors are less likely to join in the first place or to keep on giving (see Table 8.1).

Monthly giving programs are consistent with systems based on repeated special appeals, annual campaigns, and membership and may be employed simultaneously with any. Such programs are widely acknowledged to be one of the most effective (some say the *most* effective) ways to upgrade donors acquired by mail.

In the balance of this chapter, we'll explore the second and third of these four alternative approaches to securing repeat gifts from donors by mail. The first method—frequent special appeals—requires no detailed explanation. The fourth—

TABLE 8.1. Hypothetical Mailing Schedules for Four Strategies to Give Donors Opportunities to Make Repeat Gifts.

Month	(1) Appeals	(2) Annual Fund	(3) Membership	(4) Monthly**
January				
February	Appeal 1	Appeal 1	Renewal 1*	
March			Renewal 2*	
April	Appeal 2	Appeal 2	Renewal 3*	
May			Renewal 4*	
June	Appeal 3	Appeal 3	Renewal 5*	
July			Appeal 1	
August				
September	Appeal 4		Appeal 2	
October	Appeal 5	Annual 1		
November	Appeal 6	Annual 2	Appeal 3	Appeal
December	Appeal 7	Annual 3	Appeal 4	

*Repeated renewals are sent only to nonrespondents.

**In most successful monthly giving programs, payment notices are *not* sent monthly because donors have pre-authorized their giving through credit cards or EFT from their bank accounts. A special newsletter exclusively for monthly donors or occasional news bulletins might be, however, and perhaps occasional cultivation mailings as well.

monthly giving—will be the subject of the next chapter. For starters, let's examine one of the most widely used tools in the annual fund business: the renewal series.

The Annual Renewal Series

Human ingenuity has devised a seemingly limitless number of ways to measure time—everything from the nanosecond to the endless stretches represented by the eras of geological time. But we understand only three of those measurements intuitively: the day, the month, and the year. Those are concepts we have learned from the earth, the moon, and the sun, and we can feel them in our bones. We organize our lives around them. Quite naturally, then, those three benchmarks have been widely incorporated into our work as fundraisers, because those concepts are meaningful to donors, too. The rhythm of all our lives is organized into days, months, and years.

For most donors, giving an annual contribution makes sense. It's a natural thing to do. Annual campaigns, annual funds, and membership programs derive much of their power from the human tendency to think of life one year at a time.

The mechanism that lies at the heart of many such programs is the annual renewal series.

Chances are, you're familiar with the concept of an annual renewal, even if you've never sent a charitable contribution through the mail. For many decades, magazines have commonly operated on a similar annual schedule, sending renewal notices by mail at frequent intervals until you renew your subscription (although this practice is changing at many periodicals). Nowadays, those big-circulation magazines that still employ a renewal series may use as many as fifteen such notices before they (finally) recognize that you really *don't* want to renew your subscription.

The annual renewal series for an annual fund or a membership program is built on the same framework of serial reminders or notices. Donors or members receive a series of anywhere from three to ten such efforts (or even occasionally more)— usually mailings but sometimes including telephone calls. A more typical renewal series, consisting of five efforts, might follow a schedule along the lines shown in Table 8.2.

Some nonprofit organizations mail their renewals based on each donor's "anniversary date" (usually, the date on which the first annual gift or membership dues payment was received). In practice, this usually means initiating the renewal series each month for those whose memberships lapse in a given month. Many smaller organizations begin their renewal series at a fixed time of the year, starting, say, in February or June. Yet other organizations opt for a quarterly mailing schedule, consigning each donor to a particular quarter of the year.

The choice of mailing schedule is a pragmatic matter and ought to be decided on the basis of which approach is the most efficient. To my mind, it's not a question of which scheduling option is more "successful," that is, produces more net revenue. I'm very skeptical that a monthly schedule nets more money, except possibly for the very largest organizations, because the extra costs of repeating as many

TABLE 8.2. Schedule for a Hypothetical Five-Effort Renewal Series.

Effort #	Possible Theme	Maildate
1	"Early Bird Renewal"	Day 1
2	"It's time to renew"	Day 45
3	"A gentle reminder"	Day 75
4	"Have you forgotten?"	Day 105
5	"It's not too late"	Day 135

as eight different renewals in a single month are considerable. More important factors are these, I believe:

- *An annual schedule is less prone to error.* In practice, segmentation is often flawed because someone forgets to include a detail on a list order, or a data entry person is distracted and leaves out one important piece of information.
- *An annual schedule generates far fewer complaints* (once the system is accepted by the donors or members). With variable renewal dates, membership staff members waste countless hours fielding complaints from members who think their dates are screwed up.
- *An annual schedule permits more cost-effective segmentation of special appeals.* All it requires is one "window" in the appeal schedule, not twelve smaller ones.

Though a renewal series on a fixed annual schedule is generally preferred for the reasons given, there may be cases in which a monthly expire date really makes sense: a museum that acquires a lot of walk-up members year-round, for example, where members lose parking benefits (or whatever) when their membership expires.

A more important question than the timing of a renewal series concerns how well a series performs in comparison with direct mail programs based exclusively on special appeals. I've been told by several organizations that they've tested renewal series against repeated special appeals and found that the renewals didn't work. I have no idea what they meant by a test. Nor would anyone offer data to illustrate. All I know is that renewals have *always* lifted net revenue when my colleagues and I have introduced them for our clients.

There is also considerable variation in the nature of the contents of these renewal mailings from one organization to another. Some favor long letters chock full of substantive information (for at least some efforts in the series). Other organizations limit themselves to brief, businesslike notices that rely on donors' natural tendency to renew their support in the absence of some good reason not to do so. For typical examples of the briefer (and more common) sort, see Exhibit 8.1.

Donor Benefits

I'll assume that you're a generous person and that you yourself are a donor to several deserving nonprofit organizations. Why are they deserving? Why do you give them money? If you dig deeply into your motivation, you'll probably uncover a number of reasons: spiritual fulfillment, perhaps; a desire to give something back to your community; the hope of learning more about a particular issue; or simply the need to do something affirmative in a society that frustrates you in so many

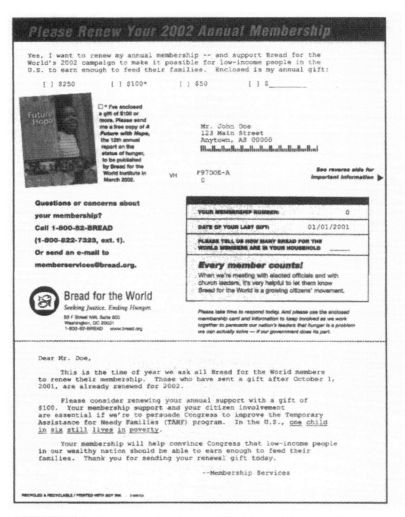

EXHIBIT 8.1. Key Elements of a Five-Effort Annual Renewal Series.

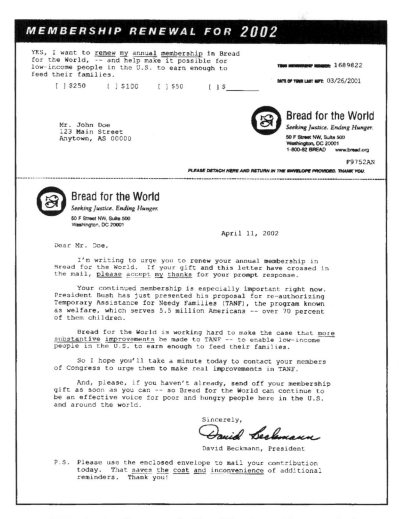

MEMBERSHIP RENEWAL FOR 2002

YES, I want to renew my annual membership in Bread
for the World, -- and help make it possible for
low-income people in the U.S. to earn enough to
feed their families.

[ ] $250   [ ] $100   [ ] $50   [ ] $_____

YOUR MEMBERSHIP NUMBER: 1689822

DATE OF YOUR LAST GIFT: 03/26/2001

Mr. John Doe
123 Main Street
Anytown, AS 00000

Bread for the World
Seeking Justice. Ending Hunger.
50 F Street NW, Suite 500
Washington, DC 20001
1-800-82 BREAD   www.bread.org

F9752AN

PLEASE DETACH HERE AND RETURN IN THE ENVELOPE PROVIDED. THANK YOU.

Bread for the World
Seeking Justice. Ending Hunger.
50 F Street NW, Suite 500
Washington, DC 20001

April 11, 2002

Dear Mr. Doe,

I'm writing to urge you to renew your annual membership in
Bread for the World. If your gift and this letter have crossed in
the mail, please accept my thanks for your prompt response.

Your continued membership is especially important right now.
President Bush has just presented his proposal for re-authorizing
Temporary Assistance for Needy Families (TANF), the program known
as welfare, which serves 5.5 million Americans -- over 70 percent
of them children.

Bread for the World is working hard to make the case that more
substantive improvements be made to TANF -- to enable low-income
people in the U.S. to earn enough to feed their families.

So I hope you'll take a minute today to contact your members
of Congress to urge them to make real improvements in TANF.

And, please, if you haven't already, send off your membership
gift as soon as you can -- so Bread for the World can continue to
be an effective voice for poor and hungry people here in the U.S.
and around the world.

Sincerely,

David Beckmann

David Beckmann, President

P.S. Please use the enclosed envelope to mail your contribution
      today. That saves the cost and inconvenience of additional
      reminders. Thank you!

EXHIBIT 8.1. Key Elements of a Five-Effort Annual Renewal Series,
Cont'd.

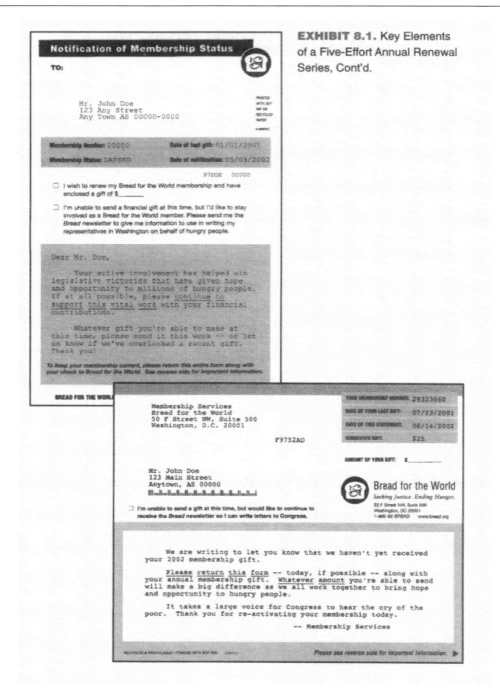

EXHIBIT 8.1. Key Elements
of a Five-Effort Annual Renewal
Series, Cont'd.

Bread for the World

Seeking Justice. Ending Hunger.

50 F Street NW, Suite 500
Washington, DC 20001
1-800-82-BREAD   www.bread.org

Your membership number: 00000

July 29, 2002

Mr. John Doe
123 Any Street
Any Town AS 00000-0000

Dear Mr. Doe,

At the June meeting of Bread for the World's board of directors, we talked about early plans for the organization's 30th anniversary in 2004.

Bread for the World has been blessed with a long history -- and has won major victories for hungry people -- because you and others have so faithfully renewed your membership.

I know personal circumstances change for each of us, but I'm concerned that your last membership gift was in January, 2001.

That's why I hope you'll take a moment to jot me a note on the reverse side of this letter. If you prefer, you may send me an e-mail message at presidentsoffice@bread.org -- or give me a call toll-free at 1-800-82-BREAD (822-7323), ext. 301.

Perhaps, though, you feel that Bread for the World has been less effective in recent years -- or that we're addressing the wrong issues. If that's the case, your comments and suggestions would be very helpful to me.

Thank you for taking time to communicate with me.

Sincerely,

David Beckmann

David Beckmann
President

P.S. I value your comments, so I hope you'll take a minute right now to respond. I've enclosed a stamped return envelope to make it easy for you to send off your note today. Thanks!

F9700E   RECYCLED & RECYCLABLE / PRINTED WITH SOY INK   2-40471E

EXHIBIT 8.1. Key Elements of a Five-Effort Annual Renewal Series, Cont'd.

Source: Bread for the World. Examples reproduced with permission.

ways. There are dozens of possibilities, perhaps hundreds. (I've described twenty-three motivations for giving in my book, *How to Write Successful Fundraising Letters* [2001].) But the common denominator among all these motives is that *giving delivers benefits to the donor.*

There may be both intangible and tangible benefits for giving to a particular cause or institution or in response to a specific appeal. The intangible ones are, I believe, by far the most powerful, because they unlock those deeper motives that most truly explain why you or I respond to appeals. But tangible benefits can be important as well, especially in a membership program (where they are typically more numerous).

The tangible benefits of giving may include any of a multitude of attractions such as the following:

- A newsletter or magazine about the organization's work or the issues it addresses
- Discounts on admission to exhibits or performances
- Opportunities to learn directly from staff members about issues or programs
- Invitations to exclusive special events
- Get-well cards to sign and send to patients in a children's hospital
- Action alerts or bulletins about fast-breaking developments in the organization's work, offering opportunities to participate directly by writing supportive letters, making phone calls, or sending e-mail messages
- A lapel pin, decal, sticker, certificate, bumper strip, or other emblem of affiliation

A well-conceived annual giving or membership program typically includes a mix of tangible and intangible benefits. In theory, the possibilities are limitless, but in practice only certain benefits will seem truly appropriate in any given set of circumstances. For instance, a donor to a university annual fund is unlikely to desire or expect to receive periodic bulletins inviting him to lobby the state legislature for additional funding for the university. Similarly, a small donor to a children's cancer center probably wouldn't appreciate the sort of elegant Lucite paperweight encasing the center's logo that a major environmental donor might enjoy. Choosing donor benefits is a matter of judgment about what is appropriate for the level of giving and for the type of organization. In Exhibit 8.2, you can see the benefits offered by several nonprofit organizations.

Membership Programs

Check your wallet or purse. How many membership cards do you find there? The automobile club? American Express? An airline frequent-flyer club? A college alumni association? A health club? A local museum? Chances are, you're a member

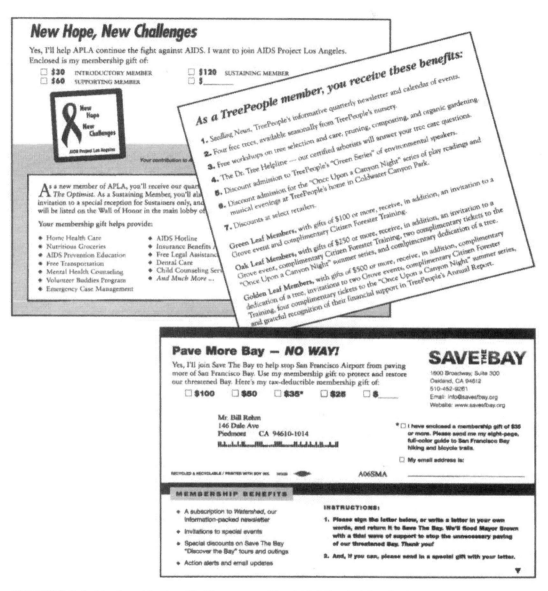

EXHIBIT 8.2. Membership Benefits Shown on a Direct Mail Fundraising Package Response Device.

Sources: AIDS Project Los Angeles, reproduced with permission; TreePeople, reproduced with permission; Save the Bay, reproduced with permission.

of several clubs or organizations, even if you don't carry their membership cards. The concept of membership has become second nature to Americans and is fast spreading worldwide because it's a useful concept that, at its best, helps us define our own identities.

Consider, for example, the art museum membership card you just uncovered in your purse. As a practical matter, it's useful for discounts on admission to the museum's shows and on merchandise for sale in the shop. But the fact that you're a museum member means more than that, doesn't it? On the most basic level, it means that you're the sort of person who goes to art museums—a person with discriminating taste and an appreciation of the sublime accomplishments of the human spirit.

Among nonprofit organizations, museums and other cultural institutions are most likely to maintain membership programs. But they're hardly alone. Over the years, thousands of other nonprofits have adopted the membership model precisely because it's so well accepted and understood and because it strengthens bonds with donors by emphasizing the intangible benefits of affiliation.

At many nonprofit organizations, the lines are blurring between membership and donor programs. The best example is the spreading use of the annual renewal series for nonmembership programs. However, two characteristics typically distinguish a membership from a donor program:

1. Explicit recognition that, by joining, a member is entitled to certain benefits and privileges
2. The presumption of a long-term relationship, with the expectation clearly stated that membership must be annually renewed

Psychologically, these are powerful distinctions, attracting some prospective donors and repelling others. But I know of no meaningful way to evaluate which approach is more advantageous from a fundraising perspective. For a substantial majority of nonprofit organizations and institutions, either a membership or a donor program might be appropriate.

In a membership program, however, there is a greater expectation of tangible benefits. The museums and other cultural institutions that pioneered the membership concept in the mid-twentieth century have led most donors to look for advantageous reasons to join a new organization. In a donor program, it might suffice to offer a periodic newsletter and little more in the way of tangible donor benefits. A membership program requires more. Marketers for some leading cultural institutions give the impression that joining entails benefits that together are worth even more than the price of membership. Be careful, then, if you elect to adopt a membership program.

However, the annual renewal model—sending notices until a donor gives—seems to work even without tangible benefits, or at least with a minimum of benefits (a newsletter, for instance). This is often the case with systems built on annual funds or annual campaigns, which I find convenient to regard as modified membership programs.

● ● ●

Aspects of membership programs have been built into both monthly giving clubs and high-dollar annual giving societies, which are the subjects of the next two chapters. First, let's look at monthly giving.

Monthly Giving

Anyone who pays a mortgage or puts monthly utility bills on an automatic payment plan understands monthly giving. In the world of fundraising, monthly giving involves a commitment to give a fixed amount—often $10 or $15—year-round, month after month, instead of merely responding to occasional appeals with $25 or $30 checks. A little fast, back-of-the-envelope arithmetic makes clear that $10 per month for a year is a lot more than two or even three $25 checks over the same period of time.

From a donor's perspective, research shows that monthly giving holds a number of attractions:

- By giving modest sums on a monthly basis, donors are able to contribute much more over time to their favorite causes and thus have a bigger impact without feeling financially pressed.
- Monthly giving, especially when it's automated, is easy and convenient. With preauthorized monthly giving using credit cards or electronic funds transfer, donors don't have to worry about writing multiple checks, getting stamps, and mailing gifts. There is virtually no paperwork.
- Because administrative costs are lower with monthly giving, a greater percentage of each gift will go directly to the cause.
- Donors appreciate how monthly giving helps them with household budgeting. It's a planned expense that helps them keep a careful check on how much they give to nonprofits.

- Many donors find it hard to say no to any solicitation request and thus especially appreciate the monthly giving option. It removes the guilt they feel when they receive a solicitation package and can't afford to give.
- People are bombarded with thousands of advertising messages, posing countless choices and decisions every day. And there are many worthy causes and issues donors would like to support. Preauthorized monthly giving to the donor's favorite organizations relieves the agony of decision making in two ways. Because monthly donors support fewer nonprofits, this lessens those frequent decisions about whether to respond to acquisition mailings. And donors often find it agonizing to decide which solicitations to respond to from their favorite nonprofits.
- Because monthly donors are too precious to exchange or rent to others, it's important always to exclude them from exchanges with other nonprofits. For many donors, this can be a strong incentive.
- Most donors receive less mail from other nonprofits because their names are not shared and less mail from the nonprofit they're supporting with monthly gifts, because it usually replaces the renewal series (and most special appeals).
- As members of a special group, monthly donors become insiders and may feel they play a leadership role in the nonprofit's work.
- In a well-managed monthly giving program, there is a named contact person at the nonprofit who can address all the questions or concerns a monthly donor may have about the organization's work or its gift processing. Donors appreciate this direct access to a real person.
- Monthly giving means less junk mail for donors to discard.
- Monthly giving saves time. There's less solicitation mail to sort, read, and respond to.
- Monthly giving helps save the environment. Less paper and less mail means fewer trees are cut down, fewer chemicals used to produce ink, and less energy consumed in transportation.
- Monthly giving allows donors to provide reliable and predictable revenue, allowing a nonprofit to budget and plan with confidence and thus accomplish more.

Exhibit 9.1 shows the business end (the response device) of a direct mail package inviting donors to join a monthly giving club. Note the payment options and the opportunity to send a one-time gift instead of joining the program.

I'm indebted to my colleague, Gwen Chapman, for the list of attractions. Gwen has two decades of experience working with monthly giving in South Africa, the United Kingdom, Canada, and the United States and has conducted extensive marketing research on the topic.

PARTNERS FOR THE EARTH   *REPLY MEMORANDUM*

TO: Lynn Pallotta
       Coordinator, Partners for the Earth

FROM:

Union of Concerned Scientists
PARTNERS FOR THE EARTH
Two Brattle Square   Cambridge, MA   02238-9105
www.ucsusa.org

Mr. John Doe
123 Any Street
Any Town AS 00000-0000

            68DOE   00000

RECYCLED & RECYCLABLE / PRINTED WITH SOY INK

☐ **YES.** I accept Howard's invitation to join PARTNERS FOR THE EARTH
by authorizing a monthly gift as indicated below.

I authorize the Union of Concerned Scientists to charge the following amount to my checking
account/credit card monthly. I understand I can change the amount or cancel at any time.

[ ] $10   [ ] $15   [ ] $_____

_____   _____
SIGNATURE   DATE

I'd like to make my monthly Partners for the Earth contributions as follows:

☐ **Please debit my checking account.** I've enclosed a VOID check so you
can note my bank account details. (Simply write "VOID" across a blank
check.) **OR**

☐ **Please debit my credit card:**   ☐ Visa   ☐ MasterCard

Card # _____ Exp. Date _____

Phone # (_____) _____

*Your monthly contributions will be
billed on the 20th day of the month
(or the closest business day). Please
remember, you may change or stop
payments at any time by notifying UCS.*

*Your gifts to UCS are tax-deductible
as provided by law. It is our policy
not to exchange or otherwise share
the names of our Partners for the
Earth with other organizations.*

☐ NO. I'm sorry, I cannot accept Howard's invitation at
this time, but I've enclosed an additional gift of:

[ ] $100   [ ] $_____

☐ My check is enclosed.

☐ Please charge my credit card (see back).

*Please return this form in the
enclosed, postage paid envelope
or mail to Lynn Pallotta,
Coordinator, Partners for the
Earth, Two Brattle Square,
Cambridge, MA 02238-9105.
Thank you!*

EXHIBIT 9.1. Response Device from a Monthly Giving Program
Invitation.

Source: Union of Concerned Scientists. Reproduced with permission.

Similarly, for a nonprofit organization with a sizable base of individual donors, a monthly giving program is (or should be) an irresistibly attractive proposition:

- Monthly giving has proven to be one of the most dramatic ways to upgrade small donors, typically eliciting cumulative annual giving that's at least three times as much as single-gift donors.
- Monthly donors are worth more. The long-term value of monthly donors in a well-managed program can be an order of magnitude greater than that of single-gift donors.
- Monthly giving can be a highly effective means to bond with donors, providing the framework for building an unusually strong, lasting relationship.
- Long-time monthly donors are the very best prospects for bequests and other planned gifts.
- Monthly giving programs can be managed much more frugally and cost-effectively than single-gift programs, offering substantial savings in administrative and mailing costs.
- Monthly giving provides steady, reliable cashflow, largely unaffected by the constant ups and downs of fundraising.

Many of the advantages perceived by donors and nonprofits alike depend on having in place a smoothly running and efficient gift-processing system. That, in turn, depends on the method or methods with which monthly gifts are accepted.

Choosing Gift Payment Options

Traditionally, monthly giving programs were labor-intensive. Because they depended on donors to mail checks in response to statements each month, any nonprofit with more than a few hundred monthly donors required a dedicated staff person to process the checks and manage the constant flow of statements, reminders, missed payments, and confused questions.

In the United States, many large monthly giving programs still involve processing large numbers of checks and fielding questions and complaints from monthly donors. However, in Canada, the United Kingdom, Europe, and elsewhere, where monthly giving (often called committed giving) has taken deep root, contributions by check are rare or nonexistent. Some payments are made by preauthorizing a monthly charge on a credit card. But most monthly gifts entail "preauthorized checking" or, in the United States, EFT. Only by employing automated systems such as these can nonprofits truly realize administrative savings and sharply reduce the need for dedicated personnel to manage a monthly giving program.

As a consequence, I routinely advise most clients not even to offer monthly donors the option of paying by check. In some cases, nonprofits choose to offer both credit card and EFT options at the outset. Others may choose to offer only monthly giving to donors only via credit card, reserving for later the effort to convert donors to EFT.

It's no secret why credit card payments are more desirable than payments by check, and preauthorized checking even more desirable still: costs are lower and loyalty much higher in either of these automated payment plans. But the costs are lowest and fulfillment rates highest of all using EFT. Fulfillment rates—the percentage of funds collected—may vary greatly from one organization to the next regardless of payment procedures, because some organizations do a much better job than others cultivating and informing their monthly donors. As a rule of thumb, however, I assume that fulfillment with EFT and credit cards will be at least 90 percent per year, whereas fulfillment by check is rarely as high as 80 percent (and I've seen it drop as low as 50 percent).

As you might imagine, the logistical arrangements involved in setting up credit card or EFT programs are challenging. However, there's not enough room in these pages to cover this important topic. Besides, you can turn instead to Harvey McKinnon's groundbreaking book on monthly giving, *Hidden Gold: How Monthly Giving Will Build Donor Loyalty, Boost Your Organization's Income, and Increase Financial Stability* (1999). Because I edited that book, I know it well and can give it my unqualified endorsement.

To get a sense of the immense value of monthly giving to a charity when gifts are fulfilled using EFT or credit cards, take a look at Table 9.1, which illustrates the revenue generated over ten years by a group of just two hundred donors who enroll in a monthly giving program. Note that this table depicts the revenue from only a group of new monthly donors enrolled in a given year. It does not take into account the monthly donors recruited either before or after that year.

In Table 9.1, I've assumed that the rate of fulfillment is 90 percent, that is, nine out of every ten gifts pledged is actually received. As Harvey McKinnon notes, 90 percent is the minimum fulfillment rate you should expect in a monthly giving program based on credit cards or EFT (unless monthly donors are recruited door-to-door or on the street, where attrition rates are substantially higher).

There's a lot to be learned from Table 9.1:

- The average monthly gift rises slightly each year, reflecting the results of at least one and often two upgrade efforts conducted during the year.
- As a result of the rise in the average monthly gift, the year-to-year decline in gross income is shallow, falling in a decade only to $20,064 from the first-year level of $32,400.

TABLE 9.1. Long-Term Income from 200 New Monthly Donors.

Year	Number in Program	Average Gift	Maximum Number Gifts	Estimated Number Gifts	Year Income	Cumulative Income	Cost per Member	Cost per Year	Cumulative Cost	Net	Cumulative Net
1	200	$15	2,400	2,160	$32,400	$32,400	$20	$4,000	$4,000	$28,400	$28,400
2	180	16	2,160	1,944	31,104	63,504	15	2,700	6,700	28,404	56,804
3	162	17	1,944	1,750	29,750	84,254	16	2,592	9,292	27,158	83,962
4	146	18	1,750	1,575	28,350	112,604	17	2,482	11,774	25,868	109,830
5	131	19	1,575	1,417	26,923	139,527	18	2,358	14,132	24,565	134,395
6	118	20	1,417	1,275	25,500	165,027	19	2,242	16,374	23,258	157,653
7	106	21	1,275	1,147	24,087	189,114	20	2,120	18,494	21,967	179,620
8	95	22	1,147	1,032	22,704	211,818	21	1,995	20,489	20,709	200,329
9	86	23	1,032	929	21,367	233,185	22	1,892	22,381	19,475	219,804
10	77	24	929	836	20,064	253,249	23	1,771	24,152	18,293	238,097

- Cumulative income over ten years from just two hundred monthly donors amounts to $253,249, with net income not far behind at $238,097. This amounts to a cost per dollar raised of about 6 cents.
- With net income over ten years of $238,097 from just two hundred monthly donors, their long-term value is $1,190, or $119 per year.

Keep in mind as you review these figures that the income doesn't stop coming in the tenth year of a monthly giving program. It will continue to grow. Harvey McKinnon estimates that it will eventually amount to about double the ten-year rate before all the monthly donors stop giving.

To gain perspective on the figures in Table 9.1, review Table 9.2, which shows the income you might expect over ten years from two hundred unusually loyal and generous donors.

Please note that, in preparing Table 9.2, I've assumed the average number of gifts per donor per year is 2.5, which is unusually high. I've also assumed much higher than usual renewal rates. Further, I've assumed that the resolicitation cost per donor per year is no more than the cost of servicing monthly donors—another highly conservative assumption. All told, Table 9.2 portrays a much more favorable picture than might be warranted.

Ignoring those caveats, let's now contrast the picture in Table 9.2 with that in Table 9.1:

- Gross revenue from multi-donors over ten years is approximately 20 percent of that from an equal number of monthly donors: $50,623 versus $253,249. And net revenue is only about 16 percent as high.
- The long-term value of the loyal and generous multi-donors in Table 9.2 is $196 over ten years, or just a trifle under $20 per year. Compare that with the $119 per year you saw in Table 9.1. The cost to raise a dollar from these multi-donors is about 23 cents, or nearly four times that for monthly donors.

Numbers like these convince me that monthly giving programs are worthwhile, no matter how much time and trouble they require and almost regardless of the amount of money needed to get them off the ground.

Building a Monthly Sustainer Program

In *Hidden Gold*, Harvey McKinnon writes about "the six essential ingredients of a successful monthly giving program." Those six elements are the following:

1. Your organization must recognize that donor loyalty is a two-way street.
2. Your organization must have an appealing mission.

TABLE 9.2. Long-Term Income from 200 New Multi-Donors.

Year	Number in Program	Renewal Rate	Average Gift	Estimated Number Gifts	Year Income	Cumulative Income	Cost per Donor	Cost per Year	Cumulative Cost	Net	Cumulative Net
1	200	—	$30	500	$15,000	$15,000	$20	$4,000	$4,000	$11,000	$11,000
2	120	60%	31	300	9,300	24,300	15	1,800	5,800	7,500	18,500
3	78	65%	32	195	6,240	30,540	16	1,248	7,048	4,992	23,492
4	55	70%	33	138	4,554	35,094	17	935	7,983	3,619	27,111
5	41	75%	34	103	3,502	38,596	18	738	8,721	2,764	29,875
6	33	80%	35	83	2,905	41,501	19	627	9,348	2,278	32,153
7	28	85%	36	70	2,520	44,021	20	560	9,908	1,960	34,113
8	25	90%	37	63	2,331	46,352	21	525	10,433	1,806	35,919
9	23	90%	38	58	2,204	48,556	22	506	10,939	1,698	37,617
10	21	90%	39	53	2,067	50,623	23	483	11,422	1,584	39,201

3. You must communicate your message effectively.
4. You must have an efficient and responsive back-end system.
5. You must be able to thank donors promptly and answer their individual concerns.
6. You need an integrated approach to building a donor program.

The first five of these six items are essentially self-evident. But the sixth calls for comment.

Monthly giving programs aren't necessarily direct-mail-driven. For many nonprofits, direct mail is the principal channel through which monthly donors are recruited and educated. But U.S. fundraisers' growing experience with monthly giving is leading us to the conclusion that our counterparts in Canada and Western Europe reached long ago: other communication channels may be more productive than surface mail. In fact, monthly donors may be recruited in any one of a great many ways as well as by mail:

- By telephone
- By television
- By newspaper or magazine ads
- With brochures distributed by staff, board, volunteers, or donors
- At special events
- Face-to-face on an individual basis
- Face-to-face using trained recruiters on city streets or canvassing door-to-door (direct dialogue)
- Through ads in your own newsletter or other publications
- By e-mail or through your Web site

U.S. charities are increasingly finding that telemarketing tends to be a more effective tool than direct mail in converting active donors to a monthly giving program. In Europe, Australia, and increasingly in other parts of the world, direct dialogue has emerged as the most productive way to recruit monthly donors, and that method recruits them from the general public, not from the much narrower pool of a nonprofit's own donor base. Meanwhile, pioneered in Latin America and Europe by Greenpeace, e-mail and the World Wide Web are showing promise as monthly giving recruitment tools as well. Also, some well-heeled charities (principally, child sponsorship organizations and religious organizations) use television and space ads to recruit new monthly donors from the public at large. It's unusual for nonprofits of other types to find television cost-effective in the United States.

However, Harvey's principal point is that you should *not* look for the single most cost-effective way to recruit monthly donors. Instead, you should use every communications channel at your disposal to promote the program, raising awareness of monthly giving as high as possible among your donors. If you want to build an active monthly giving program, place ads in your donor newsletter and in your magazine as well, if you have one; recognize new monthly donors in your newsletter and, if possible, in your annual report; include a monthly giving option in renewals and appeals to your donors. The reinforcement that comes from this repetition of your message will pay off in better response to your monthly giving invitation.

The Monthly Giving Invitation

Regardless of the medium of communications you use, you'll need to answer at least six key questions before writing an invitation to your donors to enlist in a monthly sustainer program. Those six questions follow:

1. *Are you ready to process monthly gifts on a continuing basis?* Unless your back-end operation is fully prepared to deal with the complexities of processing automated EFT and credit card gifts, you're not ready to invite donors to join your monthly giving program. Launching a monthly sustainer program may require you to contract with a bank or other gift processor—perhaps more than one. Beginning that process once the gifts start coming in is far too late!

2. *What is the name of your monthly giving club or society?* A distinctive name derived from your organization's mission or its history is ideal (Environmental Advocates or Angels of Mercy, for example).

3. *Who will you invite to join the program?* Clearly, the club will be open to all members or donors, but which segment or segments will you target in your recruitment effort? In my experience, the characteristics most commonly shared by donors who convert to a monthly giving program are longevity (at least three years of continuous giving) and above-average frequency (say, at least three gifts per year), but sometimes include newly acquired donors as well. But your segmentation could be far more sophisticated than this, and testing over time may show you that other considerations are equally important.

4. *What gift amounts will you suggest?* Some programs specify a fixed giving level, say $10 or $20 per month. Others offer a range of options ($8, $12, $16, $20). In yet other cases, the minimum suggested gift amount and any higher amounts are based on the individual donor's giving history. Take your pick, but be sure to base the dollar amounts on the patterns of giving in your own organization.

5. *What benefits will you offer?* A special sustainers' newsletter is a common feature of monthly giving programs. However, many such programs offer other tangible benefits as well, such as lapel pins or other branded merchandise (coffee mugs, T-shirts, tote bags) or donor recognition devices (certificates, plaques). Regardless of whether you elect to offer tangible benefits, be sure to emphasize the true benefits that are spelled out in the opening pages of this chapter.

6. *What are the options for payment?* Many monthly donors fulfill their gifts by credit card only, by preauthorized checking, or by mailing you checks. As I've already indicated, I do not recommend offering the check-payment option. But you'll need to decide whether to offer credit card and EFT payment, or merely one of the two. (I normally favor requesting payment only by credit card in the invitation, because that payment option requires no explanation.)

In Exhibit 9.2, you'll see a letter of invitation to a monthly giving program. As you'll note, this letter focuses on the relationship between the donor and the nonprofit rather than on its mission. Clearly conveying to donors the concept of monthly giving and the payment options available often requires more than enough words to cram into one letter!

Renewing and Upgrading Monthly Donors

One of the reasons that fulfillment rates in monthly giving are so high is that such programs don't normally require the donor to exert any effort to renew her commitment. Some organizations ask for only a one-year commitment, and others may introduce a monthly giving program for only a fixed period of time to reach some particular goal (in a capital campaign, for example). But those are the exception. In most cases, monthly donors are recruited, in the language of the commercial marketplace, "until forbid," that is, until they withdraw from the program by notifying the charity or the bank to discontinue payment.

Nonetheless, it's a common practice and a very good one to send each monthly donor an annual statement detailing her support throughout the previous year. (For tax purposes, at least in North America, the beginning of each calendar year is the best time to do this.) Sending this statement affords an opportunity to ask the donor to increase her support by adding a modest amount to each monthly payment—$2 or $3, perhaps, if her gift is in the range of $10 to 15, or $4 to $5 if it's closer to $25. It's advisable to suggest an upgrade at least once per year.

It's also a good idea to keep in mind that monthly donors are among your most loyal and generous donors and that they may be willing to contribute over and above their monthly gifts. Some nonprofits promise donors who enroll in a sustainer program that they'll be removed from the regular solicitation stream and not asked for additional gifts. In my estimation, this is a big mistake. I recommend including monthly donors in one special appeal each year—typically, the year-end mailing. Sometimes, monthly donors prove to be the most responsive segment of all!

It's all too tempting to conclude that the most cost-efficient way to treat monthly donors is to ignore them. After all, if you receive their gifts automatically via credit card or EFT, eliminating the need for monthly invoices, why should you spend money writing to them? *Don't fall prey to this specious reasoning!* Monthly donors

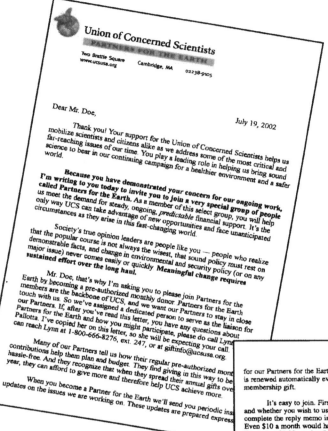

Union of Concerned Scientists
PARTNERS FOR THE EARTH
Two Brattle Square   Cambridge, MA   02238-9105
www.ucsusa.org

Dear Mr. Doe,

July 19, 2002

Thank you! Your support for the Union of Concerned Scientists helps us mobilize scientists and citizens alike as we address some of the most critical and far-reaching issues of our time. You play a leading role in helping us bring sound science to bear in our continuing campaign for a healthier environment and a safer world.

Because you have demonstrated your concern for our ongoing work, I'm writing to you today to invite you to join a very special group of people called Partners for the Earth. As a member of this select group, you will help us meet the demand for steady, ongoing, *predictable* financial support. It's the only way UCS can take advantage of new opportunities and face unanticipated circumstances as they arise in this fast-changing world.

Society's true opinion leaders are people like you — people who realize that the popular course is not always the wisest, that sound policy must rest on demonstrable facts, and change in environmental and security policy (or on any major issue) never comes easily or quickly. **Meaningful change requires sustained effort over the long haul.**

Mr. Doe, that's why I'm asking you to please join Partners for the Earth by becoming a pre-authorized monthly donor. Partners for the Earth members are the backbone of UCS, and we want our Partners to stay in close touch with us. So we've assigned a dedicated person to serve as the liaison for our Partners. If, after you've read this letter, you have any questions about Partners for the Earth and how you might participate, please do call Lynn Pallotta. I've copied her on this letter, so she will be expecting your call. You can reach Lynn at 1-800-666-8276, ext. 247, or at giftinfo@ucsusa.org.

Many of our Partners tell us how their regular pre-authorized monthly contributions help them plan and budget. They find giving in this way to be hassle-free. And they recognize that when they spread their annual gifts over the year, they can afford to give more and therefore help UCS achieve more.

When you become a Partner for the Earth we'll send you periodic inside updates on the issues we are working on. These updates are prepared express

---

Page 2

for our Partners for the Earth. As a Partner for the Earth your UCS membership is renewed automatically every year. So you won't be billed for your annual membership gift.

It's easy to join. First decide how much you can afford to give each month and whether you wish to use your checking account or your credit card. Then complete the reply memo included in this mailing and return it to Lynn at UCS. Even $10 a month would have a positive impact on what we can achieve together. That's just $0.33 per day. Less than a cup of coffee. And please remember, you can cancel or change the amount anytime. Just let us know, preferably via letter or email. That way, we have a record of your request.

I hope you will choose to become a Partner for the Earth and complete the enclosed reply memo addressed to Lynn. And if you have any questions or doubts, please do give Lynn a call. She'd be delighted to talk with you. Thank you for your continued support.

Sincerely,

Howard Ris
President

P.S.   Please review the enclosed reply form to see how easily you can make a greater impact on what UCS is able to achieve. Even a modest monthly contribution will help strengthen UCS. And don't forget, your gifts to UCS are tax-deductible.

cc: Lynn Pallotta

EXHIBIT 9.2. Letter from a Monthly Giving Program Invitation.

Source: Union of Concerned Scientists. Reproduced with permission.

are among your most important donors. They're likely prospects for legacy gifts as well as for steady annual support. In addition to sending them your regular donor newsletter and perhaps a special newsletter exclusively for monthly givers, it's also important to find other ways to keep them informed and involved. Special cultivation mailings at least once or twice a year are a very good idea. One such mailing might be a simple thank-you, recognizing their loyalty and the special role that they play in securing your finances. Another might be a clipping of a favorable newspaper or magazine story about your work, along with a note from your executive director. (If you include reply envelopes in these cultivation mailings, they'll produce additional gifts.)

● ● ●

Now that we've addressed the topic of one specialized form of giving clubs, let's turn to another specialized form—high-dollar annual giving societies, which are the subject of the following chapter.

10

High-Dollar Annual Giving Clubs

Let's be honest now. When you sort through your mail, what happens? Do you immediately reach for the direct mail appeals you've received from Save the Bandersnatch and the Institute of Cosmetology?

I don't think so. At least not unless you happen to be (1) employed by one of those two institutions, (2) deeply concerned about the plight of the bandersnatch or the challenges of cosmetology, or (3) an obsessive-compulsive student or collector of direct mail fundraising appeals.

Chances are, you sort through the day's mail in close proximity to a wastebasket, immediately tossing out credit card offers, unwanted merchandise catalogs, and appeals from organizations you've never heard of. After all, there's no real difference between unsolicited mail from a business you'd never do business with and a nonprofit you'd never support.

But wait. What happens if, say, you receive a letter from Save the Bandersnatch that doesn't look like junk mail at all? It comes in a high-quality, closed-face, 9×12-inch outer envelope, with first-class stamps and your name neatly typed, the spelling and address correct, and no teaser or other wording on the front of the envelope save the legend "First Class Mail"—a piece of correspondence, in other words—a piece of mail that contains, well, something interesting. Will you toss this letter away unopened along with all the bulk-rate junk mail? Or will you open it out of curiosity?

You'll open it, I believe. And that belief is based on two decades of experience mailing appeals in similar formats that have generated extraordinary results.

Packages like this are costly, typically many, many times as much as typical bulk-rate appeals. Under the right circumstances, however, these expensive packages pay their way over and over again. This is what I call high-dollar direct mail.

But there's a lot more to high-dollar mail than the cost and care expended on the outer envelope. Similar attention to detail is usually evident on the inside as well: at a minimum, a fully personalized letter and response device, along with a response envelope bearing a live first-class stamp. Still, the most important difference between an appeal like this and run-of-the-mill direct mail fundraising appeals lies in its *message,* not its format or high production values.

Packages like this can be used to meet a number of fundraising needs. But I've consistently found over the years that they yield the greatest rewards when used to promote annual giving clubs (or gift societies) requiring contributions of at least $500 (and often $1,000 or more) per year. For an example, please see Exhibit 10.1.

The Basic Ingredients of a Successful Annual Giving Society

Before you rush off to launch a high-dollar giving club, make sure your organization has what it takes to make a go of it. The prerequisites include the following:

- A track record that clearly demonstrates your ability to put gifts of $500, $1,000, or more to good use
- Development staff that has sufficient time, motivation, and skill to take good care of high-dollar donors (who typically require far more attention than do donors of much smaller sums)
- A large enough number of donors who have given you individual gifts of at least $100 so that you can cost-effectively mail what is likely to be an extremely expensive appeal. (In most cases, it's a mistake to use cumulative giving as a criterion to select the donors who will receive these high-dollar appeals.)

Given these circumstances, a high-dollar annual giving club may make perfect sense for you. The first step, then, is to design a giving club that's perfectly suited for your organization. This will require the following elements, at a minimum:

- An evocative name that calls to mind the essence of your organization's work or mission (such as Guardians of the Wild), identifies some attractive aspect of your work (The Science Council), or honors your founder or some other person who has made a seminal contribution to your organization (The Rachel Carson Society)

Friends of the Negev

American Associates, Ben-Gurion University of the Negev
1430 Broadway, 8th Floor
New York, NY 10018

June 24, 2003

Ms. Jane Doe
123 Any Street
Any City AS 00000

Dear Ms. Doe,

I'm writing to invite you to make an important investment today. An investment in the future of Ben-Gurion University of the Negev . . . an investment in Israel's future . . . an investment in peace and prosperity around the world.

As I'm sure you can imagine, these are very difficult times at the University. The atmosphere of fear; the economic pressures; and the demands of reserve military service are all having an enormous impact on the lives of students and faculty alike.

I want you to know that it is a great source of strength and hope for all of us here that caring Americans like yourself are standing with us through this crisis.

As a supporter of Ben-Gurion University, you have demonstrated a strong commitment to helping us achieve our two-fold mission of academic excellence and dissemination of knowledge. I am deeply grateful for your participation. Together, we are accomplishing a great deal.

Today, I invite you to join a select group of distinguished American supporters of Ben-Gurion University as a <u>Member of *Friends of the Negev*</u> with a gift of $1,250 or more to help provide scholarships for outstanding students in need.

I appreciate that this sum is greater than any single gift you've given to BGU in the past. But I know you understand that the challenges we face today are daunting — and the opportunities to nurture the leaders of tomorrow are immense.

Your membership in *Friends of the Negev* is a direct investment in a peaceful and prosperous future for generations to come.

I am the Director of the Jacob Blaustein Institutes for Desert Research. In the laboratory I

RECYCLED & RECYCLABLE / PRINTED WITH SOY INK   28101

EXHIBIT 10.1. Sample High-Dollar Invitation Package.

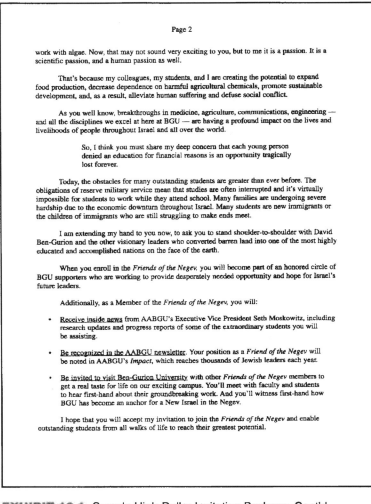

Page 2

work with algae. Now, that may not sound very exciting to you, but to me it is a passion. It is a scientific passion, and a human passion as well.

That's because my colleagues, my students, and I are creating the potential to expand food production, decrease dependence on harmful agricultural chemicals, promote sustainable development, and, as a result, alleviate human suffering and defuse social conflict.

As you well know, breakthroughs in medicine, agriculture, communications, engineering — and all the disciplines we excel at here at BGU — are having a profound impact on the lives and livelihoods of people throughout Israel and all over the world.

So, I think you must share my deep concern that each young person denied an education for financial reasons is an opportunity tragically lost forever.

Today, the obstacles for many outstanding students are greater than ever before. The obligations of reserve military service mean that studies are often interrupted and it's virtually impossible for students to work while they attend school. Many families are undergoing severe hardship due to the economic downturn throughout Israel. Many students are new immigrants or the children of immigrants who are still struggling to make ends meet.

I am extending my hand to you now, to ask you to stand shoulder-to-shoulder with David Ben-Gurion and the other visionary leaders who converted barren land into one of the most highly educated and accomplished nations on the face of the earth.

When you enroll in the *Friends of the Negev*, you will become part of an honored circle of BGU supporters who are working to provide desperately needed opportunity and hope for Israel's future leaders.

Additionally, as a Member of the *Friends of the Negev*, you will:

- Receive inside news from AABGU's Executive Vice President Seth Moskowitz, including research updates and progress reports of some of the extraordinary students you will be assisting.

- Be recognized in the AABGU newsletter. Your position as a *Friend of the Negev* will be noted in AABGU's *Impact*, which reaches thousands of Jewish leaders each year.

- Be invited to visit Ben-Gurion University with other *Friends of the Negev* members to get a real taste for life on our exciting campus. You'll meet with faculty and students to hear first-hand about their groundbreaking work. And you'll witness first-hand how BGU has become an anchor for a New Israel in the Negev.

I hope that you will accept my invitation to join the *Friends of the Negev* and enable outstanding students from all walks of life to reach their greatest potential.

EXHIBIT 10.1. Sample High-Dollar Invitation Package, Cont'd.

Page 3

Your membership in Friends of the Negev is truly an investment in a peaceful and prosperous future for Israel and, indeed, the world. You will be helping BGU grow leaders in the desert . . . a new generation of young women and men from diverse backgrounds who will share their knowledge and expertise with the world.

I look forward to hearing from you and I sincerely hope we will meet in person at Ben-Gurion University of the Negev one day soon.

With high hopes,

Avigad Vonshak
Director, Jacob Blaustein Institutes for Desert Research

P.S.   By American standards, tuition for Ben-Gurion University of the Negev is relatively inexpensive. That means your membership contribution goes a very long way in providing a real opportunity for outstanding students in need. You may want to consider making a larger gift to cover one year's full tuition. But please, know that whatever you choose to give, it will be greatly needed and deeply appreciated. Thank you.

EXHIBIT 10.1. Sample High-Dollar Invitation Package, Cont'd.

TO: Avigad Vonshak
         c/o Seth Moskowitz, Executive Vice President
         American Associates, Ben-Gurion University of the Negev
         1430 Broadway, 8th Floor
         New York, NY 10018

FROM: Ms. Jane Doe   A10DOE-B
         123 Any Street   00000
         Any Town, AS 00000

RE: MEMORANDUM OF ACCEPTANCE

         I am pleased to accept your invitation to make an extraordinary investment in a
         peaceful and prosperous future by joining *Friends of the Negev*.

         I understand that by accepting this invitation I will become an honored partner in
         advancing Ben-Gurion University's mission of excellence and dissemination of knowledge.

         Here is my first year's tax-deductible *Friends of the Negev* membership gift of:

[ ] $1,250 — Please use my membership contribution to give outstanding
         students in need the opportunity to become the leaders of tomorrow.

[ ]   I would like to provide a one-year scholarship for one student at the level indicated
         below:

            [ ] Bachelor's Degree $2,500
            [ ] Master's Degree $7,500
            [ ] Doctorate Degree $10,000

[ ]   Please list my name in your AABGU publication as:
         _____

[ ]   Please do not list my name in your AABGU publication.

[ ]   I am unable to join Friends of the Negev at this time, but I'd like to make a
         contribution of $_____.

Please return this form   "...Our plans for the future are very simple and very pragmatic. We must live
with your check in the   on and build the country, receive immigrants and put them to work, extend
enclosed pre-stamped   our education to even higher levels for an increasing mass of citizens, settle
envelope. Thank you   the desert so as to make Israel economically self-sufficient, and utilize every
very much.   effort, short of undermining our national integrity, to bring about peace."

                                           — David Ben-Gurion, "Israel Among the Nations," 1952

EXHIBIT 10.1. Sample High-Dollar Invitation Package, Cont'd.

Source: American Associates, Ben-Gurion University of the Negev. Reproduced with permission.

- An appropriate giving level or levels, whether $250, $500, $1,000, or more per year—or some combination of these amounts
- A clear understanding about the benefits to donors for enrolling in the annual giving club
- Appropriate materials ready for donor acknowledgments (and the delivery of promised benefits)
- A clear plan and timetable for the renewal and upgrading of the donors who enroll in the club

For a list of the benefits given in many high-dollar annual giving clubs, see Table 10.1.

Why go to all this trouble? Because three powerful arguments will become clear as your high-dollar giving club makes its presence felt in your organization:

1. An annual giving club at the $500 level or higher can be a very lucrative proposition in its own right, yielding substantial net revenue.
2. Many of the donors who will give you $500 or $1,000 by mail are very likely to be capable of contributing at least ten times as much when asked face-to-face. In fact, the greatest value of high-dollar donors may be that, by giving such generous gifts, they identify themselves as prospects for major gifts.
3. Whether or not these donors become major donors, they are more likely than donors at lower levels of giving to renew their support and to continue giving for a long period of time.

TABLE 10.1. Typical Benefits for a High-Dollar Annual Giving Club.

Membership Level	Benefit
$1,000	Listing in annual report
$1,000	Exclusive quarterly "insider" report from CEO
$1,000	Personalized engraved logo paperweight
$1,000	Invitation to reception with CEO
$1,000	Semiannual telephone conference calls with CEO
$2,500	All above, plus autographed book from founder
$5,000	All above, plus personal tour of project
$10,000	All above, plus luncheon with CEO and board
$25,000	All above, plus annual dinner with founder

How to Renew and Upgrade High-Dollar Donors

The process of renewing high-dollar donors is much like that of renewing other donors, and the same is true of the process of persuading them to give larger gifts. What's different is the great care used to cater to them as individuals.

For example, a direct mail renewal series is a standard feature of most high-dollar giving societies. But just like the highly personalized, high-quality packages that brought members into the society, these renewal packages bear little outward resemblance to the standard bulk-mail renewal efforts addressed to most donors at lower levels.

Similarly, the telephone can also be used to renew high-dollar donors who've failed to respond to two or more written notices. It's important, though, that the callers assigned to this project be unusually well informed and skillful and that they be prepared to devote more time to each phone conversation than they do when calling lower-dollar donors.

And the message itself in these renewal efforts must be carefully tailored to the demands of high-dollar fundraising. It's important to reinforce the "value proposition" advanced for the giving society, to recognizing the leadership role that high-dollar donors play (by serving as an example to other donors), and to treat them as very special people.

With low-dollar donors, it's common practice to seek an upgrade—frequently, a modest one—with every solicitation ("You gave $50 last year. Will you consider $60 or $75 this year?"). In high-dollar giving clubs, the upgrade request is rarely so modest. Normally, a giving society member is urged to move up to the next level of membership. A typical hierarchy of choices in a high-dollar club resembles those in Table 10.2.

Viewed in broader perspective, a high-dollar giving club plays a strategic role in an intelligently structured development program: it serves as a recruiting mechanism for major gift prospects. In only the smallest nonprofits can the development

TABLE 10.2. Giving Levels in a Typical High-Dollar Annual Giving Club.

Silver Membership	$1,000
Gold Membership	$2,500
Platinum Membership	$5,000
Diamond Membership	$10,000
The Directors' Circle	$25,000

staff reasonably hope to lavish personal attention on donors of small gifts. Typically, there's a threshold below which it isn't cost-effective to invest staff time in paying personal visits to donors. In many community-based, grassroots organizations, that threshold may be $100. At a major university or a big-budget national organization, the minimum qualifying gift may be set at $25,000. Annual giving clubs established at those levels highlight those donors who demonstrate both ability and interest in upgrading their giving.

● ● ●

In many organizations, high-dollar giving societies are also used as a means to identify planned giving prospects. However, I believe this is a mistake, as I'll explain in the following chapter, which explores legacy giving and the important role that direct mail techniques can play in promoting this truly monumental form of giving.

11

The Many Uses
of the Telephone

Now, let me guess: you don't *like* the idea of telephone fundraising. Chances are, you've got five or six objections to using what most people in the industry so clumsily refer to as telemarketing. Calling your donors on the phone seems intrusive. It's a technique widely known to be used by fraudulent charities. It puts your organization's reputation at risk because you may not be able to exert direct control over the individuals who make the phone calls. And besides, you just hate it when somebody calls *you* at dinnertime to ask for money—and so does everyone you know!

Then why do so many organizations use the telephone so extensively in their fundraising programs?

The answer I give to that question is precisely the same as my response to those who ask why so many nonprofit groups use direct mail: *It works!*

Now, please don't confuse telephone fundraisers with bucket-shops peddling tickets by phone to charitable events or the people who call you out of the blue at dinner to raise money for the police or the sheriff's department. These high-pressure operations—most of them local and some of them fly-by-night ventures that skip from one city to the next—are responsible for the lion's share of the public's complaints about telephone fundraising and for most of the fraud. Doubtless, some are honest, hardworking, and sincere, but many such operators exploit their employees, their clients (if in fact they're legitimate), and the public. To me, telephone fundraising means using the telephone as a communications tool linking a public interest organization with its supporters, almost always its current and previous donors.

It's impossible to estimate with any accuracy how much money legitimate non-profit groups and political campaigns raise by telephone in a year, but I'm certain that the figure runs to many billions of dollars. (The Direct Marketing Association estimates that the total in 2002 was more than $61 billion.) So explosive has been the growth of telephone fundraising in recent years that what was a mere handful of firms offering these services at the beginning of the 1980s has become a large industry involving many hundreds of companies. And countless charities and public interest groups—most notably colleges and universities—have established in-house phone banks operated either by volunteers or by professional staff, including students.

Whenever you contact thousands of people, whether by telephone or by mail, some of them are bound to become irritated. There's no more effective or efficient method of communicating with members and supporters than by telephone and no more efficient way to annoy at least a few of them.

Without telephone fundraising, however, many groups would raise substantially less money to support their programs. Most nonprofit organizations conclude, with varying degrees of regret, that they simply can't avoid using the telephone. Measured in a revenue-to-cost basis or in terms of sheer net profits, there's often no way to beat it.

Yes, there are complaints. And yes, individual donors *matter.* My colleagues at the Share Group have found that it's cost-effective to exert the utmost effort to mollify those few individuals—fewer than 1 percent—who become angry when they're called.

But it's a mistake to dwell on donors' complaints. Many people, especially those who don't reside on either coast, actually *enjoy* the telephone calls we make on behalf of our clients. Typically, the number of those who thank you for calling far exceeds the number who complain. Many people appreciate getting long-distance calls from groups they support. Each call is an opportunity to pass along a great deal of useful information to your members or donors, often correcting mistaken impressions or reminding them of past successes.

Whether conducted by a specialized telephone fundraising company, a commercial telemarketing service bureau, or an in-house phone bank, telephone fundraising has ten principal applications in public interest fundraising:

1. *Conducting emergency campaigns.* This is the most obvious use of the telephone in a fundraising program, because it's usually faster to get on the phones than to send a mailing. The phone is also an ideal communications channel in an emergency, because phone callers can test alternative messages easily and quickly and can adapt their conversations with donors to fast-changing events.

2. *Converting petition-signers, event-goers, and on-line activists into direct response donors.* Like it or not, direct mail is rarely effective in persuading attendees at special events or activists such as petition-signers to contribute money. Using the telephone can be much more productive.

3. *Maximizing return from an annual renewal series.* After you've reached the end of your rope through direct mail, and one more renewal notice simply isn't cost-effective, your best shot at recapturing lapsed members or donors is by phone. Normally, this is a breakeven proposition, but only in a short-term perspective. After all, now you know how much your donors are worth! Some groups find they're worth enough, and telephone reactivation is effective enough, that it pays for them to call early in the renewal cycle, as the second or third effort in a series. (Keep in mind, though, that donors who are "recaptured" by telephone tend to be more responsive to future telephone appeals than to mail.) It's not unusual for a telephone renewal effort to persuade one of every four or five donors to renew their support.

4. *Reactivating lapsed members or donors.* Although direct mail can be cost-effective in reactivating near-lapsed donors or members, say, those whose last gift was received no more than three years earlier, the telephone may be an even more efficient means to recapture their support, and it's often effective with donors whose last gift was received much earlier, sometimes even many years previously.

5. *Recruiting donors into high-dollar annual giving clubs.* Just as my colleagues and I use specialized direct mail for high-dollar donors, we also sometimes use high-dollar telefundraising. This requires employing especially talented, articulate, and knowledgeable callers and permitting them to spend longer on the phone. The higher level of the gifts they produce—often $1,000 or more—makes the effort worthwhile.

6. *Recruiting monthly donors.* In the United States, direct mail has proven to be an unreliable method to recruit monthly donors. Sometimes it works well. Usually it doesn't. Telemarketing has proven much more effective. On the phone, between 5 and 12 percent of donors contacted are likely to enlist as monthly givers in a well-managed telefundraising campaign.

7. *Upgrading donors, especially monthly donors.* I've successfully used direct mail in specialized donor-upgrade campaigns, but I've found over the years that telemarketing yields a higher proportion of upgrades and often a higher average gift as well.

8. *Issuing special appeals.* To vary the rhythm and the medium of your contact with your donors, you'll probably find it very profitable to conduct one or two special appeals each year by telephone. (Contact more frequently than every six months may be ineffective or even counterproductive.) But if your donors pledge to

contribute, it's important to follow through with several reminders to hold them to their word and not let them easily off the hook with direct mail appeals, which may request a lot less money than they've promised on the phone.

9. *Acknowledging donors.* It may well be worth your while to call at least the more generous of your donors to thank them for their support, *without asking for additional gifts.* A thoughtful gesture of this sort may increase donor loyalty over the long term. For many groups, gifts of $100 or more are big enough to justify this type of red-carpet treatment.

10. *Combining mail and phone appeals.* Especially for your most generous donors, the considerable expense of combining one or more direct mail contacts with at least one telephone call—all for a single appeal—may pay off in a very big way if it's wisely planned and well executed.

In nearly every type of professionally executed telephone fundraising campaign, donors are asked to commit themselves to contribute a specific amount of money. That amount is then cited on a follow-up mailing, sometimes called a pledge card or pledge reminder, mailed as quickly as possible after the phone call, ideally within twenty-four hours. Some firms mail slightly different versions of their pledge cards to donors who indicate support but won't commit themselves to specific amounts.

Although your specific objectives will surely vary from one type of telephone fundraising program to another, all six types have several advantages in common:

• *Net revenue.* This may be deferred revenue in the case of reactivation or prospecting efforts (since the payoff probably won't come until you receive subsequent gifts), but it's almost always the principal reason to employ telephone fundraising techniques.

• *Donor education.* By conveying a brief and clearly focused message in a comprehensive telephone "script," your donors are much more likely to *remember* you than if you mail an appeal to them, because the telephone is a warmer, more intimate form of communication. By script, I don't mean a message that callers are expected to deliver verbatim. Rather, in professional telefundraising, callers use the script as a discussion guide, and their success depends on their ability to engage donors in two-way conversations that focus on donor interests. In fact, cutting-edge telemarketers are now individually customizing scripts with such personal information, for example, as a donor's favorite animal species or what type of public television programming a donor watches.

• *Two-way communications.* Unlike all but the rarest direct mail appeal, a telephone program gives your donors a chance to talk back and to feel more involved in your work.

• *Donor loyalty.* This may ultimately be the greatest advantage of telephone fundraising. Studies show that donors who are contacted by phone tend to remain donors longer and give more generously and more frequently than those who are contacted by mail alone.

Some organizations run telephone fundraising programs independently of their other development work. This is usually unwise, unless your organization can identify a large enough number of telephone-responsive donors who can be called three or even four times per year, with limited direct mail contact. Telephone fundraising efforts are typically—and appropriately—conducted in conjunction with the overall direct mail program. The telephone is best seen as one more implement in the fundraiser's toolbox.

Currently, in state legislatures around the United States, in the Congress, and in the federal administration, legislative and regulatory pressures on telemarketers are growing rapidly. To date, the brunt of the effect has been felt by commercial telemarketers. Telefundraisers have escaped many of the more aggressive efforts to limit their freedom of operation. It's anyone's guess what the future might hold. But my advice is to make the fullest possible use of this invaluable fundraising tool, while keeping one eye on the legal and regulatory environment.

Think strategically. *Integrate* your direct mail and telephone fundraising efforts, even if you find, as some groups do, that their telemarketing efforts contribute as much as half of the net profits from the combined direct response fundraising program. The mails and the telephone are different ways to communicate a common vision and sense of purpose to your donors.

For most members of a large national organization, the only *personal* contact available is by telephone. Intelligently managed telephone fundraising can add a warm, personal dimension to the relationship between you and your members, reinforcing your donor communications and fundraising programs (including direct mail) and building individual interest and loyalty. Nothing else but face-to-face contact can match telephone fundraising as a way to *intensify* your organization's relationship with its members. The telephone is one of very few tools widely available to public interest groups that make person-to-person fundraising possible.

However, telephone fundraising is fundamentally a financial proposition. The strongest case for it is that it makes money, and it usually does so in a way that's readily predictable. The numbers tell the most important part of the story.

The Numbers That Matter Most

Like direct mail, telemarketing is a numbers-based enterprise that rests on a handful of unique fundamental concepts. The following are first among them:

• *Number of names with telephone numbers.* It's unusual for any nonprofit to have on file the telephone numbers for all its donors. Normally, the telephone fundraising agency must submit the donor file to a service bureau that computer-matches it with a compilation of all the listed numbers in the United States. It's unusual these days for that process to result in finding telephone numbers for more than 60 percent of the donors on a typical file.

• *Contact rate.* This rate is the percentage of calls attempted that result in a conversation on the phone. Contact rates tend to vary between 50 and 70 percent.

• *Pledge rate.* This rate is the percentage of contacts made that result in an affirmative declaration by the donor that he would contribute to the cause. Pledge rates typically fall into the range of 20 to 40 percent.

• *Fulfillment rate.* This rate is the percentage of pledges that actually result in the receipt of a gift. Depending on the type of telephone fundraising project, the fulfillment rate might be anywhere from 50 to 100 percent (or occasionally more, when donors who decline to pledge on the phone actually send gifts anyway!).

With that terminology nestled snugly in your vocabulary, you're ready to review the dynamics of a hypothetical telephone fundraising campaign.

What to Expect from a Telephone Appeal

Assume that your organization has 30,000 current donors on file—contributors who, in this case, have sent you at least one gift within the past twelve months. You've contracted with a professional telephone fundraising firm to conduct a special appeal designed to maximize net revenue and upgrade as many of your donors as possible. Here's what the numbers might look like:

Of your 30,000 donors, the telephone fundraising firm you've hired feels that only 20,000 qualify as good prospects for telephone contact. The rest haven't given large enough gifts at any one time.

A service bureau retained by the telephone fundraising firm will run a computer-match against your remaining 20,000 donors to find their telephone numbers. With a little luck, they'll find 50 percent, or 10,000—a decrease from previous years because of increased use of unpublished phone numbers, especially on both coasts.

Working on the basis of a script that you and the firm should devise together, paid callers will use low-cost, long-distance lines to contact those 10,000 donors, generally between the hours of 10:00 A.M. and 9:00 P.M.. Most telephone fundraising agencies today use a computer-regulated system called predictive dialing, which allows human callers to avoid reaching busy signals, answering machines, or getting no answer. Let's be generous and assume that eventually, after several tries with numbers that don't answer, the callers reach about 60 to 65 percent, or 6,500.

It's reasonable to expect that between 30 and 50 percent of these 6,500 current donors will pledge a contribution of a specific amount. (The qualifier is important, because many will also make vague promises or drop hints but not agree to specific pledges. Nonspecific pledges are much less likely to be fulfilled.) In an active donor resolicitation program, a 35 to 45 percent pledge rate is typical. That means you'll have, say, 2,600 pledges.

The fulfillment rate—the percentage of donors who actually send in checks—may range from less than 50 percent to more than 100 percent (in which case, the number of nonpayers is equal to or exceeded by the number of nonspecific pledges that are fulfilled). For a well-run telephone fundraising program, a 70 percent fulfillment rate is acceptable. For you, this means 1,820 gifts.

If the average contribution to all your direct mail resolicitations is $30, removing the 10,000 least responsive donors should raise that average by at least 10 percent, and the warmth and innate persuasiveness of telephone contact should add another 10 percent to the average gift. This means an average of about $36 for each of the 1,820 gifts you receive from this telephone fundraising project, or a gross of $65,520. (Naturally enough, the average gift almost *always* depends on whom you call.)

But don't expect all $65,520 to come in at once. Telephone contact may take time—between three and six weeks, generally, to contact all 6,500 donors. Your telephone fundraising firm then has to mail out pledge cards (within twenty-four hours of the call, if they're good), and you have to wait for the donors to respond. (See Exhibit 11.1 for a typical example.) Many don't. Most programs follow up once or twice by mail and sometimes by phone as well. Generally, 70 to 80 percent of the proceeds from a telephone fundraising program will be received within 120 days of the date of the first contact with donors. The *last* contributions should be received within 120 days of the date of the last contact. As you can see, telephone fundraising is rarely a quick way to raise a buck.

Although the length and character of the script will determine how much time each phone contact requires, it's likely that callers will average anywhere from nine to thirteen contacts per hour. The median is almost squarely in the middle of that range, or about ten or eleven contacts per hour. (At that rate, it will take about 620 hours of calling to complete the job.) If the firm is charging you $4 per contact (including direct mail follow-up costs), the cost of the effort will be $26,000. At $5 per contact, the total cost would be $32,500. Eventually, you'll net somewhere between $33,000 and $40,000.

The ratio of revenue to costs in this hypothetical project is between 2.0 and 2.5 to 1. In other words, you'll double your money. In addition, the chances are you'll

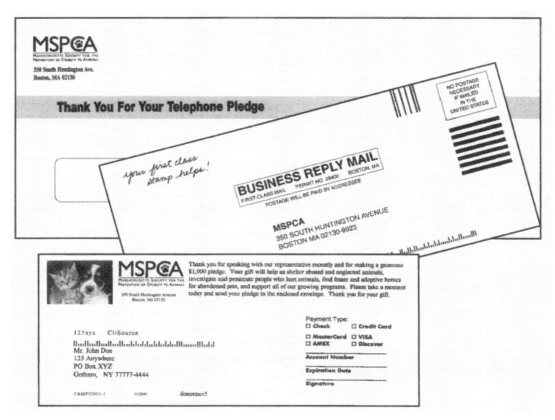

EXHIBIT 11.1. Telephone Pledge Package.

Source: Massachusetts Society for the Prevention of Cruelty to Animals. Reproduced with permission.

be getting gifts from many more than the number of donors who would respond to a direct mail appeal, you'll get larger gifts from many of them than they've ever given before by mail, and you'll have established personal contact with more than one-third of your best donors, which will educate them and build their loyalty.

Like other direct response fields, telephone fundraising has become increasingly complex. Many telefundraising firms now maintain contact records of who pledged and who didn't. In subsequent calling programs, they eliminate donors who have repeatedly refused to give in the past, thus lowering program costs and increasing pledge rates.

An especially effective telephone fundraising program—one carefully segmented to deliver the most powerful message to each segment or type of donor—can upgrade the average contribution by more than 10 percent. Some programs successfully generate major gifts: single contributions of $10,000 or more are not unknown. Careful direct mail follow-up can substantially raise fulfillment rates.

But don't be mesmerized by dollars and cents. Telephone fundraising can play a strategic role for your organization by converting many of your one-time contributors into genuine supporters, by generating real enthusiasm among many of your reliable donors and coaxing them to give much larger gifts, and by conveying the message to your supporters in the most intimate way available to you that their support really matters.

Fees charged by telephone fundraising firms vary greatly, and each firm seems to have its own peculiar list of inclusions and exclusions from the base rate. They tend to run from about $3.50 per donor contacted to $6 or more (to as much as $12 per contact in a high-dollar program. Experience and levels of talent also vary. Chances are, you'll get what you pay for. You're not likely to find any bargains.

Cost is only one of a great many issues to consider about telephone fundraising. Normally, you can lower the cost by limiting the duration of the contact (the script), by cheapening the quality of the printed materials sent to those who pledge to contribute, by avoiding "lead letters" or postcards to the donors you're going to call, and by simplifying the methods and terms of collecting payments. It may or may not be smart for you to do any of these things.

When you look around the telephone fundraising field, you should also find out whether a firm you're considering is properly registered to do business in the states where your donors live. More than forty states require fundraising firms to register. Many also require that firms file advance notices of scheduled solicitations. Regulation of telephone fundraising has become a controversial issue of considerable staying power, and I'm sure you'll agree it's essential to conduct your affairs with scrupulous regard for both legal and ethical standards.

● ● ●

OK. Now you know enough about the use of the telephone in fundraising to venture a little further along the way toward integrated, multichannel fundraising. That's the topic of the following chapter.

12

Legacy Giving

For many years now, the fundraising profession has been awash in scholarly studies, econometric projections, educated guesswork, and sheer wishful thinking about the immense sums of money that will pass from one generation to the next in the opening decades of the twenty-first century: $10 trillion? $40 trillion? $100 trillion? Just pick a number, and start scratching out on the back of an envelope how many millions *your organization* will receive in the form of planned gifts in the next ten years. The mind boggles!

Once you catch your breath, however, you'll confront a somewhat less exhilarating reality.

First, the yearbook *Giving USA 2003: The Annual Report on Philanthropy for the Year 2002* (p. 8) estimates that bequests during calendar year 2002 totaled approximately $18.1 billion—a tidy sum in anyone's book. But that figure represented just 7.5 percent of charitable giving in 2002, dramatically below the potential suggested by current wealth transfers. And *Giving USA 2002* revealed that giving by bequest generally trended upward during the previous three decades. But after adjustments for inflation, the increase averaged just 1.5 percent per year from 1971 through 2001.

Currently in the United States, according to *Planned Giving in the United States 2000: A Survey of Donors,* conducted by the National Committee on Planned Giving, only about 8 percent of those who have written wills have provided for legacy gifts, whether in the form of simple bequests in their wills or estate plans or embodied in more complex charitable trusts. To an optimist like me, this suggests an endless capacity for growth. But only a fool would suggest it's easy to persuade people to include charities in their estate plans.

Dig a little deeper into this reality, and you'll learn that professionals in the fast-growing field of gift planning lavish most of their attention on rich people—the sorts of people who might yield multi-million-dollar charitable trusts. Clearly, they're responding to Willie Sutton's insight that money isn't spread around equally in our society.

In some circumstances, that single-minded focus on people of considerable means makes a great deal of sense: for example, at a hospital with a narrow donor base, the very best use of a planned giving officer's time might well be to split his time among a few dozen wealthy prospects. But in a nonprofit organization with a broad base of donors or members acquired and cultivated by mail, that approach can be counterproductive. In such circumstances, donors of modest means may be "where the money is."

According to planned giving specialist Robert F. Sharpe Jr., the average bequest in the United States is approximately $35,000—an amount that qualifies as a major gift at just about any nonprofit organization. But few such bequests come from major donors. In fact, in-depth research conducted by Northwestern University in the mid-1990s revealed that there is *no correlation* between wealth and the likelihood of leaving a legacy. In fact, the Northwestern studies show that planned giving prospects defied detection apart from the most obvious criterion—age. And almost anyone familiar with the giving patterns revealed by computer studies of donor history knows that bequests are most likely to come from direct-mail-acquired donors who gave cash gifts of less than $100 in their lifetimes—often substantially less than $100. It's not at all unusual for a long-time $10 or $15 donor—perhaps even one who lapsed for several years just before passing away—to leave a $25,000 bequest or even one for $250,000.

The potential for raising substantial amounts of money from bequests is enormous. In a poll of donor attitudes conducted in March 2003 by Lang Research (Toronto, Ontario) for Mal Warwick & Associates, Inc., and The FLA Group, using a sample of five hundred U.S. donors and five hundred Canadian, 99 percent of American donors and 97 percent of Canadian donors asserted that they were aware of legacy giving as an option, and most of them—64 percent in the United States and 48 percent in Canada—said they thought legacy giving was a good idea. In fact, 78 percent of Americans and 47 percent of Canadians had already been asked to consider legacy gifts, and about one in three of them (23 percent in the United States, 16 percent in Canada) said they had already agreed to name a charity in their wills or estate plans. A further 29 percent of Americans and 18 percent of Canadians indicated that they are at least somewhat likely to do so in the future.

That's where direct mail comes into the picture in legacy giving.

Setting Your Strategy for Legacy Giving

Broadly speaking, there are three approaches you can pursue in hopes of securing legacy gifts:

1. *Sit around and wait.* Eventually, if your fundraising program is large enough, and if you maintain a sizable donor base, bequests are likely to float in over the transom. Depending on your organization's mission and track record, there might even be quite a few such bequests.
2. *Hire a planned giving staff.* Put them on the road to talk to your organization's major donors to discuss estate planning opportunities that will be beneficial for the donors as well as for you. If you have a big enough pool of major donors, and if your planned giving officers are both skillful and patient enough, you may eventually obtain a few truly sizable legacy gifts.
3. *Promote legacy giving throughout your donor file.* Target those whose age and giving history make them the likeliest candidates for bequests in the foreseeable future. Although this approach isn't liable to generate significant revenue in the short term, over the long haul it can prove very lucrative indeed.

Clearly, these three approaches aren't mutually exclusive. Strategy B implies Strategy A, at least so far as the overwhelming majority of the donors are concerned. And Strategy C is entirely compatible with Strategy B. In fact, that combination of B and C probably represents the soundest approach for most large, well-established nonprofits.

However, for the overwhelming majority of individual-donor-based nonprofit organizations in North America, Strategy C is the surest road to success in securing legacy gifts. And that strategy is based on putting to work specialized direct response techniques—chiefly, direct mail.

For many of the nonprofits that have been most successful in obtaining bequests from their donors, the starting point in the promotion process was to conduct research into the attitudes of legacy gift prospects. After all, you may be able to guess how your donors view your organizations, but you won't know unless you ask them. Focus groups designed to unearth their attitudes about your work and about legacy giving are an ideal way to begin the process of promoting legacy gifts.

For many nonprofits, the second step is to launch a special form of giving club called a heritage or legacy society.

Launching a Legacy Society

Donors of $1,000 or more are admitted into membership in a high-dollar giving club in many nonprofit organizations. Is it any wonder, then, that donors who commit to legacy gifts, frequently amounting to tens or hundreds of times as much money, are honored by admission to a similar group that confers special benefits and privileges?

A heritage or legacy society may offer its members any one or more of a great variety of benefits, including the following:

- A lapel pin or other emblem of affiliation
- Exclusive, members-only gatherings with prestigious speakers or members of the organization's board of directors
- An informative newsletter that honors selected members of the society and keeps them up-to-date on new wrinkles in estate planning
- Recognition in the organization's donor newsletter, annual report, or at special events

See Exhibit 12.1 for an example of a response device included in a legacy promotion mailing, which illustrates the benefits of membership in a legacy society.

It's worth giving serious thought to the name of your legacy society. Although the Brand X approach—calling it The Legacy Society or The Heritage Society—is a perfectly defensible choice, you may enhance the attractiveness of your legacy society by assigning a name with more cachet. Choosing the name of your revered founder or long-time chief executive may help to induce many donors to commit to legacy gifts that will honor an old friend. Picking a name that reminds donors of your mission may have a similar, motivating effect (Stewards of the Earth, for example, or The Beethoven Society).

If yours is a local or regional organization, and you're planning special events for the members of your heritage society, you might consider *launching* the effort at a public gathering of your donors. At such an event, you might honor those who have already notified you of their intention to include you in their wills or living trusts (with their express permission, of course).

EXHIBIT 12.1. Insert from a Legacy Society Promotion Mailing.

Source: NARAL Pro-Choice America. Reproduced with permission.

Creating a Legacy Newsletter

If a launch event isn't practical for your organization, the inaugural effort may well be the premier issue of a newsletter created for the members of your legacy society. In any case, a legacy newsletter mailed two, three, or four times annually can be a key component in an effective legacy marketing program. The contents of such a newsletter might include any or all of the following items:

- A page devoted to listing the members of the legacy society
- One or more interviews with legacy donors, along with photos
- An article illustrating how one legacy gift was put to work
- A brief message from the executive director
- Tips on estate planning from a qualified attorney or accountant
- A coupon that may be mailed to request more information or to declare interest in arranging for a legacy gift

Exhibit 12.2 shows the contents of a planned giving newsletter.

Bread for the World Members Create Charitable Bequest to Increase Over Time

Paul Harris was raised in a family that emphasized caring for poor people. He had a dramatic experience when he was 20 years old that inspired him to do what he could to bring justice to God's world. Traveling with his family in Egypt, he came face to face with starving children who he knew were not going to survive.

"Poverty with a face on it changes your heart," Paul says. He brings this compassion to his current teaching ministry at Easter Lutheran Church in Eagan, Minnesota, as he has to his various ministry positions in the past.

The Rev. Art Simon's original message for Bread for the World, that the U.S. government could do more to raise more funds for hunger concerns, is what first drew Paul to Bread for the World. When it comes to hunger and

Paul and Sally Harris

injustice, Paul believes that our responsibility to poor people is a matter of citizenship, that we must do our part.

Next year, Paul will join his wife Sally in Iringa, Tanzania, at Tumaini University. She will teach legal writing and he will teach theology. They have lived in Tanzania on two other occasions: for five months in 1990 and for four months in 1999. And they led a church group just this past May for a three-week learning tour.

Following in the tradition of his parents, who left the bulk of their estate to charity, Paul and his wife Sally have created a unique charitable bequest in their will. Before traveling in 1999, they updated their will to include 20 percent of their estate going straight to charities. Bread for the World is the largest single designee of a small group of organizations that are particularly meaningful to Paul and Sally. The unique aspect of this particular charitable bequest is that each year the percentage going straight to charity grows by one percent. Paul describes this as "proportional giving as the kids get older."

"It's an interesting exercise ... what are the causes that we care about deeply, and what percentage do they get," Paul thinks.

Both Paul and Sally realize the importance of future gifts. By placing Bread for the World in their will, they will continue to support the mission of seeking justice for hungry people for years to come. As Paul says, "both in life and in death, we can play a part to help poor people and affect public policy to have love for poor people."

EXHIBIT 12.2. One Page from the "Legacy of Hope" Newsletter.

Source: Bread for the World. Reproduced with permission.

Many, perhaps most, planned giving newsletters include articles with technical details about various forms of charitable trusts. There's no end to the legal variations on these devices, so there's lots of material you can generate. But my advice to you is simple: *don't do it!* Every bit of research I've ever encountered about the motivations of planned giving donors makes it clear that there is one overarching consideration in donors' minds when they consider a bequest, and it's not death or taxes: it's *your organization's mission.* The U.S. tax laws are full of loopholes that allow a donor with a clever tax accountant to avoid tax in myriad ways without leaving you a legacy. It's extremely unlikely that you'll secure a planned gift of any type from a donor unless she shares your passion for your mission. Let your planned giving officers discuss the arcane details of gift planning with your donors' attorneys or tax advisors, but don't befuddle them by writing about this supremely confusing field in your legacy society newsletter.

At first, there will be few legacy society members—only those who have previously committed to legacy gifts. They will, of course, receive copies of the newsletter. Equally important, however: so will those in the target group of donors you select for bequest promotion.

Selecting the Target Audience for Legacy Giving

In the broadest perspective, all donors are possible sources of legacy gifts. But just as we distinguish between "suspects" and "prospects" in donor acquisition programs, it's wise to focus our attention on those donors who are mostly likely to consider writing bequests into their wills or estate plans.

The first criterion to consider in targeting donors for bequest promotion is age. It's foolish to include anyone younger than fifty or fifty-five years old. Most organizations set the bar a little higher at sixty, sixty-five, or even seventy, depending on the size of their donor files and the amount of money budgeted to promote bequests. But a number of other criteria ought to be weighed. Experience shows that the following groups of donors have the highest propensity to leave legacies:

- Monthly donors or sustainers
- Donors who regularly give multiple gifts each year
- Donors who were sustainers or who regularly gave multiple gifts each year but lapsed in recent years
- Frequent donors who are also volunteers, including trustees
- Frequent donors who have also made use of the organization's services

Please note that the size of a donor's gifts is *not* included as a criterion here. A donor who has frequently given you $5 gifts two or three times a year for ten years is far more likely to leave you a legacy than someone who gave you $5,000 three years ago. Repeat this mantra to yourself: *there is no correlation between wealth and legacy giving!*

In reality, the selection of prospects for a bequest promotion program can be a sophisticated matter. Specialists in this area may maintain proprietary software that weighs the relative weight of a variety of variables, including such factors as giving history and the nature of previous communications from donors to the organization. With a donor base of modest size, however, it's a relatively simple matter to pick the obvious best prospects.

Cultivating and Educating Potential Legacy Donors

Prudence demands that you *do not* project current income from legacy gifts unless your organization has a long-established history of receiving multiple bequests every year. Typically, it takes at least three years, perhaps five years or longer, before a bequest promotion program begins to bring a return on its investment. Patience is the byword.

Any planned giving officer—no less than any major gift officer—will probably tell you that raising money in big chunks involves nine parts of cultivation to one part of solicitation. In most direct mail fundraising efforts, your objective is to secure funds that come from a donor's *current income* stream. A bequest comes from a donor's *assets*—a far different matter. Rich or poor, few of us are quick to part with our financial assets.

Few rules apply to legacy marketing, in part because such efforts are a relatively new phenomenon, and those who have gained experience in this specialized arena have tended not to share their experiences widely within the nonprofit sector. My own experience suggests that an optimal bequest promotion program should include the following elements:

- One or more designated staff members prepared to follow up gift planning inquiries without delay
- Printed materials linking legacy giving to the organization's mission and vision
- A carefully selected target group of prospects
- A legacy society
- A legacy society newsletter mailed two, three, or four times annually to members of the legacy society and targeted prospects
- An annual letter softly suggesting the rewards of leaving a bequest to the organization (see Exhibit 12.3 for an example)
- An annual letter suggesting that other (unspecified) gift planning options are available

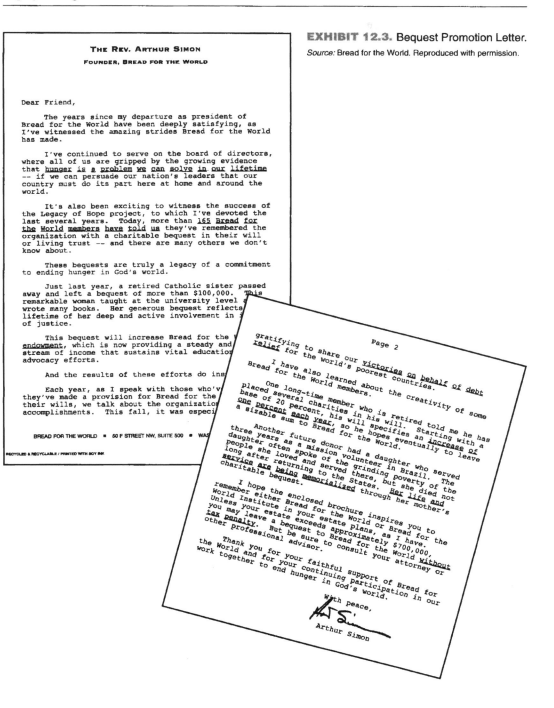

EXHIBIT 12.3. Bequest Promotion Letter.

Source: Bread for the World. Reproduced with permission.

THE REV. ARTHUR SIMON

FOUNDER, BREAD FOR THE WORLD

Dear Friend,

The years since my departure as president of Bread for the World have been deeply satisfying, as I've witnessed the amazing strides Bread for the World has made.

I've continued to serve on the board of directors, where all of us are gripped by the growing evidence that hunger is a problem we can solve in our lifetime -- if we can persuade our nation's leaders that our country must do its part here at home and around the world.

It's also been exciting to witness the success of the Legacy of Hope project, to which I've devoted the last several years. Today, more than 165 Bread for the World members have told us they've remembered the organization with a charitable bequest in their will or living trust -- and there are many others we don't know about.

These bequests are truly a legacy of a commitment to ending hunger in God's world.

Just last year, a retired Catholic sister passed away and left a bequest of more than $100,000. This remarkable woman taught at the university level and wrote many books. Her generous bequest reflects a lifetime of her deep and active involvement in issues of justice.

This bequest will increase Bread for the World endowment, which is now providing a steady and growing stream of income that sustains vital education and advocacy efforts.

And the results of these efforts do inspire.

Each year, as I speak with those who've told me they've made a provision for Bread for the World in their wills, we talk about the organization's accomplishments. This fall, it was especially

BREAD FOR THE WORLD ■ 50 F STREET NW, SUITE 500 ■ WAS

RECYCLED & RECYCLABLE / PRINTED WITH SOY INK

Page 2

gratifying to share our victories on behalf of debt relief for the world's poorest countries.

I have also learned about the creativity of some Bread for the World members.

One long-time member who is retired told me he has placed several charities in his will. Starting with a base of 20 percent, his will specifies an increase of one percent each year, so he hopes eventually to leave a sizable sum to Bread for the World.

Another future donor had a daughter who served three years as a mission volunteer in Brazil. The daughter often spoke of the grinding poverty of the people she loved and served there, but she died not long after returning to the States. Her life and service are being memorialized through her mother's charitable bequest.

I hope the enclosed brochure inspires you to remember either Bread for the World or Bread for the World Institute in your estate plans, as I have. Unless your estate exceeds approximately $700,000, you may leave a bequest to Bread for the World without tax penalty. But be sure to consult your attorney or other professional advisor.

Thank you for your faithful support of Bread for the World and for your continuing participation in our work together to end hunger in God's world.

With peace,

Arthur Simon

Additional legacy promotion efforts might include:

- Mailings, phone calls, print advertisements, and possibly other efforts to persuade allied professionals (attorneys, accountants, financial planners, bankers) to keep the organization in mind when helping clients with estate planning
- Estate planning seminars conducted by allied professionals or planned giving staff members
- Advertisements in newspapers, magazines, or a charity's own internal publications for charitable gift annuities (if the organization offers them)

A legacy marketing program can be as extensive or as limited as you wish. But keep in mind that whether your program is extensive or limited in scope, cultivation is the key. Outright efforts to "sell" planned gifts are unlikely to be effective with more than a few prospects, and they could easily persuade many others to rule out your organization as a legacy gift possibility.

● ● ●

Cultivation, in fact, is the byword of any successful fundraising program. The phrase "relationship fundraising" refers to a development program that's built on cultivation. That key concept is the subject of the following chapter.

Thank-Yous, Welcome Packages, and Cultivation Mailings

Every single donor focus group I've ever witnessed has made it unmistakably clear that a typical donor

- Expects to be thanked for her gifts
- Is peeved when she's not thanked swiftly
- Wants to know what her gifts have helped to accomplish
- Is often incensed when she receives a new solicitation before being thanked for her last gift

Extensive longitudinal research in major direct mail fundraising programs proves that, over time, the modest cost of gift acknowledgments is repaid many times over in increased donor loyalty and generosity. That's right: donors who are promptly thanked for their gifts and kept well informed about the organization's work give more gifts, more often, and they keep giving longer.

A nonlinear perspective on the donor development cycle may make clear why this is so. (See Figure 13.1.) The "Donor Loyalty Cycle" portrayed here was developed by The Domain Group, a fundraising and marketing agency with offices in Seattle, Atlanta, London, and Paris. The Donor Loyalty Cycle skillfully shows the need for never-ending communications and cultivation in relationships with donors—a principle that provides a perfect segue into the subject of "donor-centered fundraising."

FIGURE 13.1. **The Donor Loyalty Cycle.**

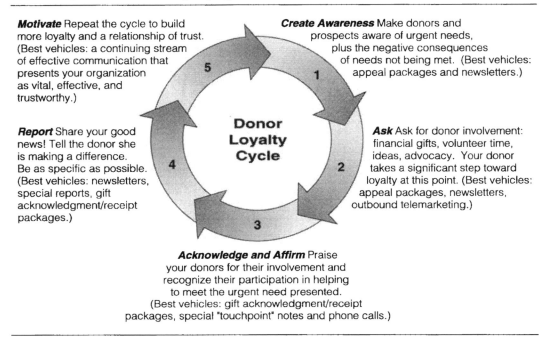

Motivate Repeat the cycle to build more loyalty and a relationship of trust. (Best vehicles: a continuing stream of effective communication that presents your organization as vital, effective, and trustworthy.)

Create Awareness Make donors and prospects aware of urgent needs, plus the negative consequences of needs not being met. (Best vehicles: appeal packages and newsletters.)

Report Share your good news! Tell the donor she is making a difference. Be as specific as possible. (Best vehicles: newsletters, special reports, gift acknowledgment/receipt packages.)

Donor Loyalty Cycle

Ask Ask for donor involvement: financial gifts, volunteer time, ideas, advocacy. Your donor takes a significant step toward loyalty at this point. (Best vehicles: appeal packages, newsletters, outbound telemarketing.)

Acknowledge and Affirm Praise your donors for their involvement and recognize their participation in helping to meet the urgent need presented. (Best vehicles: gift acknowledgment/receipt packages, special "touchpoint" notes and phone calls.)

Canadian fundraiser Penelope Burk's careful studies of donor attitudes confirm these findings. If you want an earful about the fundamental importance of speedy and appropriate donor acknowledgments, read her two books on the subject: *Thanks! A Guide to Donor-Centred Fundraising* (2000), which deals with her research in Canada, and *Donor Centered Fundraising: How to Hold On to Your Donors and Raise Much More Money* (2003), which covers the United States.

The problem this research addresses is the most fundamental in direct response fundraising today in North America. In the United States, for example, the typical direct mail fundraising program succeeds in renewing no more than one in three (roughly 25 to 35 percent) first-time donors. Is that any wonder—when that same "typical" direct mail fundraising program is likely to get thank-yous into its donors' hands no sooner than about six weeks following the receipt of a gift?

An effective direct mail fundraising program begins and ends with a prompt and heartfelt thank-you.

The Dos and Don'ts of Thank-You Letters

At first glance, you might easily conclude that sending donor acknowledgments is a simple matter. After all, what's involved but sending a postcard or a letter acknowledging a donor's gift and getting it into the mail in short order?

In practice, however, especially in a direct mail fundraising program that attracts thousands of gifts per year, sending thank-yous can be a challenging task. Any one of a number of complications might arise, such as the following:

- Gifts are processed sporadically (for example, by a volunteer who works just one day a week).
- Gifts are handled by an off-site vendor that may not be capable of sending thank-yous or not inclined to send them as soon as you'd like.
- Budget pressures require using bulk-rate postage, thus slowing down the process by requiring acknowledgments to be sent in bundles of two hundred letters or more at a time.
- Gifts from a large number of different appeals are received simultaneously.

However, the biggest complication of all is typically the reluctance of the CEO, CFO, or board of directors to spend the money necessary to deliver the sort of thank-yous donors crave. Your first challenge, then, may be to make a powerful case for the *cost-effectiveness* of a well-run donor acknowledgment program. Once you've sold the program, you can turn your attention to technical matters.

Start your planning (or your evaluation of the existing donor acknowledgment procedures) with the understanding that the ideal thank-you includes the following features. It

- Is mailed within twenty-four hours of receipt of the gift
- Is personalized (ideally is handwritten or at least contains a handwritten postscript)
- Is written with warmth, in a personal style
- Cites the amount of the gift and the date it was received
- Refers to the specific issue or project that prompted the gift
- Does *not* ask for another gift
- Promises information (to come later) about how the gift was used
- Bears the signature of the chief executive
- Is hand-signed (though not necessarily by the CEO)
- Is mailed in a closed-face envelope without a teaser
- Includes a receipt for income tax reporting
- Bears a first-class commemorative stamp

- Invites the donor to write or call with any questions or concerns and includes the signer's phone number and e-mail address

Exhibit 13.1 shows a personalized new-gift thank-you letter.

Admittedly, it's not always possible for a nonprofit organization to follow all thirteen of these guidelines in its thank-you program. For budgetary or other reasons, it may be necessary to set priorities and settle for far less than the ideal combination. If so, consider the four most important features of an effective donor acknowledgment system:

1. *Promptness:* 24-hour turnaround is better than 48, which is better than 72 or 96. A week or ten days pushes the limit. Three weeks is far too long for a donor to wait to be thanked. And don't even *think* about sending thank-yous that take longer to get into the mail.
2. *Warmth:* Show your appreciation. Acknowledge the donor's thoughtfulness, generosity, and concern. Don't send your donors a letter that could have been written by a committee of lawyers at the IRS.
3. *Personalization:* Cite the amount and the date of the gift. Be specific, and be personal.
4. *Accountability:* Explain what the gift will be used for, what feedback the donor can expect, and when.

To meet these criteria, you will likely have to adopt a system that integrates caging (recording gifts), cashiering (depositing the money), and acknowledging donors in one smooth, continuous process. The need for speed will probably rule out a separate caging and cashiering operation. (However, it may be possible for the cager to e-mail information about newly received gifts on a daily basis to whomever prepares the gift acknowledgments.)

It's most desirable to use first-class postage on thank-you letters, not only because that ensures faster delivery but because it allows for the mail to be forwarded (in the event that a donor has just moved or has used a check that contains her old address). There's another reason first-class postage makes sense: many donors are favorably impressed that you thought their gifts important enough to warrant a first-class stamp.

In many fundraising programs, the treatment accorded a donor depends on the size of his gifts. For instance, see the hypothetical program design represented in Table 13.1.

Be careful! Three questionable practices are represented in Table 13.1: (1) the use of generic rather than personalized text in acknowledgments mailed to donors

CHILDREN
INTERNATIONAL

March 26, 2003

Mr. Mal Warwick
123 Any Street
Any Town, AS 00000

Dear Mr. Warwick,

Thank you for your generous gift of $25.00, which will be used to help provide Easter
presents this year for your sponsored child. Because we feel it's important for you to
know exactly what you are helping provide, I'm writing to let you know what gifts were
selected for your child.

Though customs and celebrations in their countries may differ from ours, the children in
our program are always thrilled to receive holiday gifts from their sponsors. What's more,
your contribution will also help ensure that every child in our program receives a special
gift this Easter. Isn't it wonderful to know that no child will be forgotten because of your
kindness?

Briggitte will receive a new jacket and a pair of pants. A jacket will provide protection
during Guayaquil's rainy summer season, and is an "extra" that needy families can rarely
afford to purchase on their own. And a new pair of pants can replace old, worn-out ones.

Thank you again, Mr. Warwick. We appreciate everything you are doing on behalf of
your sponsored child.

Sincerely,

James R. Cook
James R. Cook
President

JC:ag

P.O. Box 219055 · Kansas City, MO 64121 · Sponsor Services: 1-800-888-3089 · www.children.org

EXHIBIT 13.1. Personalized New-Gift Thank-You Letter.

Source: Children International. Reproduced with permission.

TABLE 13.1. Donor Acknowledgment Levels in a Hypothetical Fundraising Program.

Amount of Gift	Nature of Thank-You
$1,000+	Personalized, hand-signed, first-class thank-you from CEO plus thank-you call from chief development officer*
$100–$999	Personalized, hand-signed, first-class thank-you from CEO
$25–$99	Generic, bulk-rate thank-you from CEO
< $25	No acknowledgment

*Would also apply if a $1,000+ donor has just sent a smaller amount than $1,000.

of $25–$99 gifts, (2) the use of bulk-rate rather than first-class postage for these donors, and (3) the omission of acknowledgments in response to all gifts of less than $25. Distinctions such as these are understandable and may even be necessary in some circumstances, and (under most circumstances) I have few qualms about omitting gifts of, say, less than $10 from a thank-you program, because I understand how powerful budget-cutting pressures may be. However, keep in mind that $10 donors can just as often leave substantial bequests as $100 donors! So, to the extent that it's possible to avoid these cost-cutting (and perhaps time-saving) measures, I recommend doing so.

Another cost-cutting measure that's sometimes employed in the name of efficiency is to use postcards instead of letters as donor acknowledgments. I regard this practice as a last resort, acceptable only if doing so is the only thing that will make possible a speedy response to a gift. The disadvantages of this technique should be obvious: postcards aren't personal, they make it impossible to cite the specific date and amount of a gift, they rarely reflect warmth, and they're not even private. Many donors are reluctant to allow the letter-carrier or other postal personnel to know whom they're giving money to. And I, for one, don't blame them. However, to even this rule, the occasional hand-signed postcard is the exception that can always be found.

If you want to express appreciation to a new donor, a thank-you letter is a natural and necessary technique. But as many fundraising practitioners have discovered in recent years, a simple thank-you sometimes isn't enough. The so-called welcome package has developed as a supplement to (and occasionally a substitute for) a thank-you letter.

The Welcome Package

You've just sent a $35 check, your first gift, to the Center for Humanity's Progress. It seemed like a good idea at the time: the Center's membership invitation was credible and compelling, giving you the impression that its work was breaking new ground in human relations. You'd never heard about the Center for Humanity's Progress before, but that was, in a way, an advantage rather than a disadvantage. It comes across as an innovative new venture addressing long-neglected needs, and $35 seems like a modest enough vote of confidence in the Center's mission.

Good enough. But now what? What will it take to persuade you to send the Center a second gift?

If the Center treats you the way so many other nonprofit organizations have treated you over the years, the chances you'll send that second gift are slim: no thank-you (or one that comes so late it's worse than none at all).

But let's assume that the Center for Humanity's Progress is starting out on the right foot and has mailed a heartfelt thank-you within a couple of days of receiving your membership contribution. The letter addresses you personally, cites the amount and the date of your gift, acknowledges your willingness to support its innovative mission, and promises that Center staff will keep in touch with you in the future. The upshot is that you know little or nothing more than you knew when you read the Center's acquisition letter, but you feel good about having given that $35.

But the next $35 will be tougher to coax from you. Typically, your next contact with the Center for Humanity's Progress is likely to be a special appeal. In this solicitation, the Center's staff requests your support—another $35, $50, $75, or more—for one of its top-priority projects. However, it just so happens that you have zero interest in that particular project. In fact, you began losing interest when you noticed it mentioned in the membership invitation. You don't regard that project as innovative—or even desirable—at all.

Under the circumstances, what are the chances you'll contribute again to the Center? Nil? Or if the Center's lucky, perhaps a little better?

What if, instead of an immediate appeal for additional funds, you received a package containing the following items?

- A second letter of appreciation and welcome as a member of the Center for Humanity's Progress, including information about the Center's Web site and an invitation to subscribe to its free electronic newsletter
- A brochure describing the Center's programs, listing its key accomplishments, and explaining how to obtain additional, up-to-date information

- A copy of the Center's most recent annual report
- A brief questionnaire about your priorities as a donor and about how frequently you wish to be solicited
- A brochure that describes the Center's legacy society and its monthly giving program, explains the ease and convenience of giving via credit card or preauthorized checking, and describes its $1,000-a-year giving society and the benefits it affords members
- A copy of the Donor Bill of Rights (see Exhibit 13.2)
- A business reply envelope in which to return the completed questionnaire and send any questions or comments you may wish to send

A welcome package like this and the contents described are just samples of innumerable possibilities that could well make the difference between persuading you to send that second gift or writing off the Center for Humanity's Progress as a lost cause. And this may well be the case, *even if you also receive that annoying appeal for funds for a program you don't respect.*

Packages like these don't come cheap. It may cost you two or three dollars or even more to send such a package. But consider this: if your acquisition cost is, say, $10 per donor, you would increase that cost by no more than 30 or 40 percent. And my experience suggests that your renewal rate would jump by a far larger percentage.

Your own welcome package will necessarily take into account your organization's unique circumstances. Ideally, it should reflect the views of your donors themselves, as revealed in focus groups or other market research efforts. The resulting package might be much slimmer than the package I've described—or much fatter. But the chances are that if you do a good job giving your donors at the outset the sort of information they want about your organization and setting the context for their giving, they'll be far more favorably disposed to you as the months and years go on. Exhibit 13.3 depicts the contents of a modest new-member welcome package.

It would be a mistake, though, to conclude that the job of cultivating your donors ends with a welcome package. In fact, the process of relationship building has barely begun at that point.

Four Phases of Fundraising

In Chapter Seven, I discussed the four stages of a donor's life. To refresh your memory and to put a slightly different spin on that matter, I'll restate those four stages in terms of the Four Phases of Fundraising, or the Four I's: (1) identify, (2) involve, (3) inform, and (4) invest.

Donor Bill of Rights

Philanthropy is based on voluntary action for the common good. It is a tradition of giving and sharing that is primary to the quality of life. To assure that philanthropy merits the respect and trust of the general public, and that donors and prospective donors can have full confidence in the not-for-profit organizations and causes they are asked to support, we declare that all donors have these rights:

1. To be informed of the organization's mission, of the way the organization intends to use donated resources, and of its capacity to use donations effectively for their intended purposes.
2. To be informed of the identity of those serving on the organization's governing board, and to expect the board to exercise prudent judgment in its stewardship responsibilities.
3. To have access to the organization's most recent financial statements.
4. To be assured their gifts will be used for the purposes for which they were given.
5. To receive appropriate acknowledgment and recognition.
6. To be assured that information about their donations is handled with respect and with confidentiality to the extent provided by law.
7. To expect that all relationships with individuals representing organizations of interest to the donor will be professional in nature.
8. To be informed whether those seeking donations are volunteers, employees of the organization or hired solicitors.
9. To have the opportunity for their names to be deleted from mailing lists that an organization may intend to share.
10. To feel free to ask questions when making a donation and to receive prompt, truthful and forthright answers.

The text of this statement in its entirety was developed by the American Association of Fund-Raising Counsel (AAFRC), Association for Healthcare Philanthropy (AHP), Council for Advancement and Support of Education (CASE), and the Association of Fundraising Professionals (AFP).

EXHIBIT 13.2. The Donor Bill of Rights.

Source: Copyright 2003, Association of Fundraising Professionals (AFP), all rights reserved. Reprinted with permission.

NATIONAL COUNCIL OF LA RAZA
1111 19th Street N.W., Suite 1000
Washington, D.C. 20036
www.nclr.org

Dear NCLR Associate,

¡Bienvenidos a la familia! You are now an Associate of the National Council of La Raza
(NCLR)—the newest member of our fast-growing community. Thank you for joining NCLR.

As an NCLR Associate, you will enjoy many valuable benefits. The most important of
these benefits is the opportunity to help ensure a better life for all U.S. Latinos.

These are crucial times for our community. Through NCLR's support for its more than
270 affiliated Latino community organizations around the country, you will also help directly
meet the needs of those in our community who are less fortunate. Through your support of
NCLR, you will help combat the short-sighted policies, the ignorance, and the bias that still face
so many Hispanic people in the United States.

As an NCLR Associate you will receive many tangible benefits, too:

- NCLR will consult you about emerging issues affecting the future of the Latino community.
- You will receive discounts on special events, including NCLR's spectacular annual conference.
- We'll e-mail you Action Alerts on current issues critical to the Hispanic community. (Please
  make sure we have your current e-mail address.)
- You'll receive NCLR's quarterly newsletter, *Agenda*, and our informative newsletter, *Boletín*.
  The enclosed complimentary brochure lists all of NCLR's publications—available to you at
  a discount.

Thank you for joining the NCLR familia. Your participation helps to build a growing
network of organizations and individuals determined to make a difference on behalf of the U.S.
Latino community. I'm looking forward to getting to know you!

Sincerely,

Darcy M. Eischens
Director, Associates Program

P.S.   Enclosed you'll find a brief survey. Please take a moment to share your answers.
        You may send the form back to me in the enclosed postage-paid envelope. We're
        eager to know more about you!

RECYCLED & RECYCLABLE / PRINTED WITH SOY INK   2-4001

EXHIBIT 13.3. New-Member Welcome Package Letter.

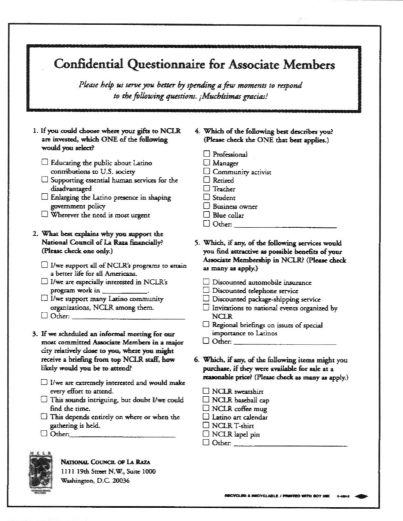

Confidential Questionnaire for Associate Members

*Please help us serve you better by spending a few moments to respond
to the following questions. ¡Muchísimas gracias!*

1. If you could choose where your gifts to NCLR are invested, which ONE of the following would you select?

☐ Educating the public about Latino contributions to U.S. society
☐ Supporting essential human services for the disadvantaged
☐ Enlarging the Latino presence in shaping government policy
☐ Wherever the need is most urgent

2. What best explains why you support the National Council of La Raza financially? (Please check one only.)

☐ I/we support all of NCLR's programs to attain a better life for all Americans.
☐ I/we are especially interested in NCLR's program work in _____.
☐ I/we support many Latino community organizations, NCLR among them.
☐ Other: _____

3. If we scheduled an informal meeting for our most committed Associate Members in a major city relatively close to you, where you might receive a briefing from top NCLR staff, how likely would you be to attend?

☐ I/we are extremely interested and would make every effort to attend.
☐ This sounds intriguing, but doubt I/we could find the time.
☐ This depends entirely on where or when the gathering is held.
☐ Other: _____

4. Which of the following best describes you? (Please check the ONE that best applies.)

☐ Professional
☐ Manager
☐ Community activist
☐ Retired
☐ Teacher
☐ Student
☐ Business owner
☐ Blue collar
☐ Other: _____

5. Which, if any, of the following services would you find attractive as possible benefits of your Associate Membership in NCLR? (Please check as many as apply.)

☐ Discounted automobile insurance
☐ Discounted telephone service
☐ Discounted package-shipping service
☐ Invitations to national events organized by NCLR
☐ Regional briefings on issues of special importance to Latinos
☐ Other: _____

6. Which, if any, of the following items might you purchase, if they were available for sale at a reasonable price? (Please check as many as apply.)

☐ NCLR sweatshirt
☐ NCLR baseball cap
☐ NCLR coffee mug
☐ Latino art calendar
☐ NCLR T-shirt
☐ NCLR lapel pin
☐ Other: _____

NATIONAL COUNCIL OF LA RAZA
1111 19th Street N.W., Suite 1000
Washington, D.C. 20036

RECYCLED & RECYCLABLE / PRINTED WITH SOY INK

EXHIBIT 13.3. New-Member Welcome Package Letter, Cont'd.

7. The National Council of La Raza is (please check ONE only):

☐ My/our principal way to address what I/we consider to be the most important issues today.
☐ One of my/our top three ways to help make the world a better place.
☐ A good cause that I/we support along with lots of others.
☐ Other: _____

8. In supporting nonprofit organizations, I/we sometimes make charitable gifts using (please check as many as apply):

☐ Check only
☐ Cash only
☐ Credit card
☐ Electronic Funds Transfer
☐ Gifts of stock
☐ Bequests in my will
☐ Charitable gift annuities or other planned giving methods
☐ Other: _____

The following information is optional.

9. Who are you? (Optional)

NAME _____
ADDRESS _____
CITY _____ STATE _____ ZIP _____
E-MAIL _____

Preferred title: ☐ Mr. ☐ Ms. ☐ Mrs. ☐ Miss
☐ Mr. and Mrs. ☐ Mr. and Ms.
☐ other _____

10. What is your age? (Optional)

☐ under 25 ☐ 25-34 ☐ 35-44 ☐ 45-54
☐ 55-64 ☐ 65-74 ☐ 75-84 ☐ 85+

11. What is your total annual household income? (Optional)

☐ Under $25,000 ☐ $25,000-49,999
☐ $50,000-74,999 ☐ $75,000-99,999
☐ $100,000-199,999 ☐ $200,000+

Please be assured that the information you supply here will be treated as confidential and used only as a means for the staff of NCLR to become better acquainted with you and your views. Thank you for helping once again to ensure a better life for all Americans. Your generosity will bear fruit for generations to come!

EXHIBIT 13.3. New-Member Welcome Package Letter, Cont'd.

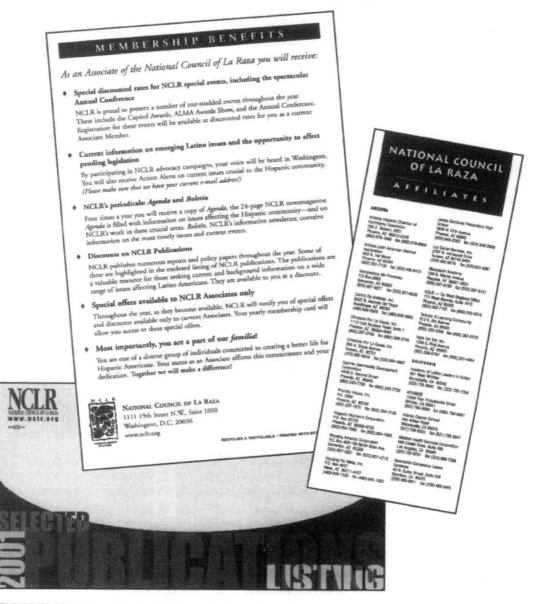

EXHIBIT 13.3. New-Member Welcome Package Letter, Cont'd.

Source: National Council of La Raza. Reproduced with permission.

Identify

This is the acquisition stage. You identify prospective donors from among countless "suspects," and, once you approach them, a certain number raise their hands to express interest in your cause or institution. In other words, they identify themselves. Naturally, what you do in response to this expression of interest is critical. If you fail to show appreciation for a donor's first gift, and promptly so, he's very likely to lose interest.

Involve

If the average direct mail donor in North America supports fourteen organizations per year, as my researches have shown, is it reasonable to assume that she will *continue* to support all fourteen nonprofits year after year? No. Because other research findings make it clear that donors frequently switch loyalties. The deplorable statistics on donor attrition alone are enough to prove that point. To lessen attrition and increase the chances that a donor will stick with you for years to come, you need to *involve* her in your organization, and that process begins with a well-crafted welcome package. Involvement might consist of volunteer work, if your organization offers volunteer opportunities; it might include some sort of activist participation, in a grassroots lobbying campaign, for example; it could entail visits to your office or field projects, briefings, tours, informal gatherings with staff, telephone conference calls to update donors on your work, dedicated members- or donors-only pages on your Web site, or anything else your imagination devises. An involved donor is immeasurably less likely to become a lapsed donor.

Inform

In simpler days, before the advent of electronic communications, the average person wasn't subjected to a seemingly endless stream of so-called information (most of it's undigested data, really) on a daily basis. (Imagine, there was even a time in human history when a single individual could hope to read every single book printed in the world during his lifetime!) Nowadays, an educated person can be pressured to read tens of thousands of words a day, including e-mail messages, electronic newsletters, Web site postings, letters, memos, magazines, newspapers, and whatever else might impinge on his world, not to mention books. Is it any wonder, then, that the fundraiser's basic tool to keep donors informed—the quarterly or bimonthly newsletter—doesn't work as well as it used to?

Please understand: I'm not suggesting that you eliminate your newsletter. In fact, testing conducted by my clients suggests that a strong donor newsletter can substantially lift renewal rates and average gifts. What I am suggesting is that a simple newsletter may not be enough. To ensure that your donors are kept fully up to date, you may need to be more creative, using some of the involvement techniques I cited immediately and not relying solely on your newsletter and the information in your special appeals. For example, a free electronic newsletter and an informative Web site are essential for most nonprofit organizations today. But you may have to go to even greater lengths to ensure that your donors are well informed, using one or more varieties of cultivation mailings. (See Table 13.2 for a guide to some common types of donor cultivation mailings and Exhibit 13.4 for an example of a letter from such a mailing.)

Invest

The ultimate gift for any nonprofit organization is a legacy gift. Such a gift represents an investment by a donor in the future of your organization. At the same time, in a well-managed nonprofit, it also represents the return on an investment in cultivating and informing the donor and in inspiring her to leave a legacy.

TABLE 13.2. Examples of Cultivation Mailings.

Format	Intended Audience
"Insider newsletter" 2–4 times annually	Monthly donors, high-dollar donors, major donors
Personalized letter from CEO or other key staff person 2–4 times annually	High-dollar donors, major donors
News-clippings highlighting major accomplishments as they occur	Monthly donors, all current active donors
Questionnaire offering donors opportunities to specify how and how often they wish to be solicited, what materials they wish to receive, and what donor services they wish to take advantage of	Any segment of the donor file, or all current active donors
Opinion surveys soliciting donors' views and preferences about the organization's program priorities	Any special segment of the donor file, or all current active donors
Complimentary copy of a book, booklet, or other product of the organization's work, along with a personal note from the chief executive or other key person	High-dollar donors, major donors

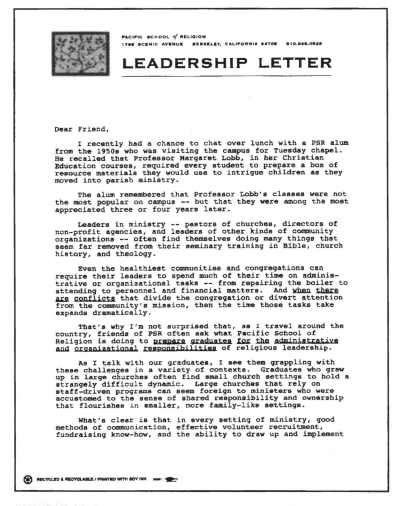

PACIFIC SCHOOL of RELIGION
1798 SCENIC AVENUE   BERKELEY, CALIFORNIA 94709   510.848.0528

LEADERSHIP LETTER

Dear Friend,

I recently had a chance to chat over lunch with a PSR alum from the 1950s who was visiting the campus for Tuesday chapel. He recalled that Professor Margaret Lobb, in her Christian Education courses, required every student to prepare a box of resource materials they would use to intrigue children as they moved into parish ministry.

The alum remembered that Professor Lobb's classes were not the most popular on campus -- but that they were among the most appreciated three or four years later.

Leaders in ministry -- pastors of churches, directors of non-profit agencies, and leaders of other kinds of community organizations -- often find themselves doing many things that seem far removed from their seminary training in Bible, church history, and theology.

Even the healthiest communities and congregations can require their leaders to spend much of their time on administrative or organizational tasks -- from repairing the boiler to attending to personnel and financial matters. And when there are conflicts that divide the congregation or divert attention from the community's mission, then the time those tasks take expands dramatically.

That's why I'm not surprised that, as I travel around the country, friends of PSR often ask what Pacific School of Religion is doing to prepare graduates for the administrative and organizational responsibilities of religious leadership.

As I talk with our graduates, I see them grappling with these challenges in a variety of contexts. Graduates who grew up in large churches often find small church settings to hold a strangely difficult dynamic. Large churches that rely on staff-driven programs can seem foreign to ministers who were accustomed to the sense of shared responsibility and ownership that flourishes in smaller, more family-like settings.

What's clear is that in every setting of ministry, good methods of communication, effective volunteer recruitment, fundraising know-how, and the ability to draw up and implement

RECYCLED & RECYCLABLE / PRINTED WITH SOY INK   04091

EXHIBIT 13.4. Letter from a Cultivation Mailing.

Page 2

a business plan can be as important for pastors as preaching skills.

PSR's Long Tradition of Leadership Development

From its beginnings in the 1860s, PSR has always taken leadership development very seriously. While some seminaries have been tempted to move in other directions, we have kept field education and coursework in preaching, the arts, and religious education at the center of our curriculum.

However, when I became President of PSR in 1996, I felt that we needed an even more explicit focus on leadership development. I believed that preparing PSR students for the day-to-day management of congregations and other religious organizations was critical to the renewal and transformation of Protestant churches.

Shortly after I arrived, the Arthur Vining Davis Foundations invited PSR to apply for a grant. There was one simple condition: the grant must respond to the president's highest personal priority for the school. We applied for and received a sizeable grant to expand PSR's faculty resources in Congregational Leadership. Gifts from other friends and supporters came forward to supplement this grant so that we were able to add a new faculty position in Congregational Leadership.

To fill this new post, we invited Speed Leas to join the PSR faculty as a half-time member for three years.

When he's not teaching at PSR, Speed serves as Senior Consultant for the Alban Institute, an ecumenical organization that supports congregations through consulting services, research, and education. You probably know of Alban's respected publications and its extensive series of workshops. For four decades, Speed has worked with churches throughout the United States and abroad. He is the nation's foremost authority on conflict resolution within congregations, judicatories, and church agencies.

Each semester, Speed teaches one course -- the first entitled "Leadership of Congregational Systems" and the other dealing with "Conflict Management in Congregational Systems." Both Master of Divinity and Doctor of Ministry students participate in these standing-room only courses.

The enthusiastic response to Speed's classes has reinforced my sense that we're making dramatic progress in helping PSR students acquire valuable leadership skills. Our role in this effort is complemented by a variety of other

EXHIBIT 13.4. Letter from a Cultivation Mailing, Cont'd.

Page 3

classes taught within the Graduate Theological Union.   A
sampling of other regular semester and summer school course
offerings includes:

Sharing the Wealth: Creating Congregations of Generous
People

Ministry in Smaller Congregations

Power, Control, and Pastoral Care

The Pastor as Community Organizer

Conflict Management for Clergy

Professional Ethics for Ministers

Art and Practice of Parish Administration

The Art of Supervision

Designing a Parish Web Site

Doing More in More Places

As you can see, students preparing for ministry have many
opportunities to sharpen their leadership skills. But we need
to do more in this crucial area.

We've found that -- as helpful as these classes are for
students training for their first positions -- the value of
these courses isn't fully understood until after seminary
graduates are in their ministry contexts. It's urgent that we
expand our offerings to provide more continuing education
opportunities.

A generous gift from PSR friends Buzz and Barbara McCoy
will fund a continued half-time faculty presence in
Congregational Leadership for at least five more years.
This half-time position will supplement our present faculty
strengths in leadership education.

The McCoys made their generous commitment in response to
our "Tradition of Boldness" campaign, which was announced in
the most recent Bulletin. One of the goals of this $12 million
fund drive is to endow permanent full-time faculty resources in
Congregational Leadership. The entire PSR faculty has recently
affirmed that training students for leadership is a principle
at the core of the M.Div. program.

EXHIBIT 13.4. Letter from a Cultivation Mailing, Cont'd.

Page 4

Searching

The 2001–2002 academic year may go down in history as PSR's "Year of the Search." Last fall we appointed John Davis as our new Chief Financial Officer. John comes to the position having served as CFO of 1-800-AIRFARE, an Internet travel company in the Philadelphia area and, in a volunteer role, as Treasurer of The Other Side magazine.

It is with very mixed feelings that I report that Riess Potterveld, PSR Vice President and Acting Dean, has been elected as the new President of Lancaster Theological Seminary in Pennsylvania. For eight years, Riess served as Vice President for Advancement -- playing a key role in rebuilding the school's base of financial support and guiding us into new initiatives like the Institute for Leadership Development and Study of Pacific Asian North American Religion (PANA) and the Center for Lesbian and Gay Studies in Religion and Ministry.

Riess and his wife Tara, an accomplished artist, will be moving over the summer. My personal thanks and the community's very best wishes go with them. Later this spring, we will be celebrating the Pottervelds' contributions to PSR.

The faculty is completing work on the all-important search for a Vice President and Academic Dean. We will also soon fill faculty positions in Educational Ministries and in Swedenborgian Studies (based in the new Swedenborgian House of Studies at PSR). And we're ready to recruit a scholar to serve in Bible and Archaeology, a new teaching post that will also enable us to expand the work of the Badè Museum. This new faculty position is made possible by another extraordinary gift to the Tradition of Boldness campaign.

Your generous financial support and your continuing interest make us bold in all we do here at PSR as we seek to serve and transform our communities of faith. I'm grateful for your involvement in the life of this seminary, and I always welcome hearing from you. These are exciting days, and I'm glad you're part of them.

May your Easter celebrations be filled with joy and hope.

Sincerely,

William McKinney
William McKinney
President

EXHIBIT 13.4. Letter from a Cultivation Mailing, Cont'd.

Source: Pacific School of Religion. Reproduced with permission.

Through all four phases of the donor development process, direct mail is an indispensable tool. The mail is most frequently used to recruit new donors; it's an excellent way to promote involvement opportunities; it's essential as a way to deliver printed information about an organization's work; and it's equally useful (in combination with efforts through other channels) in promoting legacy giving. Thus, regardless of the stage of a donor's relationship with your organization and regardless of the level of his giving, direct mail will serve you well in helping you develop a mutually satisfying relationship.

Donor-Centered Fundraising

The craft of direct mail fundraising grew out of what used to be called direct mail marketing, best known to the general public as junk mail: junk, because all too often it advertises goods or services the recipient has absolutely no interest in; junk, because more often than not it's cheaply and obviously mass-produced; junk, because in its blatant commercialism and gaudy use of color and graphics, it's frequently tasteless.

Most direct mail fundraisers (like direct marketers in general) bridle at the mention of junk mail. The truth is, however, many direct mail fundraising appeals still richly deserve to be described as junk mail. The names and addresses of the intended recipients are often misspelled or long out of date. The criteria used to select prospects are frequently fanciful, at best. The messages are poorly crafted. The appeals reek of commercialism, dominated by cheap and frequently inappropriate premiums. Any resemblance between direct mail appeals like these and the pursuit of philanthropy is strictly coincidental.

That's why I believe it's important to distinguish between the *marketer*'s approach to direct mail fundraising and the *fundraiser*'s approach. The marketer tends to think in terms of positioning, of broadcasting messages, of the organization's needs, of statistics, of market share and market penetration. The fundraiser, by contrast, focuses on building relationships with donors (see Table 13.3).

In reality, of course, my colleagues and I blend both approaches. The discipline of marketing has produced an accumulation of shrewd observations and insights about human behavior, and it offers useful guidance in analyzing results. We would be fools to reject all that. Direct mail is, after all, a form of marketing that has proven itself so useful because (1) it enables us to communicate with lots of people at the same time, and (2) many of its results are measurable. What is distinctive about the approach that we (and some other direct mail fundraisers) pursue is that we seek to put the donor at the center of our universe.

This perspective requires what Ken Burnett, the celebrated author of *Relationship Fundraising* (2002) and its sequels, calls the "90-degree shift." He is fond of

TABLE 13.3. **Two Approaches to Direct Mail Fundraising.**

The Marketer's Approach	The Fundraiser's Approach
How can I position the organization to gain the broadest possible public support?	How can I best inspire donors to provide generous, continuing support for the organization?
What message can I deliver that will maximize response within our chosen market?	How can I communicate with my donors, taking into account all that I know about them individually, to build the strongest possible relationships with them?
How can I describe the organization and its needs, its history and its mission, in the most compelling way?	How can I best relate the mission and the goals of the organization to our donors in terms of their values, beliefs, and aspirations?
How can I achieve optimum cost-effectiveness, generating the size and number of gifts that will maximize revenue at an acceptable cost?	How can I minimize donor attrition, maximize donor retention and upgrading, and nurture relationships with my donors that will maximize their loyalty?
How can I maximize market penetration and market share?	How can I provide ideal opportunities for my donors—and for prospective new donors—to validate their values, beliefs, and aspirations by supporting the work of my organization?

drawing an analogy between fundraising and marketing, citing the difference between the brand manager's challenge and that of the customer relationship manager. The brand manager at the W. K. Kellogg Company—the cornflakes people—must sell as many boxes of Frosted Flakes as he possibly can to meet his monthly or quarterly target. By contrast, the customer relationship manager's goal is to increase Kellogg's share of the eleven thousand boxes of dry cereal you may buy in your lifetime. The difference reflects a 90-degree shift in perspective, and that represents the difference between what I refer to as the marketer's and the fundraiser's approaches.

In my view, the concept of relationship fundraising popularized by Ken Burnett is based on five assumptions:

1. Most donors are generous and caring people. They want to help, and the fundraiser's job is to inspire them to avail themselves of opportunities to do so.

2. Most donors are also intelligent. They usually know when they're being taken advantage of, and they don't like it.
3. Most donors expect to be treated courteously and are offended when they're not.
4. Donors are as varied in their interests and habits. Some of them demand opportunities to express their individual preferences and to be treated as the individuals they are. All of them appreciate such treatment.
5. We are missing a huge number of opportunities if we don't operate a donor-centered approach, particularly if we persist in sending people what we want them to have rather than what they want to receive (which is not at all the same thing).

Burnett's individual perspectives aside, these five points form the basis of my thinking about fundraising. They help explain why I insist on placing such emphasis on thank-you letters and welcome packages, why I employ personalization as often as possible in appeals to current donors, and why I feel it's critical to build appeals around the benefits to the donor rather than the needs of the organization.

If you accept these five premises, then you'll think about your development program in a holistic fashion, taking into account all the communications from your organization to your donors—not just those appeals your own department produces. The bimonthly newsletter counts, too. So do the quarterly magazine, the annual report, the legacy marketing materials from the planned giving department, the invitations to special events, and whatever else might be included in the communications stream your donors may receive in the course of a year. If you want to put the donor at the center of your universe, you'll analyze this stream of messages, research which items donors want to receive and which ones they don't, and revise the fundraising and communication program accordingly.

But it's not enough to break down the vertical barriers separating your department from all the other offices that independently communicate with your donors. You'll also need to eliminate the horizontal barriers that, in so many nonprofit organizations, rigidly separate donors by giving level. Such divisions are well intended. For example, by segregating upper-level donors in a "major gifts office," extra-special donors are guaranteed extra-special treatment. However, all too often this treatment means that these donors are excluded from the benefit of the messages you have crafted so carefully to inspire them to give. I have seen countless cases in which major donors—defined as those whose individual gifts reach the $1,000, $5,000, or $10,000 level—are removed from the direct mail or membership rolls and stop receiving most of the printed materials that succeeded so brilliantly in inspiring them to *become* major donors. If you truly subscribe to the concept of donor-centered fundraising, you'll never make such a mistake.

● ● ●

Now, with the basic concepts of direct mail fundraising under our belts, we can take a more informed look at the current state of the art in raising money by mail today—and at its prospects in the decades ahead. Please join me now in Part Three, "Direct Mail Fundraising Today and Tomorrow."

PART THREE

Direct Mail Fundraising Today and Tomorrow

The next two chapters examine the evolution of direct mail fundraising. Chapter Fourteen delves into the state of the art of fundraising today, placing direct mail squarely in the center of the new multichannel communications programs that successful nonprofits are developing and describing "integrated fundraising"—the new big-picture approach that enables fundraisers to make the most of today's varied communications options. Chapter Fifteen wraps up Part Three with a discussion of twelve social, economic, and political trends that promise to affect the practice of fundraising and the development of the nonprofit sector in the decades ahead.

14

Mastering the
New Media Mix

One of the hallmarks of our age is the continuing explosion of new communications technologies. Surely, there's no end in sight to the spectacular inventiveness (and boundless greed) that has given rise to an unending stream of ever-more-amazing gadgets and devices.

Today, at least in theory, the enterprising fundraiser can use any or all of the following channels of communications with her donors, prospects, or the general public:

- *Direct dialogue.* In Europe, Australia, and elsewhere around the world, non-profit organizations are already making extensive use of solicitors trained to engage passers-by on busy city streets and in shopping malls. The technique is employed almost exclusively to enroll monthly donors, because its high overhead costs prohibit its use to solicit single gifts.
- *Co-op mailings.* There are two types of co-op mailings, neither of which has proven worthwhile for more than a handful of fundraisers: (1) packets of product promotions mailed weekly to consumers throughout the United States by Advo and other commercial companies, and (2) mailings jointly undertaken by nonprofit organizations that include appeals for all the participants.

This chapter incorporates material originally published in *Fundraising on the Internet: The ePhilanthropy Foundation.Org's Guide to Success Online,* coedited with Ted Hart and Nick Allen (2002).

- *Direct mail.* The most widely used of many direct response methods, direct mail is typically most effective when applied to donors of modest gifts.
- *Door-to-door canvassing.* This form of face-to-face solicitation was once widely employed in the United States. It has become much less common in recent years, largely because of the difficulty most nonprofits have experienced in renewing canvass-recruited donors.
- *E-mail.* Free electronic newsletters are fast becoming a standard feature in successful direct response fundraising programs. Sometimes an e-newsletter can be a useful vehicle to deliver an on-line solicitation.
- *Face-to-face contact.* Direct solicitation is the oldest and still the best way to raise money from individuals. For most nonprofits, financial realities dictate that face-to-face solicitation must be limited to major donors. However, for most organizations a major gifts program is absolutely essential.
- *Magazines.* As the magazine field has evolved from the mass-appeal magazines of the fifties (*Life, Look, Collier's, The Saturday Evening Post*) into today's highly segmented and specialized offerings, and as advertising rates have climbed along the way, it has become increasingly difficult for fundraisers to recruit new donors via ads in magazines.
- *Newspapers.* Currently, newspaper advertising is not extensively used as a fundraising device in North America, where advertising costs have become prohibitive for most purposes. The exceptions are ads placed to raise funds in response to humanitarian emergencies or (occasionally) to support action on high-profile public policy or environmental issues. In such circumstances, newspaper ads can be a cost-effective way to acquire new donors and are sometimes profitable in their own right. Otherwise, this medium is not normally effective in fundraising.
- *Newspaper free-standing inserts.* Every major Sunday newspaper includes a slew of commercial promotions—flyers, pamphlets, brochures, and other advertising matter. These items are called free-standing inserts, or FSIs, and every once in a while a nonprofit organization will create and place one to recruit new donors. The technique is not widespread in the nonprofit sector, presumably because it has never consistently worked well for any organization.
- *Package inserts.* Every once in a while, a corporate partnership will include an offer to include a small leaflet or brochure with goods shipped to customers. Occasionally, too, a utility company will consent to include a similar promotion in its monthly billing to customers. Such package inserts are rare today, however. In any case, response to package inserts is almost always vanishingly small.
- *Payroll deduction programs.* Workplace giving is the source of much of the $3 billion raised annually by the United Ways throughout North America and has been adopted by other organizations that seek to direct funds toward specialized pur-

poses such as environmental causes, African American nonprofits, and women's groups. Some larger charities pursue this channel of support on their own.

• *Radio.* There are only two widespread uses of radio as a fundraising medium in the United States, as far as I'm aware: (1) short messages appealing for old cars, boats, or other vehicles for resale by charities and (2) appeals for funds by special-interest organizations (usually religious), often not as stand-alone spots but within the stations' programming.

• *Special events.* After direct solicitation, special events are probably the world's second-oldest type of fundraising. For many organizations, especially local groups or those who operate on a wider scale but maintain local chapters, they often work well. However, in all too many cases, special events are capital-intensive and risky.

• *Telemarketing.* Like direct mail, telephone contact offers fundraisers a wide range of applications (which I'll discuss later in this chapter).

• *Television.* Although nonprofits addressing a wide range of issues have attempted to raise money through direct response television, their experience has been mixed, at best. Few organizations other than child-sponsorship groups have made a go of fundraising on television. (Direct response TV includes both "long form" infomercials, generally 30 or 60 minutes in length, and "short form" spots that are typically 60 or 120 seconds long. Both forms are typically aimed at recruiting new monthly donors.)

• *Text-messaging.* Text-messaging uses cellular telephones or other wireless handheld devices to display short messages. This twenty-first-century technique has been widely heralded for its fundraising potential but has yet to be adopted to any significant degree in the United States. In Europe, Japan, and other countries where advanced wireless technology is the rule rather than the exception, fundraisers have taken notice and are experimenting with its use.

• *Web sites.* Increasingly, donors are seeking information about the causes and institutions they support on the World Wide Web.

Increasingly, nonprofits that previously depended largely on one channel—direct mail, most notably—are learning to diversify their donor communications by employing one or several additional channels among those listed. Most commonly, they choose telemarketing, major gifts, and special events. (Table 14.1 shows a three-year schedule for the direct mail and telephone fundraising projects in such a multichannel program.)

There are several reasons for the growing popularity of this approach. First of all, the competition for charitable gifts has expanded at an eye-popping pace in the last couple of decades, not just in the United States, where the trend has gone the furthest, but in Canada, the United Kingdom, Western and Northern Europe, and

TABLE 14.1. Three-Year Monthly Schedule for a Representative Fundraising Program.

Month	Acquisition Quantity	Renewal Quantity	Special Appeal Quantity	Newsletter Quantity	Telephone Quantity	Total
Year 1						
1	50,000			500		50,500
2						
3			500			500
4				500		500
5	100,000					100,000
6			1,000			1,000
7				1,500		1,500
8						
9	150,000		1,500			151,500
10				2,000		2,000
11			3,000			3,000
12						
Year 2						
1	150,000			3,000		153,000
2		3,000	1,000			4,000
3		2,500				2,500
4		2,400		4,000		6,400
5	100,000	2,300				102,300
6			5,000		2,200	7,200
7				5,000		5,000
8			5,500			5,500
9	150,000					150,000
10				6,000		6,000
11			7,000			7,000
12					4,000	4,000
Year 3						
1	250,000			8,000		258,000
2		8,000				8,000
3		6,500				6,500
4		5,800		11,000		16,800
5	100,000	5,500				105,500
6		5,300	7,500			12,800
7				12,000	5,000	17,000
8			9,000			9,000
9	200,000					200,000
10			10,000	14,000		24,000
11			11,000			11,000
12					5,000	5,000
Total	1,250,000	41,300	62,000	67,500	16,200	1,437,000

almost everywhere else in the world where civil society is blooming. To be noticed these days, a nonprofit organization must take full advantage of all opportunities that arise to communicate its message.

In addition, the volume of commercial advertising has reached staggering proportions, flooding every sensory organ with unsolicited messages and compounding the difficulty nonprofits face to be heard above the din. And donors have personal preferences about the ways they wish to communicate with the charities they support; they're becoming increasingly vocal about expressing those preferences. One size no longer fits all.

Another factor is that electronic means of communication are rapidly moving into the mainstream of our daily lives. Some people, including many donors, are spurning traditional communication channels in favor of e-mail and the Internet.

And finally, the lower cost of electronic communications is attractive to nonprofit organizations, providing an incentive to cut back on the use of more traditional channels.

As the twenty-first century unfolds, it's foolish for us fundraisers to limit ourselves to any one, or even three, communications channels. We have to seize every available opportunity to get our messages across. The strongest response to this reality is integrated fundraising.

The New World of Integrated Fundraising

Once upon a time, a nonprofit organization could easily pigeonhole all its fundraising and marketing activities in separate, independent departments with familiar names, usually Major Gifts, Planned Giving, Direct Response (or Direct Mail or Membership), and Marketing (or Communications). When it was time to launch a capital campaign, a new Capital Campaign office sprang into being. The staff in these departments typically took little or no notice of each other's activities.

That compartmentalized model is still the rule in the nonprofit sector, but it has long since outlived its effectiveness. Discerning fundraisers today understand that we function in the context of a complex and demanding reality that's simply not amenable to such simple-minded approaches.

First of all, shrinking donor-renewal rates make the case for relationship fundraising, which demands a donor-centered approach to donor communications (see the preceding chapter). To today's well-educated donor, uncoordinated (and sometimes conflicting) messages from different departments are signs of poor planning, inefficiency, and waste. The bad impression thus created compounds the donor's displeasure at not being promptly or adequately thanked.

Second, most bequests—often the largest share of all planned giving revenue—come from donors recruited, renewed, and cultivated by direct mail. Nowadays, woe unto the planned giving office that ignores or undervalues the potential in its small-donor or membership file! And so it is with major gifts. Of course, some major donors are recruited outright, face-to-face, without any previous history of financial support for the organization. But those nonprofits that invest in donor care and careful stewardship have found, over the years, that growing numbers of donors recruited through the mail have eventually joined the ranks of their major donors.

And finally, in many organizations there's a sharp line drawn between the direct response or membership department and the major gifts office. Donors who contribute less than $1,000, say, are the business of the direct mail team. But once a donor contributes his first $1,000, he crosses the line into the domain of major gifts and is severed from the direct mail communications stream. The donor henceforth receives only those communications that come from the major gifts office. There are two problems with this: (1) it was direct response communications that nurtured his interest in the organization and prompted his $1,000 gift in the first place, and (2) major gift officers may have their hands full dealing with donors of $5,000, $10,000, or more and give short shrift to those who have given lesser amounts. All too often, those $1,000 donors are left out in the cold and receive virtually no communications. Both these factors point to the value of blurring the line between direct response and major gifts and using reformatted and personalized materials developed for direct mail to help sustain the interest of major donors.

The barriers that commonly exist among direct mail, telefundraising, and online communications cause similar problems. For example, imagine the bewilderment of a donor who receives a letter, a phone call, and an electronic newsletter within the same week from the same organization. Now imagine what she thinks when the messages delivered through these disparate channels are themselves very different.

Am I exaggerating? Unfortunately not. This scenario is all too common. The case for integrated fundraising is there in plain sight for all who have eyes to see.

What Integrated Fundraising Means

Today, integrated fundraising is a goal for most nonprofit organizations, not a reality. In fact, the concept of integrated fundraising is generally better known in the abstract—for the benefits it brings as well as its drawbacks. In theory, integrated fundraising reduces inconsistencies in communicating an organization's message, strengthens donor relationships, and yields increased revenue, especially over the long haul. The price that's paid for these considerable benefits includes added capital requirements, greater demands on management, and sophisticated skills to operate the more complex systems entailed in the process.

To describe what integrated fundraising is, it's best to examine the idea from the ground up, by cataloging the eight principles that must be built into any serious effort to implement it.

1. *Always consider the donor's point of view.* It's a cliché that fundraising is about building relationships with donors, but precious few direct response fundraising programs put this wisdom into practice in more than a perfunctory way. An integrated approach to fundraising offers hope that donors' unique interests and behaviors will form the basis of the relationships that develop between them and the causes they support.

In practice, this means that the donor's point of view must prevail. If she wants to contribute only once per year, if she doesn't want to receive your newsletter, if she's interested only in your work with cats, not dogs, if she doesn't want to get your e-mail (or visit your Web site), then those must be the rules of the relationship. Within the limits of feasibility, each donor must have the opportunity to define her own dos and don'ts.

2. *Focus on the big picture.* Integrated fundraising puts special demands on nonprofit executives. Every donor counts; every relationship is precious. But a successful fundraising program is grounded in:

- Thousands, or hundreds of thousands, of donors
- A broad array of fundraising techniques using diverse communications channels
- Management by a large number of staff persons, usually divided among several different offices or departments
- Year-round activity maintained over decades

Integrated fundraising involves all the tools and techniques for donor communications: direct mail, telemarketing, on-line communications, direct solicitations, capital campaigns, major donor fundraising, planned giving—from the bottom of the donor pyramid to the top. To succeed in integrated fundraising requires that the organization's leadership keep all this in perspective, orchestrating all these elements in an artful fashion so that the whole becomes greater than the sum of its parts. This may entail revising employee incentives, placing emphasis on organizationwide achievements rather than those of the individual department, as well as a new style of leadership and intensive staff training, so that everyone involved in development works smoothly together.

3. *Keep your message clear and consistent.* In recent years, fundraisers have begun to absorb the lessons that successful marketers in the private sector have learned about "branding." This widely misunderstood buzzword is actually a variant on the fundraising concept of relationship building. To establish a brand is to

create a total experience, for the customer or the donor alike, that's both consistent and comfortable. For a nonprofit fundraiser, the goal of this effort is to entice, retain, and upgrade donors.

Effective branding programs are designed to break through the media clutter and fix simple ideas firmly in the minds of the audiences for whom they're intended. These programs possess the following characteristics:

- They're based on shrewd and accurate positioning for the brand, that is, they stake out at least one unique benefit.
- They are reduced to the simplest ideas boiled down to their emotional core.
- They place the most emphasis on benefits to the donor or customer rather than on the features of the product or service.
- They employ distinctive themes and images that remain unchanged over a long period of time.
- They make effective use of every available communication channel to repeat the same themes and images.

4. *Segment your audience for maximum impact.* The ultimate goal of integrated fundraising is to build one-to-one relationships with donors. Unfortunately, one-to-one fundraising (talk about buzzwords!) is a long way off.

Although Internet technology could enable one-to-one fundraising, few nonprofits have put their donor data on-line or can make use of it for tailored offers. The big catalogers like Land's End are integrating their customer databases; they know what you've ordered, when, and for whom, whether you ordered by calling an 800-number, by mailing an order form, or by visiting their Web site. If you log in at their site (they use "cookies" to identify return visitors), they can access all this information in real time to present offers to you. However, only a handful of nonprofits have made the investment to put their off-line data on-line. And, in any case, it's the unusual organization that stores data deep enough to offer donors much more than gift-level options as part of the on-line experience.

For us mere mortals working for the vast majority of nonprofits, the best that we can hope for these days, with only rare exceptions, is intelligent donor file segmentation.

Effective segmentation requires using varying *marketing concepts.* For instance, as I noted in Chapter Ten, it's not often effective to solicit high-dollar donors with the same message sent to the rest of the file (albeit in a fancier package or exercising more patience on the phone). A donor who contributes $250, $500, or more at a time typically has a different sort of relationship with the cause he's supporting than does one whose highest gift never tops $30. Similarly, a long-lapsed donor is likely to feel very differently about a charity than an active one. The messages in direct mail packages, telephone scripts, or e-mail communications all need to reflect those differences.

The economies of communicating on-line make such use of variable text far easier to do in e-mail or on a Web site than in direct mail. It's considerably cheaper to refer to the date of a donor's first gift or the cumulative amount of her contributions in an e-mail appeal than in a letter. As the public grows more comfortable contributing money on-line, this advantage could become a major incentive to use on-line communications.

When nonprofits begin to integrate on-line activity into their donor databases, they will eventually be able to refer to on-line advocacy activity, what pages of a site were viewed, and even what reports were downloaded. *Then* the promise of one-to-one fundraising will be much closer to reality.

5. *Pay greater attention to cost-effectiveness than to cost.* As I explained in Chapter One, fundraisers must take into account at least five factors: (1) efficiency (the sheer cost of raising a dollar), (2) growth, (3) donor involvement, (4) visibility, and (5) stability. To some degree, these five strategic goals are mutually exclusive; emphasizing any one of those four latter goals is likely to reduce efficiency, that is, raise the cost of fundraising. This lowered efficiency (or, in other words, higher investment) may be desirable in the long-term strategic interest of the organization.

Understanding these trade-offs is critical. For example, a big current investment in on-line fundraising probably won't yield huge dividends in the short run. Strictly from the perspective of (short-term) fundraising efficiency, it's probably more advantageous to spend the same money on major donors, direct mail, or telefundraising. However, it seems equally likely that to do so would be disadvantageous to the organization in the long run, as returns from on-line fundraising efforts continue to climb.

6. *Don't give up on direct mail.* Despite all I've said about evolving technology, demographic shifts, and changing popular attitudes, most donors still prefer to communicate by mail with the causes and institutions they support.

Currently, it's not prudent to expect substantial returns on-line. It's unusual for a nonprofit to be able to secure telephone numbers for even 75 percent of its donors. And today, only the rare organization has collected current e-mail addresses for even one-third of its donors. Because people must give permission for an organization to use their e-mail addresses, virtually the only way to collect them is to ask donors directly. And even when you have phone numbers or e-mail addresses, you'll find that significant numbers of donors decline to be solicited by either medium.

However, direct mail can be used to help drive traffic to a Web site where donors can learn more, see more, and become more involved with the mission of the organization. This combination of on-line and off-line communication will provide for a deeper experience and a stronger relationship than can be built with periodic direct mail efforts alone.

As time goes on, donors may more readily volunteer their e-mail addresses. In any case, it's essential that fundraisers place a high priority on obtaining them. Eventually, those organizations that doggedly pursue such an effort will be rewarded with the key to harnessing a renewable resource in Internet fundraising.

But until that day, sustain and, if possible, expand your use of direct mail. And to get the most out of direct mail, communicate with donors and prospects through all available channels. As the world of commercial advertising and marketing has proven beyond a doubt, there is a multiplier effect in multichannel communications that frequently causes the response to a coordinated campaign to exceed the sum total of responses to uncoordinated efforts through each individual channel. This phenomenon of mutual reinforcement is one of the strongest arguments for integrated fundraising programs.

7. *Use the tools of marketing and public relations.* Whether or not your organization has a marketing or public relations department, someone within your organization is responsible for the creation of newsletters, annual reports, press releases, and other forms of written communication with the public.

Your organization's Web site address (URL) should be included anyplace the address or phone of the organization is printed. Integrating the URL into all forms of communication, fundraising or otherwise, will help drive traffic to your site. Getting supporters in the habit of using your Web site as an important source of information is essential to the long-term success of an integrated fundraising effort.

8. *Set your schedule in advance and stick to it!* Success in fundraising results from persistence and timeliness as much as it does from wisdom or creativity. After all, the fundamental law of fundraising is, "If you don't ask, you don't get" the gift. However, timing becomes doubly important in an integrated fundraising program. In a large-scale effort involving multiple departments and possibly multiple vendors as well, the demands on management can be huge. Slippage of a week or two in a fundraising appeal in January or February could well result in reducing the total number of fundraising opportunities, and thus the revenue, during the balance of the year.

If you accept the premise of integrated fundraising—that fundraising potential is maximized when we make wise, coordinated use of multichannel communications—you'll find it a whole lot easier to cope in an age when scientists and engineers continue to offer up new ways for us to communicate with one another. And you'd better be ready for yet more change. There's no holding it back.

Technology and the Future of Fundraising

To look at the future of direct mail fundraising, it's useful to review the changes we've already witnessed in the field over the past twenty years and those that seem most likely in the decade or so ahead. Take a look at Table 14.2, which reflects my own and my colleagues' experience and expectations.

If there are unfamiliar words in Table 14.2, don't fret. The details aren't important. The true significance of the pattern reflected here is that, within the limited confines of the realm of direct mail fundraising, the changes we've witnessed in two short decades seem nothing short of revolutionary. What's more, we have every reason to believe that the pace of change will continue unabated, or even accelerate, in the years ahead.

However, it's all too easy to focus on the changes in the world around us. For many of us, technology can be intoxicating. But in reality, most of these technological changes are superficial, when all is said and done. There is much more that hasn't changed and isn't likely to do so in the foreseeable future.

What Won't Change

Today, decades after the eclipse of the one-penny stamp, the fundamentals of our craft remain the same. It seems that daily changes in technology pose new challenges and new possibilities, but, so far at least, they have left the core of our work unchanged. Short of environmental collapse, nuclear war, a virulent global epidemic, or massive dislocations in the world economy, the years ahead promise more of the same.

The lion's share of public interest and charitable funding will continue to come from individuals, not institutions, even if changes in tax laws and the public mood force foundations and corporations to share more of their wealth. The generosity of American donors sets records every year. That trend is likely to continue for years to come. Lengthening lifespan and other demographic patterns are concentrating more and more of our society's disposable income in the hands of those over the age of fifty, who give most charitable contributions.

What won't change, I believe, are the fundamental realities we have always faced in fundraising:

- Most people won't give you money.
- But lots of people will give a first gift.
- Fewer people will give you second gifts.
- Even fewer will give again and again.
- Eventually, all people will stop giving you money.
- The need to recruit new donors will never end.

TABLE 14.2. How the Techniques of Direct Response Fundraising Are Changing.

Function	1980	1990	2000	2010
Copywriting and approvals	IBM Selectric, paper, U.S. Postal Service	Word processor, paper, floppy diskette, Local Area Network (LAN), Federal Express, fax machine	Word processor, CD-ROMs, e-mail and Web	Integrated officeware, Web conferencing, annotated PDFs, voice-activated word processing?
Design and typesetting	Paste-up, Linotronic	Desktop publishing, diskettes	Desktop publishing, PDF files, e-mail and Web, scanners	?
Budgeting and projections	VisiCalc	Lotus 1–2–3	Excel	Integrated officeware?
Targeting	ZIP code	ZIP+4, psychographics, demographics	Data mining	Relationship analysis and targeting?
List selection	Data cards, merge-purge	Database management, merge-purge	Multivariate analysis, data mining, demographic and other overlays	?
Database maintenance	Mainframe computer, magnetic tape	Microcomputer, hard disk drive, LAN	Networked microcomputer, on-line	Distributed processing?
Segmentation	Prospects vs. donors	Recency, frequency, monetary amount (RFM) + source; regression analysis	RFM, source, data mining	?
Printing	Sheet-fed press, web press	In-line web press, laser printer	In-line web press, laser printer, ink-jet, variable data printing	Variable data printing, selective binding and inserting?
Personalization	Cheshire label, match-fill, daisy-wheel printers	Cheshire label, laser printer, ink-jet, in-line web press, "signature" machines	Ink-jet, laser printer, in-line web press	Selective binding and inserting?
Lettershop	Cheshire label, multistation inserter	Ink-jet, laser printer, high-speed inserter	Ink-jet, laser printer, in-line web press	On-line?

TABLE 14.2. How the Techniques of Direct Response Fundraising Are Changing, Cont'd.

Function	1980	1990	2000	2010
Communication with prospects and donors	Mail, outbound phone	Mail, outbound, and inbound phone, audio, video	Mail, outbound and inbound phone, e-mail, Web, video	Mail, inbound phone, e-mail, text messaging, Web, video?
Donor involvement	Reply device, front-end premium	Reply device, front-end premium, 800-number	Reply device, front-end premium, Web, pass-through calling campaigns, phone conferencing	Reply device, front-end premium, Web, on-line conferencing?
Caging and cashiering	Manual processing, batch processing	Automated check processing, database management, barcodes, optical scanning	Automated check processing, barcodes, optical scanning, database management, barcode scanning, on-line, Electronic funds transfer	Electronic funds transfer?

Outwardly, what we know today as direct mail fundraising may no longer be recognizable to us within a couple of decades. The mechanisms by which money is transferred from donors to public interest groups may eventually bear little resemblance to current methods, either. But some close analogue of direct mail fundraising will flourish.

Today, despite occasional complaints from many donors, despite the clumsiness of our efforts to target and personalize our appeals, direct mail remains the easiest and least intrusive means for people to learn about and respond to the needs of public interest organizations. To play a part in saving lives and making history, donors needn't suffer through rote appeals delivered on their doorsteps by scruffy canvassers, eat rubber chicken and listen to boring speeches, or view documentaries in damp church basements. Direct mail fundraising is ideal for today's busy people. It's ideal, too, for elderly people, whose proportion in the U.S. population is rapidly increasing. Millions of Americans have come to rely upon direct mail as an easy and accessible way to participate in public life—even to vote.

Thirty years and more from now—in whatever direction new technology may take it—direct mail fundraising in some form will still be helping nonprofit organizations and political committees acquire, resolicit, and cultivate donors in large numbers.

Direct mail will continue to serve as the flexible tool it is. It will help charities and public interest groups implement strategies of growth, involvement, efficiency, stability, or visibility. Direct mail will continue playing a strategic role for the non-profit sector for many decades to come, helping voluntary associations serve the public interest in ever more creative and responsive ways.

● ● ●

With that said, it makes sense for us to turn our attention to the external factors that may influence our lives and our work in the decades ahead. That's the task we'll take up in Chapter Fifteen.

15

Twelve Trends
for a New Century

So, let me guess: you want to know what's in store for your future, right? Well, if you think you (or I) can predict what's going to happen ten years down the road in fundraising—or in any other field of human endeavor, for that matter—forget it.

Our hopes for predicting the future are confounded by the sheer complexity of the systems humankind has developed to govern our affairs and manage this diverse little planet of ours. Our best intentions often go awry; the Law of Unforeseen Consequences has shaped history as surely as any historian's theory. Discontinuities abound in our universe—sharp shifts in the course of human affairs caused by wars, epidemics, economic reversals, environmental change, and breakthroughs in technology. Besides, we are six billion inescapably human beings—capricious, fallible, and foolish.

If that's not enough to convince you, all you have to do to persuade yourself that predicting the future is literally impossible is to look back a few years at the predictions of some of the best-informed people on the planet.

For example, in 1929 the esteemed Yale University economist Irving Fisher made the following prediction about one month before the stock market crash that ushered in the Great Depression in the United States: "Stocks have reached what looks like a permanently high plateau."

Come to think of it, didn't we hear comments like that in the news back in the late 1990s, just months before the bottom fell out of the stock market again?

Or you could peer a little further back into American history and see what Charles H. Duell, then the U.S. Commissioner of Patents, said in 1899, on the eve of one of the most explosive periods of innovation in world history: "Everything that can be invented has been invented."

If those two examples aren't enough to convince you, check out the science fiction tales of the 1950s and 1960s to see what our world's self-proclaimed visionaries predicted for our lives early in the twenty-first century (or even long before). You'll read about rocket ships in every garage, personal robots performing just about every conceivable function (and I mean *every* function), silicon brain implants to boost your intelligence, and, well, you get the point. The harsh reality is, experts routinely fail to predict major changes. Even meteorologists can't predict next week's weather. If you think you can do better, good luck!

Caveats and excuses notwithstanding, however, we have no choice but to look ahead in hopes of anticipating new opportunities and avoiding new roadblocks. That's the immodest purpose of this chapter—not to predict but to examine today's trends and attempt to discern some of the forces that will shape our course in the decades ahead. Historic forces are guiding all our lives. We can't escape them.

History doesn't travel in straight lines. Nor does nature. So the simple, straightforward extrapolation of current realities that appeals so much to our all-too-human simple-mindedness isn't the wisest course to follow when we attempt to anticipate the future. Still, many of today's trends will continue to play themselves out in the future. The reality that will result as they mesh and morph and clash with one another is impossible to predict, partly because many current trends conflict with one another, and partly because we humans are such annoyingly unpredictable creatures. But it appears highly likely that at least twelve trends visible today will influence the experience of fundraisers in North America for many years to come. I'll touch on each of these twelve phenomena in turn.

Growing U.S. Population

Not too many years ago, demographers took for granted that the United States would go the way of Europe and Japan. Our birth rate would continue to fall, slowing and perhaps finally reversing population growth, and saddling society with increasing numbers of the aged and infirm, thus putting an ever-growing burden on a shrinking number of productive working people.

Well, guess what? It's not working out that way. Recent population studies in the United States make it clear that the country's birth rate is rising again, partly as a result of surging immigration and the higher birth rates that are common among immigrant populations. The upshot is that the American population as a whole is expanding sharply.

These days, the population of the European Union is estimated at roughly 370 million, the United States at 280 million. By mid-century, however, some demographers now estimate that the United States will be home to some 550 million people, while the European population will have shrunk to fewer than 300 million.

Like it or not, the renewed population growth in the United States will have dramatic implications for the nonprofit sector, including

- A continually growing need for education, health, and other human services
- The continuing expansion of the nonprofit sector in response to this growing need (unless political trends are sharply reversed and government rises to the challenge)
- Growth, more growth, and growth again in the U.S. economy, providing an ever-expanding resource base to support society's growing needs

All in all, the future of the U.S. economy and of its nonprofit sector may be brighter than you think.

Longer Lives for Young and Old

Less than a century ago, when the radical concept of retirement was introduced into American society, it was widely assumed that a retiree would live a mere few years. After all, in 1935 when President Franklin D. Roosevelt signed the Social Security Act, life expectancy in the United States was 61.7 years and the retirement age the Act fixed in law was 65. The Social Security system was designed with this demographic reality in mind.

In 2000, U.S. life expectancy at birth was 76.9 years. More to the point, for Americans aged 65, life expectancy was 17.9 years. In other words, the average American could reasonably expect to live nearly another 18 years after retirement! Is it any wonder there's such intense debate today about the future of Social Security? We live in a changed world. (These figures are from the National Center for Health Statistics of the U.S. Centers for Disease Control and Prevention.)

No longer, then, is old age considered to begin at 65. Demographers now speak of the "old old," those who are 85 years of age or older, and this number has become the true threshold to old age. The United States in 2000 counted some 4.2 million people 85 or older, as well as an estimated 70,000 who were 100 or more (according to a 1999 report by the U.S. Census Bureau). That was nearly double the estimated number (37,000) of centenarians in 1990, which shows how sharply inclined is the trendline.

Not only are we living longer, we're healthier and more active, too. The non-stop medical revolution is not just extending our lives, it's changing our lifestyles as well.

Nowadays, the life expectancy of a healthy five-year-old girl in the United States is approaching one hundred. Triple-digitarians are still the exception—barely 1.1 percent of our population. Not too long from now, they may become commonplace. Think what that means: your daughter or granddaughter—or, with a little more luck, your son or grandson—could well live to witness the twenty-second century. Think, too, about all the living those young people will do between now and then and how much that will cost.

In tandem with longer lives, we'll witness a continuing rise in the demand for health care and education—health care, obviously, because we live longer primarily because of medical science, and education, because "lifelong education" is becoming not just a buzzword among education professionals but will soon be the only route to survival in our dynamic, fast-changing society.

This reality has several obvious implications for fundraising. First, when we speak of long-term relationships with donors, we have to recognize that the long term is getting a whole lot longer. One of my clients has several hundred donors who have contributed annual gifts for fifty consecutive years or longer. With a proper devotion to stewardship and a sensitive appreciation of the requirements of relationship fundraising, we can gain life-long friends whose cumulative giving will dwarf our traditional notions of long-term value.

On the other side of that coin, however, we must take into account the ever-rising cost of health care. As our donors age, and the demands on their increasingly slender resources mount year after year, they may find it impossible to continue giving generously, no matter how much they want to do so. All the more reason, then, to sustain our relationships with them despite the lack of ongoing support: the potential for legacy giving remains.

And finally, the continuing growth in demand for health care and education spells opportunity for the nonprofit sector, given that (at least in the United States) health care and education are by far our two biggest areas of activity outside of religion.

The Emerging Ethnic Majority

It's no surprise to a Californian, a New Yorker, or a Texan that American society is growing more diverse. On both coasts, as well as in the Sunbelt, the proportion of foreign-born residents is mushrooming, and the new immigrant populations, chiefly from Latin America and Asia, are bringing with them new habits and assumptions about society, new ways of relating to one another, new vitality, and new ideas that enrich life in the United States.

However, if you travel widely in the United States, as I do, you know that growing ethnic diversity isn't limited to the states where immigrants have traditionally settled. In recent years, I've encountered large numbers of new Americans in New England, all around the Great Lakes, throughout the Plains states, and everywhere in the South—rural areas as well as urban. Our society is changing faster than most of us realize.

I happily welcome this change, because I recognize that the United States, for all our military and economic power, is but one among hundreds of nations, and we Caucasians who still dominate the U.S. population are a tiny minority on a globe that teems with people of color. (The Chinese and Indians alone constitute well over one-third of the world's population. We Americans—all of us—account for about 5 percent.) However, I recognize, too, that our growing ethnic diversity complicates my job as a fundraiser, and, inevitably, it will make your job harder, too, if it hasn't already.

The habits of philanthropy differ from one culture to another. Having traveled in more than seventy nations and worked with fundraisers in an even greater number of countries, I know that the impulses of philanthropy are universal. There is something deeply seated in the human psyche that, sooner or later in life, moves most of us to do what we can to help those who are less fortunate than we are and to support activities that nurture the mind and the soul and celebrate the human spirit. But we have many different ways of expressing these impulses. It's clear that the approaches and techniques we've honed to inspire philanthropy in the established majority population in the United States don't necessarily work in communities of color.

The philanthropic habits I've observed in Asian and Hispanic communities predominantly composed of immigrants, as well as among lower-income African Americans, revolve around family and religion. People help people they know and support the institutions (chiefly churches and mosques) that are the centers of their community life. Lack of familiarity with mainstream charities is compounded by distrust of large institutions acquired in the old country (or, in the case of African Americans, the new one). Add the ingredient of limited funds and typically large families, and the chances that established nonprofits will be successful in raising funds in these communities are limited.

That's not to say that it's impossible to conduct successful fundraising in immigrant communities. There is no lack of generosity among Hispanics, Asians, and African Americans. Indeed, some studies show that people in such communities are more generous than the average American in comparison with their income.

Though traditional fundraising techniques such as direct mail and telemarketing won't work well in these circumstances, other efforts—tied to family or religious centers—may do very well, indeed.

It's also critical to note that by no means are all Asians or Hispanics newcomers. Some Latino families in California and the Southwest trace their ancestry back to Spanish settlements that were well established before the Mayflower crossed the Atlantic. Large numbers of Asians—now third-, fourth-, and fifth-generation Americans—are descended from waves of Chinese, Japanese, and Filipinos who emigrated to the United States in the nineteenth and early twentieth centuries. Among millions of Americans who fall into these categories, the melting pot has worked its ways. It would be downright stupid to assume that any individual won't respond to a charitable appeal simply because he happens to fall into a particular ethnic category.

The Supremacy of the Corporation

Just two centuries ago, the corporation was a creature of the state (or, in monarchical societies, the crown). To become incorporated, thus (in most cases) shielding individual investors from liability, a company had to gain the state's approval for its charter. In theory, only companies that served the public interest could become corporations. In fact, in the United States, it was not until late in the nineteenth century that most corporations could legally operate outside the borders of the states in which they were incorporated. For that change—a sea-change in the potential power of corporations—we can thank the Robber Barons of that era and the power they accumulated over state legislatures and the federal courts. This redefinition of the corporation helped multiply the fortunes of the railroad barons, J. P. Morgan, and John D. Rockefeller Sr., whose Standard Oil was among the first and one of the most spectacular beneficiaries of the newly granted freedom to corporations. But it is the latter-day successors to the Robber Barons—the managers of the major national and multinational corporations—that have reaped the greatest benefits.

The limited power of the corporation in the nineteenth century is now hard to grasp in the early years of the twenty-first. Today, corporations are the dominant force in the world. The biggest multinational companies have greater economic clout than all but a handful of nations. The corporate agenda—social stability over social equity, private ownership of natural resources, free trade, protection for intellectual property, and privatization of state-owned enterprises—holds sway almost everywhere in the world. Corporate interests steer the political process in much of the world, decidedly including the United States.

There are those (including me) who think this development is unfortunate. Others strenuously disagree. Tempting though it is, I can't debate the point here. As a fundraiser, I simply recognize that this is the reality in which we operate and that it has many implications for our work, including those that follow.

The Role of Corporations

The traditional view of the corporation is that its sole purpose is to earn a return on investors' dollars. Though this cramped and shortsighted perspective is now widely questioned, it still dominates thinking on both Wall Street and Main Street, and it still plays itself out in an ever more frenzied effort to persuade consumers to buy products and services we don't necessarily need. As a result, we lucky few who inhabit the prosperous nations of the Global North are treated to increasingly loud media noise—the flash, dazzle, and tempting promise of marketers and advertisers, vying for what they think of as their rightful share of our income, inundating each of us with thousands of promotional messages every day of our lives. In the midst of this cacophony, launching a fundraising campaign has become a daunting task. All but the most modest efforts now require us to use many of the same attention-getting devices as the major marketers.

The Corporate Ethos

Today's corporate ethos is based on the self-righteous assumption that the earth's resources are humankind's to plunder. Though more than a century has passed since the closing of the last habitable frontier in the Global North, our corporations act as though the biosphere—land, water, air, and all life on our planet—is limitless. Collectively, the nations of the world, under corporate leadership, are devouring resources at a rate that is so dramatically unsustainable that we will face dangerous shortages within a very few years. Fish stocks in the oceans are dramatically depleted, and many species have been driven to extinction. Our once-majestic forests are mere shadows of their former selves. The diversity of plant and animal life has been sharply curtailed, and species are dying out at an alarming rate. The very water that is our staff of life is becoming scarce in many regions, with that scarcity widely expected to trigger regional wars as the twenty-first century unfolds—a problem that will be greatly exacerbated by continued global warming, which, in turn, will result in droughts in many parts of the world. Everywhere we turn in the biosphere, we can see the destructive impact of humanity's greed and shortsightedness. So, if you think the environmental movement was powerful in the last four decades of the twentieth century, stick around. It's difficult for me to believe that environmental, conservation, and wildlife organizations won't soon start attracting much more than the 2.7 percent of charitable donations they received in the United States in 2002 (*Giving USA 2003*, p. 10).

Corporate Dominance

The steady increase in corporate dominance of the political process and corporate overconsumption of natural resources is one of the root causes of growing poverty around the world. The increasing grassroots anger in the Global South about social and economic issues has already begun to increase the demands on North American and European funders. These demands can only grow further if multinational corporations maintain their control of the levers of power.

Shift in Decision-Making Power

The concentration of wealth in the hands of a shrinking number of large corporations has steadily moved the seat of decision-making power farther and farther from the communities where we live and work. Many companies that built reputations over decades as pillars of community support have been absorbed by larger firms. In all too many cases, the civic-minded spirit that animated their leaders has gone out the window along with many of the leaders themselves. It has become more difficult as the years have gone by for local nonprofits to secure support from local companies that have become subsidiaries of larger entities—not just financial support but support in the form of executives on loan, high-level placements on nonprofit boards, in-kind contributions, and community engagement in general. But the implications of this shift in decision-making power reach beyond the nonprofit sector itself: the power of our communities is undermined, making local solutions to local problems more difficult to attain.

The Shifting Cultural Context

Perhaps Alexis de Tocqueville, the famous Frenchman whose insights about American democracy early in the nineteenth century are still celebrated, has no counterparts in today's America. I suspect, however, that there are several. And one of them, I believe, is the sociologist Paul Ray.

Ray's studies over the past two decades have led him to posit a new analytical model of American society, cutting across the traditional lines that draw sharp distinctions such as liberal and conservative; rural, urban, and suburban; black, white, Hispanic, and Asian; working class and middle class. After extensive soundings of public sentiment and lifestyles in the closing years of the twentieth century, Ray found that about one-quarter of the U.S. adult population—some 50 million people—subscribes to varying degrees to a new postconsumer ethos. He calls this subculture the Cultural Creatives.

You can read about Ray's insightful approach in *The Cultural Creatives: How 50 Million People Are Changing the World* by Paul H. Ray and Sherry Ruth Anderson (2000).

Cultural Creatives share a distinctive set of values that contrast with those of the Americans Ray describes as Traditionals or Moderns. The five most widely cited values, according to Ray's research (p. 29), are as follows:

- A desire to rebuild neighborhoods and communities
- A fear of violence against women and children
- A liking for what is foreign and exotic
- A view of nature as sacred
- A strong commitment to the environment

Cultural Creatives tend to distrust traditional institutions—government, the military, established religion, multinational corporations—and find virtue in individuals and local, human-scale organizations that "walk their talk." They seek to live their lives in accord with their personal values, which include a deeply felt desire for personal (often spiritual) fulfillment and a passionate commitment to the notion that the human race shares a common destiny.

Cultural Creatives believe that to solve society's social and environmental problems, we must significantly reinvent our business, governmental, and cultural institutions, hence the term *Cultural Creatives*. Although Modernists and Traditionalists often agree with Cultural Creatives about the problems (including environmental challenges and the growing divide between haves and have-nots), they differ in what the solutions need to be. Modernists believe that the current system is the best there is and just needs some tweaking to address the problems. Traditionalists believe that the problems could be solved if only we could return to how things were fifty years ago.

The rise of Cultural Creatives coincides with and reinforces other trends that are more visible to the naked eye: (1) socially responsible investing (SRI) and (2) social responsibility in business.

Socially Responsible Investing

Just thirty years ago it was almost unthinkable that any investor, whether individual or institutional, might allocate funds based on any criteria other than risk and return. As of 2001, more than $2 trillion was invested in the United States in a socially responsible manner, up from $1.5 trillion ten years earlier, according to the nonprofit Social Investment Forum. The precise criteria for SRIs vary greatly from one investor and one fund to another, but they tend to share three important attributes: (1) potential investments are *screened* to eliminate those that run counter to the investor's values or those that match the investor's values; (2) SRI shareholders use their votes as owners to pressure the companies they own to improve their social and environmental practices; and (3) social investors earmark a portion of their portfolios to community investments outside the stock market. Community investments go directly into economically hard-hit communities to create affordable housing, child care, jobs, and new, community-based businesses. (Note that the $2 trillion represents not only SRI assets invested in screened portfolios but assets active in shareholder advocacy and community investing.)

When it comes to screening, the most commonly excluded investments are those in tobacco companies, heavily polluting industries, arms manufacturers, and companies that exploit sweatshop labor. But some SRI negative screens are much more finely honed, ruling out corporations with offensive subsidiaries, a history of labor conflict, or a poor record of environmental compliance.

Positive screens may identify promising companies such as those engaged in developing new environmental cleanup technology, renewable energy resources, or inner-city enterprises.

SRI has joined the mainstream investment community, with America's best-known mutual fund companies now offering socially responsible mutual funds to compete with those from the smaller, specialized companies like Pax World Fund (the first SRI fund), the Calvert Group, Domini Social Investments, and Trillium Asset Management. Every year, Cultural Creatives pour billions more into these funds, helping to establish a new paradigm on Wall Street.

Social Responsibility in Business

Meanwhile, on the other side of the coin, social responsibility is fast taking hold, even in some of the most traditional precincts of the business world. In the 1970s and 1980s, pioneering companies such as Ben & Jerry's, The Body Shop, Tom's of Maine, Working Assets, and Patagonia were laughed (or sneered) at by their peers in business and derided in newspaper business pages.

These companies, committed to the "triple bottom line" of social and environmental returns as well as shareholders' profits, had set out to prove that values-driven businesspeople could "do well by doing good." In the years that followed, hundreds and then thousands of companies followed suit, fueled by patronage from the fast-growing Cultural Creative population. By the mid-1990s, Big Business started catching on. The new popularity of socially responsible business practices followed groundbreaking survey research spotlighting the marketplace value of social responsibility. The 1999 Cone/Roper Cause-Related Marketing Trends Report—the first national longitudinal study to identify changes in consumer attitudes toward cause-related marketing—revealed that, when price and quality are equal, 76 percent of U.S. consumers reported that they would be likely to switch to a brand associated with a good cause. This figure was up ten points since 1993. In addition, 83 percent of Americans have a more positive image of companies supporting a particular cause that they care about. And for companies with cause programs, 87 percent of all employees report having a stronger sense of loyalty to their employer. Companies without cause programs report approximately 67 percent of employees having strong loyalty to their company.

Meanwhile, the organization, Business for Social Responsibility, hatched by visionaries in the Social Venture Network in 1992, had begun signing up one after another of the Fortune 500, including many Fortune 50 companies—united in the understanding that consumers were leading a revolution of expectations. No longer was it enough to produce and sell a quality product at the lowest possible price. More and more consumers, led by Cultural Creatives, wanted to know whether you exploited your employees and despoiled the environment in the process. At the same time, socially responsible investors, including some of the largest pension funds in the country, were bringing further pressure to bear on corporate leaders through increasingly visible shareholder resolutions challenging some corporate practices. For example, by 2003 shareholder resolutions on the risks represented by global warming had polled one out of four votes at the annual meetings of some of the world's most prominent companies, forcing some corporate boards to re-examine their cavalier attitude about the environmental impact of their decisions.

Of course, for some major corporations the emerging postconsumer values merely occasion "greenwashing," that is, making cosmetic changes or simply using new marketing ploys without making substantive changes in their operations. More and more frequently, however, some of the world's biggest companies are adopting significant socially responsible business practices, having concluded that their long-term survival requires them.

Meanwhile, inspired by Ben & Jerry's, The Body Shop, and Patagonia, a whole new generation of "green" businesses with social and environmental missions at their core has emerged and is growing rapidly. Many of these are cataloged annually in Co-Op America's *National Green Pages, 2002 Edition* and have grown from a handful of companies two decades ago to a thriving sector encompassing thousands of companies that offer everything on the list of today's selective consumer.

This newly emerging reality has a number of implications for the nonprofit sector and for fundraisers in particular. First of all, the Cone/Roper data about the marketplace value of association with good causes have produced an upsurge in cause-related marketing. High-profile companies, eager to burnish their brands, have partnered with some of America's best-known nonprofits. The companies provide free advertising, access to customers, and sometimes cash as well, in exchange for public recognition. In dollars and cents, the impact of cause-related marketing has been modest, but the promotional value of these partnerships has proven substantial indeed for some charities.

Another implication is that investors' demands for SRI policies are increasingly being felt in the institutional funds that possess a large share of America's wealth, including the endowment funds of many large nonprofits. As organizations chartered to serve the public interest, not-for-profits are especially vulnerable to these demands and are likely to feel them more and more intensely as the years go by.

Third, for decades the nonprofit sector has operated under the assumption that the psychic rewards of serving the public interest are sufficient to compensate for low pay and often difficult working conditions. To some degree, this is true, at least in the minds of many nonprofit employees, but times are changing. Many young people entering the sector nowadays come with a different set of expectations than did their parents' generation. It has become increasingly difficult to persuade recent entrants to the nonprofit world that their employers can't offer competitive pay, desirable working conditions, *and* the satisfaction that comes from serving noble ends. (If you've recently tried hiring new entry-level development staff, you may have observed this. I have.) Increasingly, too, today's more aggressive labor unions are capitalizing on these higher expectations. The trend, then, seems to be toward higher operating costs in the nonprofit sector, compounding the challenge we fundraisers face—not just because we must raise a lot more money but because many donors are shocked by the real costs of running an effective nonprofit organization today.

And finally, while support from the corporate sector in general appears to be shrinking, there is lively and growing interest among the new wave of "green" businesses to enter into partnerships with nonprofits. Most green businesses are rooted in their communities. Some have even been founded with the express purpose of building their communities by providing jobs, offering cause-related marketing opportunities, becoming active as companies in civic and cultural affairs, and sharing their profits with worthy causes.

Implications of Climate Change

Don't be misled by the naysayers in the corporate sector and in the U.S. government. There is near-unanimous agreement in the mainstream scientific community that global warming is under way, that much of it is caused by human activities, that it has already made itself felt in changing weather patterns and shifting wildlife habitats, and that its long-term effects on human civilization will be severe if its growth isn't reversed. In fact, the most recent estimates by the International Panel on Climate Change make it clear that earlier projections were far too conservative. Under the most likely scenarios, summer temperatures worldwide are estimated to be between 12 and 20 degrees Fahrenheit higher by the end of the century than they are now. Civilization as we know it will not survive such a dramatic change in our environment. More to the point, at this rate of change, the near-term effects of climate change will be far more severe than previously envisioned, and even the modest cutbacks in greenhouse gas emissions set under the Kyoto Protocol (the global treaty negotiated to combat climate change) are insufficient to forestall many of these effects. The implications of this trend for the nonprofit sector are substantial.

Health

First, the massive environmental changes that now appear all but inevitable will affect our health and well-being. Climate change does *not* simply mean that our winters will become warmer. In fact, the most recent studies suggest that the greater effects will be observable in summertime. Climate affects wind patterns and ocean currents, which in turn govern cloud formation, rain and snowfall, the boundaries of deserts, and the temperature and density of the polar icecaps. Human life thrives within a narrow range of temperatures; our most vulnerable people—the old and infirm, the sick, the very young—often find it especially difficult to adjust to severely high temperatures. Furthermore, as a result of the climate change already in progress, tropical diseases are gradually spreading through the planet's temperate zones and bringing such threats as malaria and dengue fever to U.S. shores. Over time, these developments will further tax an already overburdened health care system, increasing their demands for funds.

Economic Disruption

And climate change is bringing economic disruption in its wake. Crop patterns are already affected in some parts of the world because of shifting atmospheric temperatures and changing rainfall patterns. But the growing impact on agriculture, however severe it may become, pales beside the crushing blow that climate change will wreak on many parts of the world where clean water is already scarce and will become much scarcer. For example, projections show diminishing winter snowfall in California's mountains, threatening drought so severe that it may not just cripple the state's abundant agricultural production but parch its cities as well. Meanwhile, climate change is compounding the impact of poor farming and animal husbandry practices in other parts of the world, expanding already extensive desert lands into once-fertile territories. To cope with the human impact of these devastating changes will take massive financial resources, as well as intensive, long-term efforts by nongovernmental organizations not presently well equipped to deal with disaster on such a scale.

Rising Waters

Many of the globe's biggest cities, containing more than two-thirds of the world's population, are located in a relatively narrow band of land within a few miles of ocean waters. Most of us, then, are vulnerable to the rise in sea levels, a direct result of global warming that is already in evidence. In the absence of gargantuan public works projects to hold back the rising waters, major cities such as New York could be partially submerged as the twenty-first century unfolds. Oceanfront properties the world over face a similar fate. Many island communities will simply be drowned. The slow-moving disasters in store for us are no less threatening than hurricanes or earthquakes, and they will surely place a greater burden on disaster-relief efforts as the years go by.

Shrinking Habitats

Biologists are already monitoring a pronounced shift in the growing season of plant life and the habitat range of wildlife in North America and elsewhere in the world. Many species will adapt to these changes. Some will not. The planet's shrinking biodiversity will shrink further as a result, adding to the urgency of the efforts of conservation and environmental organizations that seek to preserve the wilderness, protect endangered species, safeguard the biological treasures of rainforests, conserve and restore commercial fisheries, and defend our rights to unfettered access to the glories of nature.

Divergence in Communications

Some take comfort in the notion—hyped for years by corporate dreamers and their acolytes in the media—that the ever-growing array of communications channels will eventually merge, or converge, into one all-encompassing network. Soon, they say, the telephone, the television, the personal computer, and all their many components and peripheral devices will morph into a single, all-purpose communications device. Humanity everywhere will be bound together by a ubiquitous wireless network that will allow us all to cast off the limitations imposed on us by time and distance.

Nonsense!

Perhaps someday this science fantasy will come to fruition but not in my life-time, and I expect to live for a good many more years. Reality intrudes in too many ways on this fanciful dream. For starters, only about one billion out of our planet's current population of six billion could reasonably be described as belonging to the world of telephones and television, let alone personal computers, and the fast-widening income and asset gap between rich and poor nations makes it vanish-ingly unlikely that this condition will change quickly. Also, as it turns out, the technology itself isn't cooperating as smoothly as the visionaries had hoped. But, most important, people in even the most technology-dependent societies simply aren't buying what the dreamers are offering; the world's telecommunications com-panies have lost hundreds of billions of dollars through unwise mergers and heed-less market ventures in pursuit of this impossible dream.

To my mind, our current reality is defined much more accurately by divergence than convergence. For the foreseeable future, we fundraisers—along with every-one else in what is misleadingly called civilized society—will face a proliferating array of communications choices. Our challenge will be to choose the right ones and use them wisely.

Venture Philanthropy and Donor Choice

Today's donors demand increased control over the use of their gifts. We see this trend expressed in many ways, every one of them having significant implications for fundraising practices and the evolution of the nonprofit sector.

Donor-Advised Funds

The most explosive growth among U.S. foundations lies in the nation's nearly seven hundred community foundations. A very substantial portion of that growth comes from the emergence of donor-advised funds as many donors' preferred vehicle for philanthropy. The rules that govern the operations of donor-advised funds vary from one foundation to the next. A few restrict their donors' choices to locally based nonprofits or otherwise limit the range of choice. Most, however, operate donor-advised funds along classical lines, allowing anyone who establishes a fund with a minimum amount (often $50,000 or $100,000) to exercise full freedom of choice about which nonprofits will receive gifts made from the fund.

Another fast-growing phenomenon is the emergence of charitable giving mech-anisms offered by some of the nation's biggest investment companies. In 2002, the Fidelity Investments Charitable Gift Fund was ranked number two in the *Chron-icle of Philanthropy's Philanthropy 400*, having raised more than $1 billion the previous year. Fidelity was one of four commercial donor-advised funds on the Philanthropy 400 list that year.

Many donors are unsatisfied with the hands-off role offered them by donor-advised funds. They want to become more directly involved in the affairs of their grantees, as board members, consultants, or even unpaid staff members. Their gifts come with strings attached—sometimes lots of strings.

Venture Philanthropy

Other donors—sometimes alone, sometimes in groups—are developing the concept of *venture philanthropy.* This term can mean either or both of two things: (1) using philanthropic gifts as seed capital to help launch new public interest ventures, or (2) (more often) investing funds in profit-making ventures run by nonprofit organizations to diversify their funding base. Either way, venture philanthropy blends capitalism with the nonprofit ethic, producing an amalgam that is helping to foster a more entrepreneurial spirit in the independent sector. That's all to the good, as far as I'm concerned, and I hope it foretells a more venturesome approach and a greater willingness to assume risk in fundraising.

Gift Designation

Just as wealthy donors are looking for—and finding—ways to assert continuing control over their contributions, less-well-heeled donors are demanding more opportunities to designate their gifts. In recent years, the United Way has succumbed to this pressure in many communities, allowing its donors to assign their gifts to specific charities. Similarly, nonprofits themselves are finding that donors often respond better when offered the opportunity to earmark their gifts for certain projects rather than for general support. For direct response fundraisers, this development poses a challenge, because one of the major virtues of small-donor fundraising is that it normally generates unrestricted gifts. This is yet another adjustment in our traditional practices that we may have to set aside as the years go by.

Donors in general reflect the prevailing attitudes of a distrustful age and are demanding increased scrutiny of nonprofit finances. No longer is it sufficient to build a strong brand and a reputation for frugality and effectiveness. Nowadays, many donors want to be shown how their gifts are used and how effective charities' work has been. Fundraisers must be prepared to demonstrate transparency in financial matters and to shape our appeals around demonstrations of our organizations' effectiveness.

Rising Concern with Privacy

For at least the past two decades, public concern about privacy has been rising steadily, fed by widespread publicity about the ways financial institutions share information among themselves and with the public, as well as growing awareness of list-usage policies in direct mail, both commercial and not-for-profit. This development has already had substantial impact on fundraising in general and direct response fundraising in particular. As a result, professional telefundraisers have been forced to change the ways they communicate with donors in many states, and direct mail fundraisers have adopted new practices, clarifying how we will or won't make use of information supplied by donors and offering them the opportunity to "opt out" of list exchange and list rental arrangements. However, we may find that further changes are in store for us.

First, the privacy movement continues to gather steam. It finds its most visible expression in the introduction of restrictive legislation at both the federal and state levels and in the rapid increase of registration requirements in states, counties, and municipalities across the country. Everyone seems to be getting into the act, which is testament to the public appeal of the privacy issue. To date, privacy legislation in the United States is still far less rigorous than it is in Germany and many other European countries, but times are changing.

So far, the biggest burden imposed on nonprofit organizations and on fundraising consultants has been the number of state-level requirements for registration with offices in the states' attorneys general or secretaries of state. The paperwork, bonding requirements, and registration fees—a thinly veiled fundraising effort by the states themselves—have created resentment and unnecessary work and have driven some small consulting firms out of business. (Unfortunately, these requirements have never been demonstrated to deter fraud, the ostensible purpose for which they were enacted.)

Until now, Congress, legislatures, and state charities regulators have concerned themselves primarily with fundraising via direct response—by mail and phone, and, more recently, via the Internet—because those programs have been more visible. However, fundraisers using other techniques are also covered. My fear is that growing preoccupation with privacy will eventually lead to restrictions on one of the mainstays of major gift fundraising: donor research. If that occurs, and some of fundraisers' most favored sources of donor information are declared out of bounds (Securities and Exchange Commission records and property tax rolls, for example), the impact will be felt on direct response fundraisers as well. As our methods become more sophisticated, we are ranging farther and farther afield in search of information that can help us target donors and prospects more accurately.

Continuing Globalization

Globalization has become one of the buzzwords of our time. In its narrow sense, the phenomenon encompasses free trade in goods, services, intellectual property, and financial instruments, which has made its impact felt on the people of every continent and practically every nation. Clearly, though, globalization in the broader sense has been under way for millennia, tracking the development of new technologies in transportation, communications, and the growth of business and industry. (Even in the prehistoric Neolithic Age, trade and population movements from continent to continent were widespread.) It's that broader view that is relevant to the nonprofit sector, because the impact on us comes as much from "internationalization" as it does from the economic consequences of free trade. The implications are several. For example, some U.S. charities discovered fundraising opportunities overseas many years ago. Others have been learning quickly in recent years. The attractiveness of raising money outside the United States first became evident to nonprofits dedicated to international aid and development, such as CARE, Save the Children, and World Vision. More recently, domestic nonprofits such as People for the Ethical Treatment of Animals and Habitat for Humanity have branched out overseas, raising local funds to support their extended operations. Other organizations are likely to follow, barring economic disaster or other historical discontinuities.

At the same time, overseas charities have been entering the U.S. market. Many foreign universities and other nonprofits are registered as tax-exempt, not-for-profit organizations and maintain offices in the United States for the express purpose of raising money here to support their operations at home. Other organizations simply mail appeals directly to selected members of the American public. Either way, they intensify what is already fierce competition for philanthropic support in the nonprofit sector.

The explosive growth of multinational corporations, along with the concomitant trend toward mergers and acquisitions in many spheres of business, has lessened the numbers of home-based corporations with direct ties to their communities. The net effect to date is that corporate support for local charities has declined. In the future, as corporations increasingly recognize the public relations value of local community involvement, that trend may shift.

I would like to think that the shrinking of the world as globalization marches on would increase the U.S. public's interest in international work. Unfortunately, at just the point when the country's leaders in Washington are aggressively extending their reach across the globe, I've seen no signs that public support for international aid and development is rising sharply. The data in *Giving USA 2003* [p. 45] show that public support for nonprofits engaged in international affairs did, indeed, continue its decade-and-a-half-long rise averaging nearly 10 percent per year, but the total still amounted to only 1.9 percent of total funds contributed.

Today, some of the most innovative fundraising work anywhere in the world is under way overseas. I've taught fundraising to nonprofit executives, volunteers, and board members from more than one hundred countries on six continents, and I can tell you from personal experience that the nonprofit sector is vibrant and growing virtually everywhere on the globe. And I've learned a great deal from the resourceful efforts undertaken to raise funds for nonprofit ventures in some of the world's poorest countries. We North Americans can learn a lot from the experience of our counterparts, not just in the United Kingdom, Australia, and other English-speaking countries but on every continent.

The Growing Gap Between Rich and Poor

It's no secret: the gap in income and wealth between the world's richest nations and the poor countries, collectively called developing nations, has widened in recent decades. Despite high-profile United Nations conferences to highlight the problem and well-publicized international aid and relief efforts by industrialized countries and nongovernmental organizations alike, much of the world's population remains mired in desperate poverty, with little or no hope for a better future. According to the U.N.'s 2001 Human Development Report, some 1.2 billion people—one out of every five human beings—live on less than one dollar per day. All told, 2.8 billion people—almost one of every two—live on less than two dollars per day. And the numbers are going up, not down. A trickle of "foreign aid" is overwhelmed by streams of cash coming from the other direction: payments for industrial goods, interest on loans from commercial banks as well as the World Bank, and capital flight to more stable countries.

Analysts have sliced and diced U.S. economic and tax data every conceivable way to prove—or disprove—the widening gap in wealth and income between our own poorest and richest citizens. Statistics never lie, but people do. But if the data are unconvincing, the reality is stark. Within the United States, the rich are getting richer and the poor aren't. After more than two decades of regressive tax policies and cuts in human services, ballooning salaries and bonuses for corporate executives, sports stars, and top entertainers, the number of America's rich has exploded. There were 2,100,000 high-net-worth individuals in the United States at the end of 2001, according to Cap Gemini Ernst & Young and Merrill Lynch in their 2002 World Wealth Report. (High-net-worth individuals are people with financial assets of at least $1 million, excluding real estate.)

For the nonprofit sector, there are several consequences of these economic trends. First, as poverty grows—even relative poverty in the face of an increasingly affluent upper class—its social costs mount, too. Crime. Alienation. Alcohol and drug abuse. All these factors place a special burden on nonprofits, which are often alone on the margins of society, struggling to provide human services.

Meanwhile, demand for services throughout society rises as the middle class is squeezed. Nonprofits increasingly face needs far surpassing their abilities. The burden then shifts to fundraisers, who must attempt as best they can to meet ever-more-ambitious budgets.

Commentators on philanthropy sometimes speak of "compassion fatigue." Certainly, as the need for social services grows, and as larger and larger numbers of nonprofits turn to new channels to boost their fundraising efforts, donors are besieged by more and more solicitations. Is compassion fatigue under way as I write? Some think so. I believe it's too early to tell.

At the same time, the growth in the ranks of American millionaires has led to a huge increase in the number of philanthropic foundations. Every year, thousands more join the more than 58,000 U.S. foundations listed by the Foundation Center in 2002. Some recent entrants, such as the Gordon E. and Betty I. Moore Foundation and the Omidyar Foundation (based on fortunes built at Intel and eBay, respectively), are multi-billion-dollar enterprises. The money contributed through foundations accounted for nearly one in every eight philanthropic dollars received by U.S. nonprofits in 2001, representing a continuing increase in the proportion of funds from foundations.

The Permanence of Change

With all that said, there is, however, one more, overarching trend: the seeming permanence of change itself. It's said that the six billion people now inhabiting planet Earth create more scientific knowledge in any passing year than all of humankind previously generated in ten thousand years of history. This staggering claim, which is based on estimates about the continuing acceleration of scientific inquiry, is beyond my comprehension. All I know is that no matter how widely I travel or how much I read, I am flabbergasted by how much less I know each passing year.

For unnumbered centuries, humankind slowly evolved in a society that, to all appearances, was static and unchanging. Change came in fits and starts, at widely separated intervals. In fact, during the first nine thousand years of human history, the very concept of change was alien to most people. Life proceeded in cycles, marked only by the passage of the years and the progression of the seasons. The notion of change as progress became widely familiar to the human race only within the past five centuries.

How little we know about how our forebears lived, or how radically different our own lives have become! If you were an American teenager in the 1950s, as I was, your view of the world was indelibly shaped by the attitudes that prevailed in the Eisenhower era. The assassination of President John F. Kennedy and, later, both his brother and the Rev. Dr. Martin Luther King Jr.; the Cuban Missile Crisis, the Vietnam War, the Generation Gap, the War on Poverty, the walk on the moon— these seminal events of the 1960s were profoundly shocking and unsettling. The launching of the Internet and the invention of the microprocessor during those years went largely unremarked, leaving their impact to be noted two or three decades hence. Yet to those who were teenagers in the 1960s, these events were world-shapers, and now they're memories that color their experience of more recent events.

The 1970s saw Watergate, the end of the Vietnam War, the OPEC oil embargo, the Iranian Revolution, the Soviet invasion of Afghanistan, and the advent of sharp inflation in the U.S. economy. In the 1980s, we witnessed the Reagan tax cuts, the creation of the Macintosh computer, U.S. intervention in Central America, the go-go years on Wall Street, the collapse of the Soviet Union, and the fall of the Berlin Wall. The 1990s brought the first Gulf War, the birth of the World Wide Web, the adoption of the cellular telephone, the Internet boom, and, finally, the collapse of the U.S. stock market.

At whatever point you came of age during those four decades, your views were forever altered by the life-changing events of your time. In looking back on all those years, all that we truly have in common is the inescapability of change. Are you ready for more? You'd better be. Welcome to the twenty-first century!

● ● ●

Now, to gain some perspective on the road ahead—and on the contents of this book—let's venture together into a close examination the four-year experience of one direct mail fundraising program. That's the topic of this book's final chapter, which follows immediately.

PART FOUR

Four Years in the Life of a Successful Direct Mail Program

I n Chapter Sixteen, the book's final chapter, you'll get an inside look at the direct mail fundraising program of a remarkable nonprofit organization, the Union of Concerned Scientists (UCS). In the course of four years, UCS reconceived and reinvigorated its dormant direct mail fundraising program, achieving dramatic growth in membership and revenue. In many ways, the UCS program is a textbook example of how to apply the concepts and techniques discussed in this book.

The statistics and the sample packages that appear in the pages that follow are reproduced with the kind permission of Howard C. ("Bud") Ris, president of UCS, and David Whalen, its director of development. The numbers included here are compiled from reports and analyses prepared by Emily Ferman and Marie Minardi of the UCS staff, the good people of the Target Analysis Group of Cambridge, Massachusetts, and Mwosi Swenson and Dan Suzio of Mal Warwick & Associates.

The managers of this sustained effort were Emily Ferman at UCS and Mwosi Swenson at Mal Warwick & Associates, who share much of the credit for the program's success. Many other staff members at both my firm and at UCS contributed as well. Another who deserves special note is Sheila Dennis, who served as UCS's director of development during the program's first three years.

16

The Union of Concerned Scientists, 1999–2003

By 1998, Bud Ris knew it was time to take action to resuscitate his organization's once-lucrative direct mail fundraising program. As the long-time executive director (and later president) of the Union of Concerned Scientists (UCS), Ris vividly recalled the heyday of the program a decade and a half earlier, when the organization's high profile during the Reagan years had allowed it to increase its member and activist file to more than 100,000. Since then, however, the file had shrunk by over two-thirds, and the revenue it produced was declining.

Though little known outside the environmental and peace movements and the scientific community, UCS had played a pivotal role for nearly thirty years in many of the nation's most critical and controversial national security and environmental issues. Merging the power of sound science with citizen activism and the active support of Nobel Prize-winning scientists and other top researchers, UCS had been instrumental in moderating both federal and state policies on a wide range of critical issues. UCS's long list of achievements recalls some of the benchmark victories in the history of the environmental movement. Here are a few of those achievements.

Three-Mile Island. Remember Three Mile Island in 1979? In the wake of the worst nuclear disaster in U.S. history, UCS provided critical technical leadership to local citizens' groups pressing for tougher safety standards at nuclear power plants. Two decades later, millions of Americans are safer because the organization's work led to comprehensive regulatory change throughout the nuclear industry.

Star Wars. Do you recall the highly charged debate in the 1980s over President Reagan's "Star Wars" proposal? Evidence brought to light by UCS played a critical role in scaling back this ill-advised and potentially disastrous military adventure.

Drive for renewable energy resources. At the beginning of the 1990s, UCS reinvigorated the drive for solar, wind, and other renewable energy sources by providing new analysis, technical support, and training to dozens of local and state environmental groups in the Midwest, New England, and the Far West. Now states all across the country are launching new and creative renewable energy programs. Indeed, wind power is now the fastest-growing energy source in America.

During the 1990s, UCS expanded its program to include a number of cutting-edge issues, ranging from climate change to controversies around the application of biotechnology in agriculture. Throughout this period, the organization's revenue and the scale of its activity grew steadily, thanks in large part to successful efforts to enlist support from foundations and the loyal commitment of donors who had been with the organization since the late seventies and early eighties.

UCS became much more visible in the major news media in the 1990s, rising to the point that it was the third most-cited environmental organization in the *New York Times* during a twelve-month period ending in 2002. And it substantially expanded its activity outside of Washington, focusing on key states and regions where important policy precedents could be set.

But despite the lengthening list of the organization's accomplishments, its base was shrinking, along with the financial support through direct mail that had played such a large role in earlier years. In the course of a multiyear organizational planning process, it also became apparent that UCS was in danger of becoming overly dependent on foundation support and that it required a substantially broader base of grassroots activist support for its efforts in advocacy and public education.

For these reasons, and because staff resources were limited, UCS resolved to contract with a direct mail consulting firm. By the happy coincidence of good timing and good chemistry, UCS chose my firm, Mal Warwick & Associates, Inc. After competitive presentations and discussions, we began work together in February 1999.

Here was the challenge we confronted:

- Donor acquisition efforts had virtually come to a standstill. The numbers of new donors recruited fell short of the numbers lost to attrition.
- Donor resolicitations were mailed to far too many donors, including lapsed donors, and were thus not consistently cost-effective.
- Although the organization was going to great lengths to focus its positioning in the media, its positioning in direct mail was unclear, and messaging was inconsistent. Many long-time donors thought of UCS as an arms-control organization, but with the ending of the Cold War that focus no longer made sense.

During the 1990s, UCS made the transition from arms control to a broader approach to the environment. The mail needed to reflect that critical shift.

- A disproportionate number of active donors—nearly one-third of the total—had never given any gift of $25 or more.
- For an organization with a stellar history and the large numbers of loyal, long-time donors to prove it, UCS possessed a disappointingly small number of high-dollar donors.

It was clear from the outset that these challenges couldn't be met overnight. Together, my colleagues and I and the UCS staff resolved to tackle them methodically, one after another, in a concerted, long-term effort to regain the program's momentum and generate the added revenue the organization needed to expand its many promising programmatic initiatives.

In the pages that follow, I'll describe the progress of our efforts, year by year, over the ensuing four years. First, however, it's worth gaining perspective on the program as a whole by examining some of the benchmarks we have tracked to monitor our progress.

A Four-Year Overview

In Table 16.1, you'll see a summary of the UCS direct response fundraising program from 1999 through 2002 (with figures for 1998 included to establish a baseline).

A word of caution about these numbers: they include revenue from tele-fundraising, e-mail and Web fundraising, and other activities managed in-house by UCS, as well as the direct mail results summarized in the following pages. The

TABLE 16.1. Four-Year Summary of UCS Direct Mail Fundraising Results.

	1998	1999	2000	2001	2002
Total 12-month donors	28,540	30,152	34,322	40,134	45,125
Total new donors	1,247	2,075	6,768	9,287	11,804
Total revenue	$1,610,592	$1,905,101	$2,400,438	$2,754,512	$3,061,984
Revenue per donor	$56.43	$63.18	$69.94	$68.63	$67.86
Number of $500+ donors	263	336	452	542	583
1st year retention rate	38.1%	45.1%	38.1%	45.5%	42.3%
Multiyear retention rate	68.1%	69.5%	70.6%	74.4%	73.5%

Note: These figures were based on the UCS fiscal year, October 1 through September 30, and exclude all donors who made individual gifts of $5,000 or more.

figures cited here, then, do not match those cited next, which are drawn from reports compiled by Mal Warwick & Associates and refer only to direct mail.

As you can see at a glance, the numbers delineate a successful direct mail fundraising program, with revenue doubling in four years. But that took a lot of doing, as you'll learn.

Year 1: Converting to a Membership Program

As we—both the consultant and the client—saw things early in 1999, three tasks took on the highest priority:

1. Getting a handle on the organization's messaging
2. Resuming donor acquisition activities
3. Building a stronger base for long-term loyalty by introducing a membership program with a more efficient, annual renewal system in place of the monthly system then in place

Those three tasks absorbed much of our energy in 1999.

Messaging

Messaging came first. Despite our best efforts, it quickly became clear that UCS's mission wasn't singular and unambiguous. Though linked intellectually in myriad ways, the two poles of the organization's work—national security and the environment—touched different (though overlapping) constituencies and couldn't be easily conflated into a single, appealing catch-phrase. Instead, bowing to the pressures of reality, we settled on a tagline of sorts: "a cleaner, healthier environment and a safer world." (At the time, UCS was in the early stages of a systematic positioning exercise, but its outcome, including a new logo and tagline, wasn't expected for nearly a year.) This fence-straddling solution allowed us to encompass both realms of activity, emphasizing the environmental issues that lay at the core of UCS's work during those years while acknowledging the continuing importance of national security issues to the organization's leadership.

Acquisition

Once the messaging debate had ended, we turned our attention to developing themes that could be tested in acquisition. Three issues fought for consideration, and in the end we elected to test all three. We divided a mailing of approximately 100,000 letters into three segments, in hopes that at least one of the three letters would draw a 1 percent rate of response and thus point the way to a viable direct mail donor acquisition program on a larger scale. (One percent would be substantially higher than recent UCS in-house prospecting efforts, none of which had topped 0.60 percent.) In fact, *every one of the three letters* drew more than 1 percent. The aggregate rate of response for the mailing as a whole was 1.24 percent, with an average gift of $30 (which was also substantially higher than in recent UCS acquisition mailings). We thus set in motion a second prospect mailing to test the top two packages against each other and to expand the list of lists we could explore.

Exhibit 16.1 illustrates one of the three initial test packages we mailed in 1999—one that proved to have great staying power and is still in use today (after necessary revisions).

EXHIBIT 16.1. UCS Direct Mail Membership Acquisition Package.

Union of Concerned Scientists
Citizens and Scientists for Environmental Solutions
Two Brattle Square   Cambridge, MA 02238-9105
www.ucsusa.org

Dear Friend of the Environment,

As a person who is concerned and informed about the environment, you know that the effects of oil consumption reach far and wide:

Oil spills pollute the seas and threaten our most treasured wilderness areas.

Tailpipe emissions foul our air.

Carbon dioxide causes global warming.

Crises in the Middle East—where a lot of our oil comes from—threaten our security.

You also probably know that the simplest, most cost-effective way to reduce our consumption of oil in the United States is to **increase the fuel economy of motor vehicles**.

Indeed, **the technology exists right now** to make all passenger vehicles significantly more fuel-efficient.

The auto manufacturers know that. So do our representatives in Congress.

What's more, consumers want it. Scientists have made the case for it. And concerned citizens are demanding it.

So what's the hold-up?

As you might have guessed, the Big 3 automakers and their friends in Washington just don't want to change their ways. They have resisted every single opportunity to implement new standards or provide consumers with better choices.

That's why I'm writing you today. You and I—along with thousands of other concerned individuals around the nation—have to increase the pressure for meaningful solutions.

You can start taking effective action today.

Just **send the enclosed action postcards** to UCS right away. And please join the campaign to get more fuel-efficient cars and SUVs on the market and on the roads—by becoming a member of the Union of Concerned Scientists.

Because the Union of Concerned Scientists is leading the campaign for cleaner, more fuel-efficient vehicles, you can be confident you will be taking high-impact action for the environment.

RECYCLED & RECYCLABLE / PRINTED WITH SOY INK   41721C

EXHIBIT 16.1. UCS Direct Mail Membership Acquisition Package, Cont'd.

Page 2

Americans are exposed to lots of hype. That makes it hard to sort out which actions really help, and which are just feel-good gestures that don't make any significant difference. But the Union of Concerned Scientists conducts solid scientific research. We reveal the most serious and widespread causes of environmental damage—and work to promote long-lasting solutions.

Then, UCS's 60,000 members—leading scientists working together with thousands of concerned citizens—campaign for changes that will make the most difference for the environment.

Your support as a member now will **help UCS mount an effective campaign to win more fuel-efficient cars.**

Our research shows that when Americans understand the damage gas-guzzling vehicles do, they favor tougher standards. We also know that Americans are deeply concerned about our nation's dependence on foreign oil and drilling in wilderness areas and other environmentally sensitive areas.

But many Americans are unaware of how these problems can be solved. With your support, UCS will get the word out through the news media, through the Internet, through individuals like you, and into the halls of Congress. We'll combine the best available science with strong and effective citizen action—just as we have done many times in the past.

And when you join our campaign to get fuel-efficient vehicles on the road faster, you will support UCS's collaborative work with many other environmental groups. Collaboration and coalition efforts are hallmarks of UCS action. We marshal our resources carefully and avoid duplication of other organizations' work. And we provide highly credible technical information that everyone can use.

Your support is especially important now, because Congress—with its friends in Big Oil and the auto industry—is dragging its feet on tougher regulations.

We've got to go directly to the American people, the media, our elected representatives—and the car manufacturers themselves—to demand cleaner, more efficient vehicles!

So much is at stake here!

The impact on our health, our planet, our economy, and our national security can be dramatically lessened by increasing the fuel economy of new passenger vehicles.

Our studies have shown that the major automakers could produce new vehicles averaging more than 40 miles per gallon—using cost effective technologies already "on the shelf." Hybrid electric-vehicle technologies could bring all passenger vehicles to 55 miles per gallon or more. These improvements could save consumers thousands of dollars in fuel costs over the lifetime of their vehicles.

Emissions of carbon dioxide—caused by the combustion of gasoline in cars and SUVs—could be reduced by millions of tons. Burning less gasoline would mean that hundreds of millions of pounds of toxic emissions and smog-forming pollutants would never reach our lungs.

EXHIBIT 16.1. UCS Direct Mail Membership Acquisition Package, Cont'd.

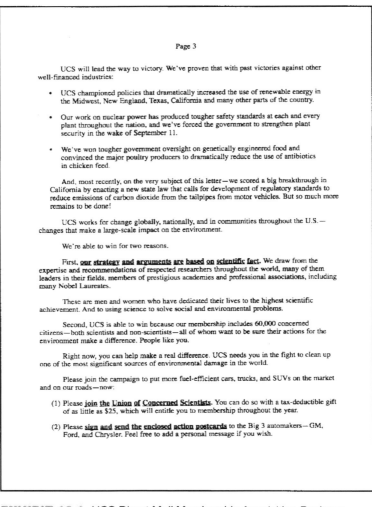

Page 3

UCS will lead the way to victory. We've proven that with past victories against other well-financed industries:

- UCS championed policies that dramatically increased the use of renewable energy in the Midwest, New England, Texas, California and many other parts of the country.

- Our work on nuclear power has produced tougher safety standards at each and every plant throughout the nation, and we've forced the government to strengthen plant security in the wake of September 11.

- We've won tougher government oversight on genetically engineered food and convinced the major poultry producers to dramatically reduce the use of antibiotics in chicken feed.

And, most recently, on the very subject of this letter—we scored a big breakthrough in California by enacting a new state law that calls for development of regulatory standards to reduce emissions of carbon dioxide from the tailpipes from motor vehicles. But so much more remains to be done!

UCS works for change globally, nationally, and in communities throughout the U.S.— changes that make a large-scale impact on the environment.

We're able to win for two reasons.

First, **our strategy and arguments are based on scientific fact**. We draw from the expertise and recommendations of respected researchers throughout the world, many of them leaders in their fields, members of prestigious academies and professional associations, including many Nobel Laureates.

These are men and women who have dedicated their lives to the highest scientific achievement. And to using science to solve social and environmental problems.

Second, UCS is able to win because our membership includes 60,000 concerned citizens—both scientists and non-scientists—all of whom want to be sure their actions for the environment make a difference. People like you.

Right now, you can help make a real difference. UCS needs you in the fight to clean up one of the most significant sources of environmental damage in the world.

Please join the campaign to put more fuel-efficient cars, trucks, and SUVs on the market and on our roads—now:

(1) Please **join the Union of Concerned Scientists**. You can do so with a tax-deductible gift of as little as $25, which will entitle you to membership throughout the year.

(2) Please **sign and send the enclosed action postcards** to the Big 3 automakers—GM, Ford, and Chrysler. Feel free to add a personal message if you wish.

EXHIBIT 16.1. UCS Direct Mail Membership Acquisition Package, Cont'd.

Page 4

With your help, we'll keep the heat on until they make real changes. Then we'll evaluate their progress with rating studies such as the "Pollution Lineup" report you can find on our website (www.ucsusa.org). And we will keep pushing for regulatory changes at the federal level to realize fuel-economy advances that are much more ambitious than what has been proposed so far.

If you join the Union of Concerned Scientists with a membership contribution of $25 or more, you'll receive complimentary subscriptions to our information-packed magazine, *Catalyst*, and our practical, down-to-earth newsletter, *earthwise*.

But, most importantly, as a member of UCS you'll be adding your voice to those of tens of thousands of scientists and other concerned citizens who bring scientific fact to the forefront in the ongoing debate about environmental policy.

Working together, as scientists and citizens, we can and will persuade the automakers to continue improving their products—and we'll make headway, step by step, in strengthening government environmental policies.

Together, we can and will protect our planet and our health by dramatically decreasing our dependence on oil.

I look forward to welcoming you soon as UCS's newest member!

Sincerely,

Howard Ris
President

P.S.   UCS studies have shown that fuel-economy standards can be raised to over 40 mpg over the next 10 to 15 years while enhancing vehicle safety and maintaining performance. The National Academy of Sciences has reached a similar conclusion. Please help UCS get to the root of the many problems caused by gas-guzzling vehicles—by demanding cars, trucks, and SUVs that are more efficient and less polluting. Take action today!

EXHIBIT 16.1. UCS Direct Mail Membership Acquisition Package, Cont'd.

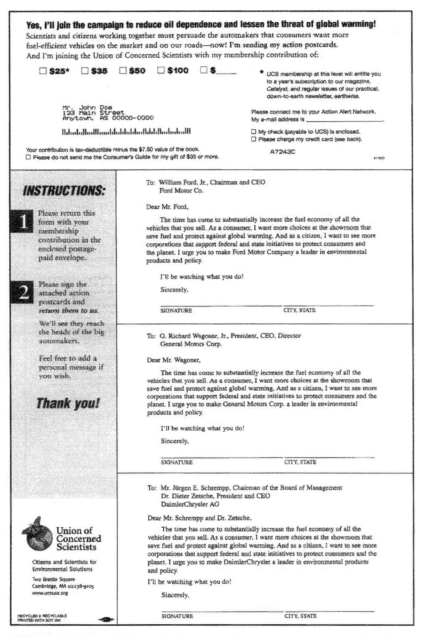

Yes, I'll join the campaign to reduce oil dependence and lessen the threat of global warming!

Scientists and citizens working together must persuade the automakers that consumers want more fuel-efficient vehicles on the market and on our roads—now! I'm sending my action postcards. And I'm joining the Union of Concerned Scientists with my membership contribution of:

☐ $25*   ☐ $35   ☐ $50   ☐ $100   ☐ $_____

* UCS membership at this level will entitle you to a year's subscription to our magazine, Catalyst, and regular issues of our practical, down-to-earth newsletter, earthwise.

Mr. John Doe
123 Main Street
Anytown, AS 00000-0000

Please connect me to your Action Alert Network. My e-mail address is _____

☐ My check (payable to UCS) is enclosed.
☐ Please charge my credit card (see back).

A7243C

Your contribution is tax-deductible minus the $7.50 value of the book.
☐ Please do not send me the Consumer's Guide for my gift of $35 or more.

INSTRUCTIONS:

1 Please return this form with your membership contribution in the enclosed postage-paid envelope.

2 Please sign the attached action postcards and *return them to us.*

We'll see they reach the heads of the big automakers.

Feel free to add a personal message if you wish.

Thank you!

Union of
Concerned
Scientists

Citizens and Scientists for
Environmental Solutions

Two Brattle Square
Cambridge, MA 02238-9105
www.ucsusa.org

RECYCLED & RECYCLABLE
PRINTED WITH SOY INK

To: William Ford, Jr., Chairman and CEO
Ford Motor Co.

Dear Mr. Ford,

The time has come to substantially increase the fuel economy of all the vehicles that you sell. As a consumer, I want more choices at the showroom that save fuel and protect against global warming. And as a citizen, I want to see more corporations that support federal and state initiatives to protect consumers and the planet. I urge you to make Ford Motor Company a leader in environmental products and policy.

I'll be watching what you do!

Sincerely,

_____   _____
SIGNATURE   CITY, STATE

To: G. Richard Wagoner, Jr., President, CEO, Director
General Motors Corp.

Dear Mr. Wagoner,

The time has come to substantially increase the fuel economy of all the vehicles that you sell. As a consumer, I want more choices at the showroom that save fuel and protect against global warming. And as a citizen, I want to see more corporations that support federal and state initiatives to protect consumers and the planet. I urge you to make General Motors Corp. a leader in environmental products and policy.

I'll be watching what you do!

Sincerely,

_____   _____
SIGNATURE   CITY, STATE

To: Mr. Jürgen E. Schrempp, Chairman of the Board of Management
Dr. Dieter Zetsche, President and CEO
DaimlerChrysler AG

Dear Mr. Schrempp and Dr. Zetsche,

The time has come to substantially increase the fuel economy of all the vehicles that you sell. As a consumer, I want more choices at the showroom that save fuel and protect against global warming. And as a citizen, I want to see more corporations that support federal and state initiatives to protect consumers and the planet. I urge you to make DaimlerChrysler a leader in environmental products and policy.

I'll be watching what you do!

Sincerely,

_____   _____
SIGNATURE   CITY, STATE

EXHIBIT 16.1. UCS Direct Mail Membership Acquisition Package, Cont'd.

Source: Union of Concerned Scientists. Reproduced with permission.

Membership

Meanwhile, we initiated our effort to breathe new life into the donor resolicitation program by designing and launching a five-effort annual membership renewal series. This sequence of appeals, mailed to all donors at the same time, requested renewed support "for the year 1999." It was based on the assumption—a correct one, as it turned out—that few long-time donors would object to the characterization of their support as "membership." The renewal series did its job and more, generating half a million dollars in revenue and renewing nearly fifteen thousand donors.

However, a fourth challenge confronted us early in the year because of the tragically untimely death of UCS's long-time chairman, Henry W. Kendall. Kendall's loss was a personal tragedy for many on the UCS board and staff and for many of the donors. He had been a part of the organization since its beginnings in 1969 and its chairman for a quarter of a century. A Nobel Laureate in physics (he was the codiscoverer of the quark), Kendall was also an energetic and skillful leader. He had loomed large in every aspect of UCS's work for two-and-half decades.

Naturally, UCS members had to be informed of Kendall's passing, and Kendall's many friends in the organization needed an opportunity to memorialize him. The result—after an unusually intensive copywriting process—was the launch of the Henry Kendall Society, allowing members and friends to make gifts of $1,000 or more per year that would enable UCS to fulfill Kendall's vision that sound science could help policymakers create a safer and healthier planet.

Table 16.2 sums up the UCS mailing program for the year 1999.

Year 2: Focusing on Member Involvement and Upgrading

In 2000, with a successful first year—far over projections—behind us, we launched several additional elements in the UCS membership development program. These included lapsed member reactivation, member cultivation, and high-dollar renewals.

Lapsed Member Reactivation

In any long-term direct mail fundraising program, lapsed and former donors are likely to dwarf in numbers the active, current donors. UCS was no exception. Our efforts to mine the large file of lapsed and former members included both a mailing and telemarketing. (The telephone fundraising program was conducted, very ably, by the Share Group, Somerville, Massachusetts.) From the outset, we had known that reactivation of previous members had to figure as a standard feature of our program. Our second year of collaboration finally gave us the opportunity and the resources necessary to launch this effort.

TABLE 16.2. UCS Membership Development Program, 1999.

Project	Mailed	Quantity	Revenue	Gifts	Percent	Average
Acquisition 1	06/99	99,179	$36,581	1,228	1.24%	$30
Acquisition 2	09/99	149,924	48,358	1,824	1.22%	27
Subtotal		249,103	84,939	3,052	1.23%	28
High-Dollar 1	07/99	2,830	96,315	124	4.38%	777
High-Dollar 2	09/99	2,472	50,305	143	5.78%	352
Subtotal		5,302	146,620	267	5.04%	549
Renewal Series*		119,631	560,171	14,948	12.50%	37
Special Appeal 1	09/99	36,902	45,695	1,222	10.14%	37
Special Appeal 2	11/99	10,393	229,471	3,938	10.67%	58
Special Appeal 3	12/99	9,935	50,812	815	7.84%	62
Subtotal		57,230	325,978	5,975	10.07%	55
Total		431,266	$1,117,708	24,242	5.59%	$46

*In 1999, the renewal series consisted of five efforts. All numbers shown reflect the aggregate results of the series as a whole.

Member Cultivation

In the course of 2000, we mailed four cultivation letters. These included the UCS annual report and a donor survey but no solicitation for funds, although reply envelopes were inserted in the first three. Our objective was not to raise net money but merely to inform donors about the work their gifts had helped make possible. In fact, the four mailings, taken together, raised $86,000, considerably more than enough to cover their costs.

High-Dollar Renewal and Upgrading

After successfully enlisting several hundred members in the Henry Kendall Society in 1999, we faced the need to renew—and, if possible, upgrade—their support in 2000. This called for an expanded program of high-dollar solicitations. It also allowed us to launch a lower-level high-dollar society—The Friends of UCS—requesting annual gifts of $250 or more.

Exhibit 16.2 depicts a high-dollar appeal of the type that we began mailing in 2000.

Table 16.3 details the direct mail program during 2000.

Union of Concerned Scientists
Citizens and Scientists for Environmental Solutions

KURT GOTTFRIED, CHAIRMAN OF THE BOARD

October 12, 2001

Mr. John Doe
123 Any Street
Any Town, AS 00000

Dear Mr. Doe,

As a member of the Henry Kendall Society, you are one of our most generous supporters. That's why I'm writing you personally.

As you're aware, we launched the Henry Kendall Society to generate unrestricted funds so that we could promptly meet unforeseen threats and unanticipated opportunities. I am hoping you will help us sustain and expand the work we have initiated with your help—by renewing your membership for 2001 with another generous gift.

I'm writing you today with a special sense of urgency about an issue on which our staff has recently done groundbreaking work: the overuse of human antibiotics to fatten healthy cows, pigs, and chickens for sale.

Giant poultry and meat producers routinely feed enormous quantities of antibiotics to healthy animals—frequently antibiotics developed for human use. They do so to speed up the animals' growth, increase profits, and avoid diseases caused by crowded, unsanitary conditions. This practice poses a grave threat to human health, because bacteria passed to humans through the food we eat often acquire resistance to antibiotics needlessly administered on the farm. As a result, a little child sick from *salmonella* food poisoning, or another deadly but common disease, may have fewer and fewer options for treatment. With the effectiveness of antibiotics compromised, the child could die.

Concerns about resistance have recently led the American Medical Association to come out in opposition to the use of antibiotics in healthy farm animals.

We are all at risk. But children, the elderly, and those with weakened immune systems, such as cancer and transplant patients and people with AIDS, are most susceptible to illness and death from antibiotic-resistant bacteria.

Each year, millions of pounds of valuable antibiotics—well *over one-half of all antibiotics produced in the U.S.*—are fed to healthy chickens, pigs, and cows. Many of these drugs are the same ones humans depend on to fight infectious disease. Overuse of these drugs in agriculture, along with their excessive use in human medicine, threatens to breed "superbugs" that could take us back to the days when thousands died yearly from pneumonia, tuberculosis, and a host of other infectious diseases.

UCS has been at the forefront of this important issue. We founded, and are a leading member of, *Keep Antibiotics Working: The Campaign to End Antibiotic Overuse*, a national coalition of health, consumer, and environmental groups working to reduce antibiotic use in

WWW.UCSUSA.org | Two Brattle Square · Cambridge, MA 02238-9105 · TEL: 617.547.5552 · FAX: 617.864.9405
1707 H Street, NW · Suite 600 · Washington, DC 20006-3919 · TEL: 202.223.6133 · FAX: 202.223.6162
2397 Shattuck Avenue · Suite 203 · Berkeley, CA 94704-1567 · TEL: 510.843.1872 · FAX: 510.843.3785

RECYCLED & RECYCLABLE / PRINTED WITH SOY INK   41461D

EXHIBIT 16.2. UCS High-Dollar Giving Club Special Appeal.

livestock. We are also working on Capitol Hill to introduce important legislation that will ban the use of medically important antibiotics in healthy animals.

I am asking you and other members of the Henry Kendall Society to help us expand our new campaign to address the dangerous, unnecessary use of antibiotics vital to human health.

In fact, there are two things you can do right now to help UCS and a coalition of collaborating organizations stand up to agribusiness and put an end to this risky practice:

(1) Sign the enclosed petitions to the CEOs of Tyson Chicken and Perdue Farms, two of the nation's largest poultry producers. Tell them you want them to stop the unnecessary use of antibiotics in chicken and livestock production.

(2) Renew your membership in the Henry Kendall Society with a gift to match—or, if possible—exceed your gift last year.

If you would like to receive a copy of our report on the overuse of antibiotics on the farm, I would be happy to send you one. You can also find it on our website (http://www.ucsusa.org/food).

Please lend us a hand. This threat to human health is not sometime in the future. It is here now. Today, there is mounting worry in the medical community about the over-prescription of antibiotics for human beings. The indiscriminate use of antibiotics in U.S. livestock production is compounding the problem. In just the last 20 years, our study estimated there has been over a 300% increase in the use of antibiotics per bird by poultry producers—not to combat disease but for reasons such as promoting growth and increasing the growers' profits.

Other nations have already taken action to address this critical problem. In 1998, fearing a rise in untreatable infectious diseases, the European Union banned the use of antibiotics that are medically important for humans from use as growth promoters in livestock production. And in Sweden, where growth-promoting antibiotics have been banned for over a decade, they've turned to alternative methods, like better cleaning and ventilation of livestock facilities to reduce animal stress and the need for antibiotics. Contradicting the arguments made by American livestock producers, animal health didn't suffer, and consumer food prices didn't substantially increase.

UCS believes immediate action is necessary at the national level:

- The Food and Drug Administration (FDA) must compel companies that sell antibiotics to provide an accurate, annual accounting of use in livestock production.
- The U.S. Department of Agriculture must improve the thoroughness and accuracy of its periodic surveys of antibiotic use in livestock production.
- Both agencies, as well as the Centers for Disease Control and Prevention, must fast-track our government's antibiotic resistance action plan.
- The FDA should withdraw approvals for medically important antibiotics used as growth promoters.

Please join us in our fight to stop the indiscriminate use of antibiotics by livestock producers. Help us get our message out by signing the enclosed petitions. And please return them with your membership renewal in the Henry Kendall Society today.

Sincerely,

Kurt Gottfried

Dr. Kurt Gottfried
Chairman of the Board

P.S.   Thank you for your continuing generosity. Your renewal gift funds our public education and advocacy work. Think of this request as an investment in the future of our nation and our planet.

EXHIBIT 16.2. UCS High-Dollar Giving Club Special Appeal, Cont'd.

Union of Concerned Scientists
Citizens and Scientists for Environmental Solutions
www.ucsusa.org

URGENT RESPONSE MEMORANDUM

To: Dr. Kurt Gottfried
       Chairman of the Board
       Union of Concerned Scientists

From: Mr. John Doe
       123 Any Street
       Any Town, AS 00000

                                      00000
                                      45DOE-A

Re: <u>Campaign Against the Unnecessary Use of Antibiotics</u>

Yes, Dr. Gottfried, I'll help underwrite the campaign to stop the unnecessary use of antibiotics in livestock . . . *because it's putting my health and my family's health at risk!* Breeding antibiotic-resistant bacteria is very risky business.

I'm signing the petitions below and am enclosing my tax-deductible renewal gift to the Henry Kendall Society to help fund this campaign and UCS's other urgent public education and advocacy work on issues affecting my health and the environment in the amount of:

                 [ ] $1,000   [ ] $1,500   [ ] $_____

We gratefully acknowledge your gifts this year totalling $250. The Henry Kendall Society is composed of individuals contributing $1,000 or more in a calendar year.

[ ]   Please list my name in your Annual Report as: _____.

[ ]   I wish to remain anonymous.

Please return this form with your check in the enclosed pre-stamped envelope, or mail to Kurt Gottfried, Chairman, Union of Concerned Scientists, Two Brattle Square, Cambridge, MA 02238. Thank you.

To: **John H. Tyson, Chairman and CEO**
        Tyson Chicken

Dear Mr. Tyson,

      As an American consumer and supporter of the Union of Concerned Scientists, I strongly oppose the unnecessary use of antibiotics in poultry production to promote animal growth and simply increase corporate profits. Compelling new scientific evidence recently published by UCS shows that the quantity of antibiotics used on healthy animals is significantly larger than the amount used in human medicine. This practice could be putting my family's health at risk.

I urge you to stop the unnecessary use of antibiotics in your poultry and livestock production.

<u>SIGNATURE</u>
Ms. Sheila Bell, Any Town, AS

To: **Jim Perdue, Chairman and CEO**
        Perdue Farms

Dear Mr. Perdue,

      As an American consumer and supporter of the Union of Concerned Scientists, I strongly oppose the unnecessary use of antibiotics in poultry production to promote animal growth and simply increase corporate profits. Compelling new scientific evidence recently published by UCS shows that the quantity of antibiotics used on healthy animals is significantly larger than the amount used in human medicine. This practice could be putting my family's health at risk.

I urge you to stop the unnecessary use of antibiotics in your poultry and livestock production.

<u>SIGNATURE</u>
Ms. Sheila Bell, Any Town, AS

RECYCLED & RECYCLABLE / PRINTED WITH SOY INK   414880

EXHIBIT 16.2. UCS High-Dollar Giving Club Special Appeal, Cont'd.

Source: Union of Concerned Scientists. Reproduced with permission.

TABLE 16.3. UCS Membership Development Program, 2000.

Project	Mailed	Quantity	Revenue	Gifts	Percent	Average
Acquisition 1	02/00	224,955	$77,213	2,769	1.23%	$28
Acquisition 2	04/00	49,976	4,189	122	0.24%	34
Acquisition 3	06/00	295,870	80,178	2,831	0.96%	28
Acquisition 4	10/00	301,929	93,734	3,065	1.02%	31
Subtotal		872,730	255,314	8,787	1.01%	29
Annual Report	04/00	3,871	0	0	0	0
Cultivation 1	05/00	3,846	24,131	45	1.17%	536
Cultivation 2	10/00	4,950	16,044	298	6.02%	54
Cultivation 3	11/00	3,654	45,846	46	1.26%	997
Cultivation 4	11/00	39,085	0	0	0	0
Subtotal		55,406	86,021	389	0.75%	221
High-Dollar 1	03/00	2,487	108,695	326	13.11%	333
High-Dollar 2	05/00	2,161	77,826	179	8.28%	435
High-Dollar 3	09/00	1,625	60,275	200	12.31%	301
Subtotal		6,273	246,796	705	11.24%	350
Renewal Series*		159,075	717,731	16,901	10.62%	42
Special Appeal 1	07/00	10,621	31,598	874	8.23%	36
Special Appeal 2	09/00	12,676	32,771	1,187	9.36%	28
Special Appeal 3	11/00	52,410	326,907	4,322	8.25%	76
Special Appeal 4	12/00	15,006	93,630	982	6.54%	95
Subtotal		90,713	484,906	7,365	8.12%	66
Total		1,184,197	$1,790,768	34,147	2.88%	$52

*Late in 2000, UCS mailed a postcard offering members an incentive to supply their e-mail addresses. The incentive was the chance to win a gift certificate for books.

Note: In 2000, the renewal series consisted of six efforts plus a lapsed member reactivation mailing. All numbers shown reflect the aggregate results of the series as a whole.

Year 3: Beginning Legacy Promotion

While our direct mail membership development program was unfolding, UCS steadily expanded its efforts to secure major and legacy gifts. Development staff approached members of the Henry Kendall Society, seeking face-to-face opportunities to discuss larger gifts. And a newly hired planned giving officer began reaching out to selected UCS members to promote bequests and other forms of legacy gifts.

In 2001, in addition to expanded membership acquisition, renewal, special appeal, and high-dollar programs, we launched our first legacy promotion mailing. This was a limited effort, targeting just twelve thousand carefully selected members because of budgetary limitations. (UCS staff members continued cultivation mailings on their own.) Though viewed as an investment in cultivating selected members as prospective planned gift donors, the legacy mailing produced $57,000 in revenue, mostly in the form of charitable gift annuities.

The major event of the year 2001 was, of course, the series of terrorist attacks that struck the United States on September 11. In an unprecedented outpouring of philanthropic fervor, Americans contributed $2 billion to the relief effort that followed, triggering apocalyptic predictions from far and wide that charities addressing other issues would be grievously hurt. Although this was, in fact, the case with certain organizations based in the New York City and Washington, D.C., areas, as well as with arts organizations in general, these predictions proved to be alarmist. Year-end fundraising efforts for UCS were extremely successful, far outstripping those in 2000. And an acquisition mailing that arrived in mailboxes the week of September 10 was one of the most successful in 2001.

In most major respects, however, 2001 was a year much like other years for the UCS membership development program. Exhibit 16.3 shows a year-end mailing of the sort sent in November 2001.

Table 16.4 sums up the results for the year 2001.

Year 4: Continuing Growth in Challenging Times

Economists later confirmed that the U.S. economy dipped into recession in the fall of 2001, a development that was accelerated by the events of 9/11. By early 2002, the recession was in full bloom, with unemployment rising, retail sales slowing, consumer confidence on the wane, and the stock market tumbling to lows last seen before the Internet bubble. It was inevitable that our membership development program for UCS would reflect this reality. In fact, the impact was severe:

- By the summer of 2002, the response rate in membership acquisition efforts had dropped significantly. It fell further in early fall, recovering to the level of a year earlier only by year-end.
- Response to special appeals was also down somewhat, even at year-end. (The inclusion of an invitation to the Partners for the Earth program artificially makes the special appeal results as a whole appear lower than they were.)
- Membership renewal results, while strong, were essentially flat compared with 2001.

Happily, these numbers rose again to earlier levels in the opening months of 2003.

Union of Concerned Scientists
Citizens and Scientists for Environmental Solutions
Two Brattle Square   Cambridge, MA 02238-9105
www.ucsusa.org

Howard Ris
President

November 2002

Dear UCS Member,

As we conclude a year in which the fundamental mission and goals of our programs have been challenged as never before, your support of the Union of Concerned Scientists is more important than ever. Your commitment to protecting the global environment, enacting smart national energy policies, and reducing the threat of nuclear weapons is key to protecting the future of our planet.

The power of your membership is evident when we review what UCS has achieved over the past year—despite the Administration's attempts to roll back a host of environmental laws and regulations, and despite its unwillingness to cooperate with other nations to protect the environment and our security. Let me tell you about just some of the **accomplishments your support made possible in 2002**:

- We focused our legislative efforts in 2002 on an **Energy Policy** that reduces our nation's dependence on foreign oil and cuts global warming gasses. Much of our effort went into damage control against the national energy bill. We were able to contain some of the worst elements put forth by the Bush Administration—like drilling in the Arctic National Wildlife Refuge and subsidies for the fossil fuel industry. We also succeeded in gaining the inclusion of a first-ever 10% Renewable Energy Standard in the Senate's version of the bill, as well as tax incentives to encourage development of fuel-efficient vehicles and renewable energy.

  Further, we set important precedents at the state level by passing landmark legislation in California mandating the reduction of global warming gasses emitted from new vehicles and setting goals and timelines for major increases in renewable energy.

- UCS brought the issue of global warming and the related impacts and solutions close to home in the Gulf Coast states (AL, FL, LA, TX, MS). Our intensive **Climate Solutions** campaign included the release of a major report that garnered region-wide media coverage, an interactive web feature, and a strong curriculum guide. This campaign explained a complex issue to the general public and directly resulted in state initiatives in Louisiana, Florida, and Texas to address global warming.

- In the area of **Food and the Environment**, UCS, working in coalition with several other groups, convinced leading poultry producers, including Tyson Foods, Perdue, and Goldkist, to voluntarily eliminate the non-therapeutic use of antibiotics in their livestock production. And we convinced the U.S. Department of Agriculture and the Environmental Protection Agency to implement a number of improvements to their oversight and regulation of genetically engineered crops.

None of this would have been possible without your support. I am deeply grateful to you for your steadfast commitment enabling UCS to work for a healthier environment and a safer

RECYCLED & RECYCLABLE / PRINTED WITH SOY INK   41791A

EXHIBIT 16.3. UCS Year-End Appeal.

Page 2

world. Concerned men and women like you, in partnership with leading scientists, make it possible for us to make real gains against significant odds.

It's clear that in the current political and economic climate, we'll have to work even harder in the year ahead. We will advance our major campaigns to promote solutions to climate change, through renewable energy, cleaner vehicles, and sustainable forestry, and to reduce the abuse of antibiotics in livestock agriculture. We will advocate for sound alternatives to the Administration's destabilizing nuclear weapons policy, which places higher priority on U.S. nuclear flexibility than on controls to guard against terrorist access to nuclear weapons and materials.

Specifically, your support will allow UCS to:

- Expand our successful climate solutions campaign that integrates new analytical reports, media, and local outreach to the Great Lakes region, while continuing our educational programs and policy work in California, New England, and other key states;

- Reduce the abuse of antibiotics in livestock agriculture through federal legislation and persuade the pork industry to adopt voluntary reductions;

- Increase the pressure on Capitol Hill to counter the aggressive, unilateral policies of the Bush Administration by strengthening programs to keep nuclear weapons out of the hands of terrorists and supporting multilateral inspection and control through the United Nations.

While we work to improve our effectiveness in the nation's capital, we will expand our work in key states and regions. We'll increase our direct engagement with auto companies, electric utilities, and food producers and retailers, while strengthening our partnerships with organized labor and continuing our longstanding efforts to mobilize the scientific community nationwide. We will stand with concerned citizens, public officials, and organizations that share our values and our goals.

It is only with your continued support that we can continue to make significant progress on our agenda for a safer world and healthy environment. In these challenging times, I'm counting on your partnership more than ever.

Please send your tax-deductible, year-end contribution to the Union of Concerned Scientists today. Together we will use the power of sound science combined with grassroots activism to protect the earth and all of its inhabitants.

Sincerely,

Howard Ris
President

P.S.   **Please be sure to complete and return the 23rd Annual Membership Survey** enclosed with this letter. Your answers will help us keep our member communications relevant to your concerns and our public education efforts well-targeted. I look forward to hearing from you. Thank you for your support!

EXHIBIT 16.3. UCS Year-End Appeal, Cont'd.

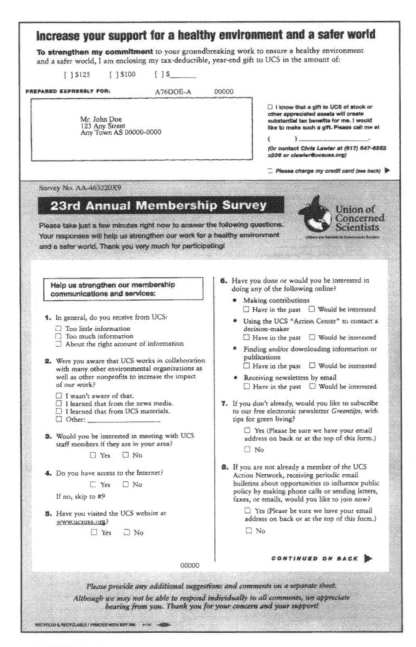

EXHIBIT 16.3. UCS Year-End Appeal, Cont'd.

☐ Please charge my:

☐ Visa ☐ MasterCard

Amount $ ________

Exp. date ________

Card # ________________

Signature

____

We are proud of the way we manage our funds. Our financial report is sent free to anyone requesting a copy and certain states require us to advise you that a copy is also available from them. If you desire a copy of our official registration or financial information, please contact UNION OF CONCERNED SCIENTISTS, Two Brattle Square, Cambridge, MA 02238-9105, or any of the following state agencies:

FLORIDA: A COPY OF THE OFFICIAL REGISTRATION AND FINANCIAL INFORMATION MAY BE OBTAINED FROM THE DIVISION OF CONSUMER SERVICES BY CALLING TOLL-FREE [illegible] WITHIN THE STATE. REGISTRATION DOES NOT IMPLY ENDORSEMENT, APPROVAL, OR RECOMMENDATION BY THE STATE. [illegible] **ILLINOIS:** Charitable Trust and Solicitations Bureau, [illegible] **MARYLAND:** For the cost of copies and postage: Office of the Secretary of State, State House, Annapolis, MD 21401. **MICHIGAN:** [illegible] **MISSISSIPPI:** The official registration and financial information of the Union of Concerned Scientists may be obtained from the Mississippi Secretary of State's office by calling [illegible]. Registration by the Secretary of State does not imply endorsement. **NEW JERSEY:** INFORMATION FILED WITH THE ATTORNEY GENERAL CONCERNING THIS CHARITABLE SOLICITATION MAY BE OBTAINED FROM THE ATTORNEY GENERAL OF THE STATE OF NEW JERSEY BY CALLING [illegible]. REGISTRATION WITH THE ATTORNEY GENERAL DOES NOT IMPLY ENDORSEMENT. **NEW YORK:** Office of the Attorney General, Department of Law, Charities Bureau, 120 Broadway, New York, NY 10271. **NORTH CAROLINA:** FINANCIAL INFORMATION ABOUT THIS ORGANIZATION AND A COPY OF ITS LICENSE ARE AVAILABLE FROM THE STATE SOLICITATION LICENSING BRANCH AT [illegible]. The license is not an endorsement by the state. **PENNSYLVANIA:** The official registration and financial information of the Union of Concerned Scientists may be obtained from the Pennsylvania Department of State by calling toll-free, within Pennsylvania, [illegible]. Registration does not imply endorsement. **VIRGINIA:** State Division of Consumer Affairs, Department of Agriculture and Consumer Services, PO Box [illegible], Richmond, VA [illegible]. **WASHINGTON:** Charities Division, Office of the Secretary of State, State of Washington, Olympia, WA [illegible]. **WEST VIRGINIA:** Residents may obtain a summary from: Secretary of State, State Capitol, Charleston, WV 25305.

REGISTRATION WITH ANY OF THESE STATES DOES NOT IMPLY ENDORSEMENT, APPROVAL, OR RECOMMENDATION BY THE STATE.

9. Do you regularly read our quarterly newsletter, *earthwise*?

☐ Yes ☐ No

If not, why not?

☐ I don't have time.
☐ It's not interesting to me.
☐ The articles are too complicated.
☐ The articles are too elementary.
☐ Other: ________________

10. Do you regularly read our magazine, *Catalyst*?

☐ Yes ☐ No

If not, why not?

☐ I don't have time.
☐ It's not interesting to me.
☐ The articles are too complicated.
☐ The articles are too elementary.
☐ Other: ________________

11. Have you ever contacted one of the UCS offices with a question about our work or your membership?

☐ Yes ☐ No

If yes, did you receive a response that was:

☐ Very satisfactory
☐ Satisfactory
☐ Unsatisfactory

Additional comments:

____

____

____

____

____

____

Help us get to know you better (optional):

12. Do we have your current email address (please check at the top of this form)?

☐ Yes ☐ No

☐ I do not have an email address.

If no, or if incorrect, please write here:

____

13. What daily newspapers do you read regularly (at least two times per week)?

☐ New York Times
☐ Wall Street Journal
☐ Washington Post
☐ USA Today
☐ Other daily newspaper: ________

14. What magazines do you read regularly? (Please exclude professional journals.)

____

____

15. Please indicate your age:

☐ Under 27	☐ 28-37
☐ 38-47	☐ 48-57
☐ 58-67	☐ 68-77
☐ 78-87	☐ 88+

16. Are you a scientist?

☐ Yes ☐ No

17. If yes, what is your field?

☐ Life/environmental science
☐ Physical science
☐ Engineering
☐ Physician/Healthcare
☐ Other: ________________

Please return this survey in the enclosed self-addressed envelope, or mail to the
Union of Concerned Scientists
Two Brattle Square
Cambridge, MA, 02238-9105.
Thank you very much!

FOR OFFICE USE ONLY:

A	B
C	D
E	F
M	R

EXHIBIT 16.3. UCS Year-End Appeal, Cont'd.

Source: Union of Concerned Scientists. Reproduced with permission.

TABLE 16.4. UCS Membership Development Program, 2001.

Project	Mailed	Quantity	Revenue	Gifts	Percent	Average
Acquisition 1	01/01	300,349	$101,553	3,446	1.15%	$29
Acquisition 2	05/01	296,634	95,863	3,112	1.05%	31
Acquisition 3	08/01	299,972	108,156	3,312	1.10%	33
Acquisition 4	11/01	297,739	102,420	3,397	1.14%	30
Subtotal		1,194,694	407,992	13,267	1.11%	31
Annual Report	04/01	4,538	48,100	78	1.72%	617
High-Dollar 1	03/01	2,483	100,230	328	13.21%	306
High-Dollar 2	06/01	1,824	52,455	174	9.54%	301
High-Dollar 3	10/01	1,392	58,040	210	15.09%	276
Subtotal		5,699	210,725	712	12.49%	295
Renewal Series*		185,353	842,096	19,311	10.42%	44
Planned Giving	11/01	11,702	57,360	15	0.13%	3,824
Special Appeal 1	05/01	33,728	227,365	4,337	12.86%	52
Special Appeal 2	06/01	8,016	27,161	797	9.94%	34
Special Appeal 3**	08/01	2,969	6,264	244	8.22%	26
Special Appeal 4	11/01	41,580	405,138	5,194	12.49%	78
Special Appeal 5	12/01	14,978	100,046	1,058	7.06%	95
Subtotal		101,271	765,974	11,630	11.48%	66
Total		1,503,257	$2,332,247	45,013	2.99%	$52

*In 2001, the renewal series was expanded to eight efforts plus two lapsed member reactivation mailings. All numbers shown reflect the aggregate results of the series as a whole.

**Special Appeal 3 was an invitation to join the UCS monthly giving program, the Partners for the Earth. The results reported here take into account only the first gifts received, not later income from sustainer payments.

Despite the difficult economic environment, we forged ahead in our membership development program, maintaining the volume of prospecting at the previous year's level, expanding legacy promotion, and bolstering the monthly giving program by mailing both to upgrade existing members and to invite new ones.

The workhorse of the UCS program continued to be the membership renewal series. A summary of the year's results can be seen in Table 16.5.

To regain perspective on this picture, take another look at Table 16.1, which appears early in this chapter. Note that, ups and downs along the way notwithstanding, the end result of all this activity after four years was to double annual revenue from membership, increase the number of twelve-month active donors by 58 percent, boost revenue per donor per year by 20 percent, increase the first-year

TABLE 16.5. UCS Membership Development Program, 2002.

Project	Mailed	Quantity	Revenue	Gifts	Percent	Average
Acquisition 1	02/02	300,094	$98,564	3,392	1.13%	29
Acquisition 2	05/02	299,972	77,617	2,753	0.92%	28
Acquisition 3	08/02	299,972	74,500	2,385	0.80%	31
Acquisition 4	11/02	296,889	101,353	3,253	1.10%	31
Subtotal		1,196,927	352,034	11,783	0.98%	30
Annual Report	05/02	4,985	25,308	74	1.48%	342
High-Dollar*	03/02	4,391	232,336	545	12.41%	426
Renewal Series**		233,276	879,519	20,385	8.74%	43
Planned Giving 1	06/02	11,648	10,788	15	0.13%	719
Planned Giving 2	10/02	12,248	25,929	27	0.22%	960
Subtotal		23,896	36,717	42	0.18%	874
Special Appeal 1	04/02	8,500	29,138	728	8.56%	40
Special Appeal 2	07/02	15,649	84,501	1,309	8.36%	65
Special Appeal 3	10/02	27,353	89,102	1,909	6.98%	47
Special Appeal 4	11/02	53,561	337,464	4,638	8.66%	74
Special Appeal 5	12/02	25,000	110,977	1,466	5.86%	76
Subtotal		130,063	651,182	10,050	7.73%	65
Partners Upgrade***	04/02	2,524	21,072	417	16.52%	51
Partners Invitation	07/02	5,999	2,413	87	1.45%	28
Subtotal		8,523	23,485	504	16.91%	47
Total		1,602,061	$2,200,581	43,383	2.71%	51

*The three high-dollar mailings dropped in 2002 were a three-part renewal series for the Henry W. Kendall Society and the Friends of UCS.

**In 2002, the renewal series consisted again of eight efforts plus two lapsed member reactivation mailings. All numbers shown reflect the aggregate results of the series as a whole.

***This mailing was designed to upgrade some members of the Partners for the Earth monthly sustainer program and to persuade others to convert from check payments to EFT. The results shown include a projection of all income received during the first twelve months from newly upgraded members. The mailing is shown in Exhibit 16.4.

retention rate by 11 percent and the multiyear retention rate by 8 percent, and enlarge the number of $500-and-up donors by 74 percent.

So, if anybody ever says to you, "Direct mail is dead," you know what to say.

I can't guarantee that your direct mail donor development program will work as well as UCS's. (Of course, it might work even better!) But I can assure you that you will maximize the potential of direct response for your organization by putting into practice the principles laid out in this book.

Union of Concerned Scientists
PARTNERS FOR THE EARTH

Two Brattle Square   Cambridge, MA   02238-9105

April 5, 2002

Mr. John Doe
123 Any Street
Any Town, AS 00000

Dear Mr. Doe,

You are among our most important allies, and I'd like to thank you. As a member of this select group, you help us meet the demand for steady, ongoing, *predictable* financial support. It's the only way UCS can take advantage of new opportunities and face unanticipated circumstances as they arise in this fast-changing world.

Society's true opinion leaders are people like you — people who realize that the popular course is not always the wisest, that sound policy must rest on demonstrable facts, and change in environmental and security policy (or on any major issue) never comes easily or quickly. **You know that meaningful change requires sustained effort over the long haul.**

That's why I'm asking you to please increase your Partners for the Earth contribution by whatever amount you can afford. An additional annual amount of $120 is only $10 a month, or a mere $0.33 per day. Even a modest increase in your regular pledge amount will have a positive impact on what we can achieve together.

And you can make your money work harder for UCS by switching to a pre-authorized payment method, using either your bank account or credit card. (Pre-authorized payments from your bank account are the most efficient method — allowing more of your contribution to go directly to UCS program work.) It's costly for UCS to send out statements and process checks every month. So when you switch, we will stop sending you reminder statements. Please see the enclosed reply form for details.

Partners for the Earth members are the backbone of UCS, and we want you to stay in close touch with us. So we've assigned a dedicated person to

www.ucsusa.org | Two Brattle Square · Cambridge, MA 02238-9105 · TEL: 617.547.5552 · FAX: 617.864.9405
1707 H Street, NW · Suite 600 · Washington, DC 20006-3919 · TEL: 202.223.6133 · FAX: 202.223.6162
2397 Shattuck Avenue · Suite 203 · Berkeley, CA 94704-1567 · TEL: 510.843.1872 · FAX: 510.843.3785

RECYCLED & RECYCLABLE / PRINTED WITH SOY INK   47811

EXHIBIT 16.4. UCS Monthly Giving Program Conversion and Upgrade.

Page 2

serve as the liaison for our Partners. Perhaps you've already had the opportunity to talk with Lynn Pallotta. If you have any questions about Partners for the Earth, please do give her a call. You can reach Lynn at (800) 666-8276 ext. 247.

Many of our Partners tell us how their regular pre-authorized monthly contributions help them plan and budget. They recognize that when they spread their annual gifts over the year, they can afford to give more and therefore help UCS achieve more. And please remember, you can cancel or change the amount anytime. Just let us know, preferably via letter or email. That way, we have a record of your request.

Thanks to your commitment, UCS achieved impressive gains over the last year. In every field where UCS is active — energy policy; national missile defense; antibiotic resistance; the impact of cars and trucks on the environment and on our health; climate change and biodiversity — the past year has been productive.

It's a great comfort to know that we can count on your sustaining support in the coming year as a Partner for the Earth. Thank you for joining in partnership with us to bring sound science to bear in our continuing campaign for a healthier environment and a safer world.

Sincerely,

Howard Ris
President

P.S.   Please review the enclosed reply form to see how you can make a greater impact on what UCS is able to achieve. Even a modest increase in the amount you regularly contribute will help strengthen UCS. And don't forget, your gifts to UCS are tax-deductible.

EXHIBIT 16.4. UCS Monthly Giving Program Conversion and Upgrade, Cont'd.

REPLY MEMORANDUM

YES, I want my money to work harder for the earth. PLEASE CANCEL MY MONTHLY REMINDER STATEMENTS. I'd like to make my Partners for the Earth contributions as follows:

[ ] **Please debit my checking account each month.** I've enclosed a VOID check so you can note my bank account details. (Simply write "VOID" across a blank check.) OR

[ ] **Please debit my credit card each month:** [ ] Visa [ ] MasterCard

Card # ______________________ Exp. Date __________

Signature ______________________ Phone # (___)__________

[ ] I'd like to increase my monthly contribution from $20.00 to $22.00.

[ ] $22.00 is not enough. **I'm really proud to be a Partner for the Earth!** Please increase my monthly contribution from $20.00 to

[ ] $30.00 [ ] $______

Mr. John Doe
123 Any Street
Any Town, AS 00000

61DOE-A
00000

Union of Concerned Scientists
PARTNERS FOR THE EARTH
Two Brattle Square Cambridge, MA 02238-9105
www.ucsusa.org

Please return this form in the enclosed, postage paid envelope or mail to Lynn Pallotta, Coordinator, Partners for the Earth, Two Brattle Square, Cambridge, MA 02238-9105. Thank you!

You may change or stop payments at any time by notifying UCS. Your gifts to UCS are tax-deductible as provided by law.

EXHIBIT 16.4. UCS Monthly Giving Program Conversion and Upgrade, Cont'd.

Source: Union of Concerned Scientists. Reproduced with permission.

If you need encouragement, keep in mind that about three out of every four Americans contribute money to not-for-profit organizations during any given year. After all, the funds to support the country's more than one million nonprofits has to come from somewhere!

And when all is said and done, good direct mail fundraising respects the basic precepts of fundraising:

- Presented with opportunities in the right way at the right time, most people respond to appeals for financial support for causes and institutions that make a positive contribution to society.
- Treated consistently with respect and appreciation for their generosity and concern, most people will give again and again to support their values and beliefs.

Follow those principles, and you can't go wrong in direct mail fundraising.

Glossary

Account Executive. The individual who manages a client's direct mail fundraising activities on behalf of a consulting firm (also known as a *Client Consultant*)

Acquisition Mailing. A mailing to prospects to "acquire" new donors, members, or subscribers (also called *Prospect Mailing*)

Active Donor. A *Donor* whose last gift to an organization was received within the past twelve months (in some organizations, within thirteen, eighteen, or twenty-four months)

Annual Appeal. For organizations with inactive direct mail fundraising programs, the year's single or principal fundraising appeal, typically mailed at the end or the beginning of the calendar year

Ask, or ask amount. Generally, the minimum (or most heavily emphasized) individual gift suggested in a fundraising *Package;* not the total amount asked of all *Donors*

Attrition. The loss of donors due to death, illness, address changes, changing fortunes, or changing priorities

Back-End Premium. A free gift offered in exchange for a donation (generally, a donation above a certain minimum amount)

Back-End Services. The part of the direct mail campaign concerned with *Caging, Cashiering,* tabulating the results, sending *Donor Acknowledgments,* or fulfilling promises made in the mailing, as well as with storing and updating the list of respondents

Buckslip. A small slip of paper ($3\frac{1}{2} \times 8\frac{1}{2}$ inches is a common size) that fits into the *Package* and dramatically illustrates some particular feature of the *Offer,* such as a free calendar or book (usually promised for gifts above a certain minimum amount)

Bulk Mail. Third-class mail, which requires a minimum of two hundred identical pieces per mailing; discount rates available for qualified nonprofits, currently about half of those paid by business mailers

Business Reply Envelope (BRE). A self-addressed envelope that guarantees payment of postage on receipt by the organization that prints it (also called *Postage-Paid Envelope*)

Caging. Recording and tallying the raw information from direct mail, telephone fundraising, or other *Direct Response* campaigns so that the responses may be analyzed and decisions made about future campaigns, including identity of each donor, the date and amount of each gift, and its source (called caging after nineteenth-century post office desks, with their multiple cubbyholes or "cages" into which mail was sorted and classified)

Carrier Envelope. The outside envelope that contains the appeal letter and other components of the direct mail *Package* (also known as an outer or carrier)

Cashiering. Processing and depositing contributions mailed in response to a direct mail, *Telephone Fundraising* effort, or other *Direct Response* campaign

Cheshire Label. A strip of plain paper on which the addressee's name and address are imprinted by computer; usually printed four across a sheet; named after the machine that addresses, cuts, and glues the labels onto envelopes or *Response Devices.*

Client Consultant, or *Account Executive.* An employee of a consulting agency who manages a client's direct mail fundraising activities on the firm's behalf

Closed-Face Envelope. An envelope that does not have a window (see *Window Envelope*)

Compiled List. A mailing list derived from publicly accessible sources such as directories, telephone books, or city and county records; contrast with *Donor List*

Continuation Mailing. A mailing to larger numbers of prospective donors on lists that have been tested first in modest quantities (see *Rollout*)

Control Package. A direct mail acquisition *Package* that has performed successfully and against which any new acquisition package is tested

Copy Platform. A concept on the basis of which a direct mail *Package* is to be written; usually spells out the *Ask,* the *Offer,* the opening lines of the appeal letter, and the envelope *Teaser* language, if any

Copywriting. The creative process involved in conceiving, designing, and writing a fundraising *Package*; alternatively, the actual wording of the fundraising appeal

Database. A *List* of names, addresses, and other information (in fundraising, especially the giving history) maintained on a computer in such a way that selections may be made or the list ordered on the basis of numerous criteria;

sometimes combines several lists on the basis of some common factor, such as source, into one merged, master list from which duplicates are eliminated

Demographics. The study of statistical data about groups of people, especially such characteristics as age, income, gender, religious affiliation, and educational level

Direct Response. A form of advertising that elicits a direct action by the recipient of the message; may be a letter, telephone call, newspaper or magazine ad, or radio or television spot; normally asks for response by mail or telephone

Donor. An individual who has contributed money to a nonprofit organization or political committee

Donor Acknowledgment. Acknowledges a *Donor's* contribution with a receipt or a thank-you letter or note, possibly with other inserts

Donor Acquisition Cost. The difference between the cost of the mailing and the amount it generates in contributions, divided by the number of *Donors* acquired; expressed as dollars and cents per donor acquired

Donor Base. The list of an organization's contributors

Donor Conversion. The process of persuading *Donors* who have responded to an organization's *Prospect Mailings* with an initial gift to become active, regular, or frequent donors to the organization

Donor Cultivation. A long-term process through which a nonprofit organization or political committee acquaints selected *Donors* with its work and becomes better acquainted with the donors' needs and preferences, in hopes of eventually securing large donations

Donor File, or donor list. A computer listing, or *Database,* of the names, addresses, sources, and contribution history of an organization's donors; sometimes contains additional information, if available

Donor Recognition. Any means by which a nonprofit organization or political committee publicly acknowledges a *Donor's* support, for example, plaques and certificates, listings in newsletters or annual reports, screen credit in films and video presentations, and mention at public events

Donor Research. Generally refers to the process of searching through information available to the general public (from such sources as newspapers, magazines, and directories) to unearth facts about an organization's best specific, individual prospective *Donors* of *Major Gifts*; contrasts with *Market Research,* which aims at *groups* of donors rather than individuals

Donor Resolicitation. An organization's letter or phone call requesting additional support from individuals who have previously supported its work (also called *Special Appeal* or *Renewal*)

Donor Retention. The ability to maintain individuals as active and continuing *Donors* to an organization; also the process of seeking that end

Donor Survey. An in-depth, quantitative study of the beliefs, attitudes, *Demographic,* and *Psychographic* characteristics of an organization's *Donors* by means of statistically valid survey research techniques applied to a small sample of the *Donor Base*

Dupe Rate. The percentage of names identified as duplicates or invalid addresses; also known as the *Merge Factor*

80–20 Rule. The maxim that the top 20 percent of an organization's *Donors* contribute approximately 80 percent of its revenue, while the bottom 80 percent of the donors contribute just 20 percent

Electronic Funds Transfer (EFT). A method whereby individual *Donors* may instruct their banks to make automatic monthly or quarterly deductions from their accounts, which are transferred electronically to the accounts of the charitable organizations of their choice

Electronic Mail. A computerized system that prints, personalizes, and distributes written fundraising appeals with great speed; usually used for urgent appeals

Fiber Optics. A telecommunications medium that transmits digital information in the form of pulses of laser light through minute strands of transparent cable; now coming into wide use across the United States and expected to be the predominant form of transmitting both voice and data over long distances

File. A computerized *List*

Flashcount. A periodic statistical report of the results of an individual mailing that summarizes the returns for each list or *Keycode* by percent response, average contribution, and other measures during a particular period of time, usually no more than a few months

Focus Group. A method of qualitative research in which groups of up to twelve *Donors* or *Donor Prospects* are methodically interviewed about their attitudes and reactions toward an organization or the materials it produces

Format. The size, shape, and color of the envelope, the character of the inserts, and the extent (or lack) of *Personalization* of a direct mail *Package*

Former Donors. Donors who have not contributed to an organization in two or more years (three or more years, for some organizations)

Frequency. The number of times an individual has contributed to an organization, either cumulatively or within a specific period of time

Front-End Premium. An item included in a direct mail *Package* as an up-front free gift in order to encourage response; typically, membership cards, stickers, decals, stamps, key chains, address labels, letter-openers

Fulfillment Rate. The percentage of *Donors* who actually send in checks in response to a *Telephone Fundraising* campaign or other fundraising effort that elicits *Pledges* rather than immediate cash gifts

Fundraising Ratio. The ratio of cost to revenue, expressed as a percentage; the cost of a dollar raised expressed in dollars and cents; traditionally, used to evaluate the efficiency of fundraising programs

Geodemographics. In fundraising, a method of targeting *Prospective Donors* based on the demographic characteristics revealed in census data for residents of specific geographic areas, selected on the basis that their demographic profile closely matches that of an organization's previous *Donors* (see *Psychographics*)

Gift Club or *Giving Club.* An association or category established by a nonprofit organization or political committee that is limited to *Donors* who contribute frequent or generous gifts, often receiving special benefits or *Donor Recognition*

Gift Level. Generally, a measure of an individual *Donor's* capacity for future gifts based on the size of past contributions; may include the amount of the highest previous contribution, the total cumulative amount of all gifts received to date, or the amount of the most recent contribution

High-Dollar Mailing. Direct mail fundraising *Packages* specifically designed to elicit above-average gifts by using larger envelopes, extensive personalization, and a high *Ask*; mailed to very selective lists

House File, or house list. The names and addresses of an organization's active and recently lapsed *Donors,* members, supporters, and subscribers

Impact Printer. A computer-driven printing mechanism in which metal or plastic characters directly strike the paper; including "daisy-wheel" machines that make a typewriter-like impression and "line printers" that operate at very high speed and leave an often sketchy impression on the page that is commonly associated with computer printers

Independent Sector. The term denoting the nonprofit world, that is, organizations that are neither governmental nor profit-making businesses; a coalition of nonprofit organizations is INDEPENDENT SECTOR; also called *Third Sector*

Ink-Jet Printing. Printing (generally of a name, address, and *Keycode*) executed by a high-speed printer that produces an image by spraying ink through small jets to imitate typewriter print

Inquiries. In fundraising, individuals who have responded to an advertisement or a direct mail package with a request for information or a response to a survey but have not sent contributions

Involvement Device. An element in a direct mail *Package* used to heighten interest in the package and to provide recipients with opportunities to use their hands or to participate in some way to assist the mailer; for example, petitions, surveys, postcards addressed to decision makers, stamps, and stickers

Keycode. A code consisting of letters or numbers assigned to a specific *List* or segment of a list for the purpose of tracking responses so the list's effectiveness relative to other lists may be evaluated; usually printed on the mailing label or *Response Device* (see *Source Code*)

Lapsed Donors. Donors whose last gift arrived at least a year to eighteen months ago but no longer than two to three years ago; sometimes called Lybunts (Last Year But Unfortunately Not This Year)

Laser Printing. In direct mail fundraising, a *Personalized* process of reproducing printed material that combines photocopier technology with computerized *List Maintenance* techniques, permitting each sheet or printed impression to include information unique to one individual on a *Donor File*

Lettershop, or mailhouse. The shop in which the individual components of a mailing are collated, inserted, and packaged for delivery to the post office; frequently address and affix postage to the mailing *Packages*

Lifetime Value. Refers to the long-term value of a *Donor,* member, subscriber, or buyer from an organization's perspective; calculated by one of several methods; provides guidance when setting investment levels in *Acquisition Mailing*

Lift Letter. A second or supplementary letter included in a fundraising *Package* to reinforce the message of the main letter or present an argument for a contribution from a different point of view; often signed by a celebrity or other influential individual

List. In direct mail, a *Database* of names and addresses of individuals who share one or more characteristics, such as membership in or support of a given organization

List Broker. An agent who brings together *List Owners* and mailers (users) to arrange the rental or exchange of mailing *Lists* (in whole or part); acts on behalf of the *List Owner* and list user to make all necessary arrangements with the *List Manager,* who acts as the agent for the list user

List Exchange. An exchange of donor, member, or subscriber *Lists* between two organizations, generally on a name-for-name basis, with the two organizations usually mailing at different times

List Maintenance. The ongoing process of updating and correcting a *Donor File* or other computerized mailing *List.*

List Manager. The organization or individual, often a *List Broker* or direct mail consultant, who is responsible for the promotion and record keeping necessary for the regular exchange or rental of a mailing list

List Owner. The organization or individual that owns rental or exchange rights to a mailing *List*

List Rental. The arrangement through which a *List Owner* furnishes names to a mailer for one-time use only

List Test. A random sampling of a *List* used to determine the cost-effectiveness of mailing to the entire list; usually based on samples of between 3,000 and 10,000 names

Live Stamp. An actual postage stamp affixed by hand or machine, usually either to a *Carrier Envelope* or to a reply envelope

Magnetic Tape. An early but now universally accepted electronic storage medium favored in the direct mail industry to record and reproduce via computer the data on a mailing *List*

Mail-Responsiveness. The propensity for an individual to respond to a sales offer or funding appeal sent by mail.

Major Gift. A significant and out-of-the-ordinary gift, which may be as little as $100 for some organizations or upwards of $1,000,000 for others

Market. The intended audience of an appeal; the likely or potential supporters of an organization; the prospect *Lists* that together comprise an organization's *Universe*

Market Research. In fundraising, refers to *Donor Surveys, Focus Groups,* and other methods used to study the beliefs, attitudes, and *Demographic* and *Psychographic* characteristics of previous or potential donors, in order to understand how to devise and deliver more effective appeals for support

Marketing Concept. The concept on which a fundraising *Package* is based; a capsule statement of the connection between the *Offer,* the *Market,* and the signer of the appeal letter

Maxi-Donors. Those *Donors* who have recently or frequently given generous contributions

Membership Renewal. A *Resolicitation,* used by organizations with formal membership structures, requesting payment of an individual's annual dues; alternatively, a response to a dues notice or a system to collect dues from the membership as a whole

Merge Dupes, or *Multi-Donors. Donors,* members or subscribers found on more than one *Prospect List;* in commercial direct mail, called *Multi-Buyers*

Merge Factor. The percentage of names identified as duplicates or bad addresses (also known as the dupe rate)

Merge-Purge. A computer operation that combines two or more mailing *Lists* in a matching process to produce one *File* that is relatively free of duplicates and to measure the degree to which the component lists overlap with each other

Multi-Buyers. See *Multi-Donors*

Multi-Donors, or *Merge Dupes. Donors,* members, or subscribers found on more than one *Prospect List;* in commercial direct mail, called *Multi-Buyers*

Offer. In fundraising, the programmatic action or individual benefits promised by an organization to those who send contributions, dues, or subscription payments; also known as the pitch; commercially, the terms under which a specific product or service is promoted by a mailer; in fundraising, the set of needs, promises, or assurances that justifies the *Ask*

On-Line Packaging. A production method that integrates printing, *Personalization,* and bundling for the post office into one continuous process on an assembly line

Package. A direct mail appeal, its wrapping, and all its contents; commonly consists of a *Carrier Envelope,* a letter, a *Response Device,* a *Business Reply Envelope;* may include other items, such as a brochure, news clipping, or a *Front-End Premium*

Package Test. Testing one direct mail *Package* (or one of its features or characteristics) against those of another by mailing both to statistically equivalent groups of individuals chosen at random from the same *List* or lists

Personalization. The reproduction of a message on individualized materials that bear the recipient's name and (often) other unique, personal information; methods include *Laser Printing, Ink-Jet Printing,* and other computer-driven technologies

Planned Giving. Using estate planning methods to formulate and schedule contributions by an individual *Donor,* generally involving large or long-term gifts or bequests

Pledge. In fundraising, a promise made by a *Donor* or *Prospect* to contribute money at a later time, with the amount and date when the gift will be made either specified or unspecified; used as either noun or verb

Pledge Card, or pledge reminder. In *Telephone Fundraising,* a notice sent to remind those who *Pledge* to contribute to an organization, with *Reply Envelope* usually enclosed

Pledge Program. A system, often a *Gift Club,* through which ardent supporters of a nonprofit organization or political committee may give regular, generally monthly, donations and often receive special benefits in return; can be implemented through *Electronic Funds Transfer* (sometimes called *Sustainer Program*)

Postage-Paid Envelope. A self-addressed envelope that guarantees payment of postage on receipt by the organization that prints it; also called *Business Reply Envelope)*

Premium. A product offered or given to a prospective *Donor,* member, or subscriber as an incentive to respond to a direct mail *Package* (see *Back-End Premium* and *Front-End Premium*)

Pressure-Sensitive Labels. Mailing labels, generally affixed by hand, that do not require water; colloquially called peel-off or peel-and-stick labels

Prospect. In direct mail fundraising, a prospective new *Donor;* in *Major Gift* fundraising, any prospective donor, including an organization's previous contributors

Prospect Mailing. A mailing to prospective new *Donors,* members, or subscribers to ask for their support; also called *Acquisition Mailing* or cold mail

Psychographics. In fundraising, a method of targeting prospective *Donors* based on their demonstrated (or predicted) lifestyle choices or behavioral traits (see *Geodemographics*)

Recency. The date (or time period) during which a *Donor's* latest contribution was received

Resolicitation, or renewal mailing. An organization's letter or phone call requesting additional support from individuals who have previously supported its work; also called *Special Appeal* or *Donor Resolicitation*

Response, or reply device. A form, generally restating the *Offer* and bearing the addressee's name and address and a *Keycode,* on which the recipient is asked to indicate the size of her gift and sometimes other information as well

Rollout. Generally, a mailing to larger quantities of prospective *Donors* on *Lists* that have been tested first in modest quantities; more precisely, using all available names remaining on one or more pretested lists in a *Continuation Mailing*

Salting or *Seeding Lists.* A practice employed by *List Owners* and *List Brokers* for protection against misuse or theft; insertion of names and addresses, usually fictitious, on the *List* so that the owner or broker receives copies of all mailings sent to the list

Segmentation. The process of subdividing a *List* into subdivisions or "segments," usually defined by such variables as *Recency, Frequency,* or *Gift Level*

Self-Mailer. A direct mail *Package* that requires no separate *Carrier Envelope;* usually either a piece of paper with multiple folds or a booklet format

Service Bureau. A company that offers *Back-End Services,* typically including a variety of data processing services

Source Code. A *Keycode* denoting the specific *List* or segment of a list from which a *Donor's* name and address were originally derived

Special Appeal. An appeal for funds from previous *Donors* or members that is not a *Membership Renewal* notice; often sent several times per year

Split Test. A test of any variable in a mailing (such as *Package* variations, the *Ask,* or different postage rates) by splitting one or more *Lists* or segments into equal numbers of statistically identical names and addresses to determine which approach works better than others; also called an A/B split

Sustainer Program. A *Gift Club* through which ardent supporters of a nonprofit organization or political committee may give regular, generally monthly, donations and often receive special benefits or *Donor Recognition;* can be implemented through *EFT;* also known as *Pledge Program*

Teaser. A brief message on the *Carrier Envelope* used to pique the reader's interest or curiosity and thus increase the likelihood that the envelope will be opened

Telephone Fundraising. Sometimes (to the author's annoyance) called telemarketing; a practice of calling previous *Donors* or prospective donors by phone to ask for donations

Test Mailing. An organization's initial effort to gauge its potential to mount a cost-effective direct mail fundraising program

Testing. The process of comparing results for dissimilar items by simultaneously mailing each item to an equal number of statistically identical names; for statistical validity, changing only one variable in any one test, such as different rates of postage, different suggested minimum gift amounts, different *Teasers,* different-colored envelopes, or the like

Third Sector. The term denoting the nonprofit world, that is, organizations that are neither governmental nor profit-making businesses (also called *Independent Sector*)

Unique Names. Those names and addresses remaining on a merged or combined mailing *List* for a *Prospect Mailing* after a *Merge-Purge* has identified and eliminated duplicates and invalid addresses

Universe. The total number of names and addresses that comprise a mailing *List;* also the total number of names and addresses judged to be good prospects to support a nonprofit organization or political committee

Updating. Adding, changing, or deleting information on a *Donor List* to increase its accuracy

Upgrading. The process of inducing previous *Donors* to increase the *Frequency* of their gifts

Window Envelope. An envelope that reveals the name and address through a die-cut hole, or window, with possibly more than one window showing other features of the enclosed material

Word Processing. In direct mail, generally refers to *Personalization* that employs *Impact Printers* to mimic individually typed letters

Working with a
Direct Mail Consultant

I admit it: I'm biased. As a direct mail fundraising consultant, both self-interest and experience lead me to believe that you'd probably be well advised to hire a consultant to help you launch and manage your direct mail fundraising program. I've made every effort in this book to explain clearly how our business is conducted. Nonetheless, you can see that it's very complicated and makes lots of demands on your time and managerial expertise. Chances are, you'll need help—a great deal of it.

Too often, I've seen direct mail fundraising programs that are managed in-house by nonprofit organizations or political campaigns fail to realize their full potential for the following reasons:

- Staff was distracted by other priorities.
- They lacked the time or resources to meet maildates on a consistent basis, month after month.
- The attitudes they conveyed in their mailings were parochial, overly self-serving, or simply uninteresting.
- They didn't have the depth and scope of experience to know how to respond quickly when creative challenges arose.
- They just didn't have the breadth of experience to see opportunities for what they were or to know what to do about them when they surfaced.

Frequently, these organizations chose to manage their programs in-house, either because they wanted to save money or because they felt they knew better than anyone else how best to present themselves to the world. In most circumstances, neither reason holds water.

The savings from in-house management are often illusory. Even if returns on individual mailings are as good as any consultant might obtain, an in-house organization rarely can achieve the consistency and frequency of a mailing schedule managed by outside professionals.

A public interest group rarely has the full range of skills and resources necessary to survive in the Darwinian marketplace of public interest fundraising. Public interest marketing demands a lot more than an intimate understanding of your organization and its work. It's not enough to tell the world what you need. You have to convey your message—cost-effectively—in a way that connects on a visceral level with your constituents and *motivates* them to act generously and immediately. This calls for a special set of marketing and communications skills that are not common in managers, whether nonprofit, political, or otherwise. It also calls for an ability to work with specialized suppliers or vendors: a network of list brokers, printers, lettershops, and other vendors that will enable you to produce your mailings on time and cost-effectively.

Moreover, nowadays the difference between success and failure in a mailing can result from very subtle changes in list selection, copy, design, packaging, or other factors. *An organization's competitive advantage in direct mail fundraising lies on the margins*—in very small numbers. For example:

- Lowering the cost of printing by 2 cents per package could allow you to mail a million donor acquisition letters *and recruit 10 or 20 thousand new members* instead of mailing 100,000 and generating only 2,000 gifts. A consultant's clout with printers could make this much difference in the price.
- Mailing eight donor resolicitation letters next year instead of six could increase your organization's net direct mail revenue by 12 to 15 percent. If your staff is stretched thin, a consultant's attention to the mailing schedule could make the difference.
- Enhancements in copy and design derived from experience with many other public interest groups could lift the response rate in each of your donor resolicitations from 5 percent to 8 or 10 percent. When the year's at an end, you could find yourself with an active donor base that is 20 or 30 percent larger.

Differences of this magnitude could make or break your strategic plan.

With all this said, however, *some* organizations are better off managing their programs in-house. This may be the case for your group under the following circumstances:

- If your agency's annual budget is less than $100,000, you're unlikely to be able to afford professional help on a continuing basis.
- If your constituency or market is too small to permit aggressive donor acquisition by mail, you're unlikely to gain enough benefit from an ongoing relationship with a consultant.
- If you've been in the mails for years and your strategy calls for a modest, continuing program along well-established lines that your staff is competent to handle, chances are slim that you'll need anything more than copywriting, technical assistance, or an occasional bit of advice.
- If—on the other end of the spectrum—your direct mail fundraising program is so large and lucrative that you can afford to hire a staff of full-time, top-flight fundraising professionals, you're probably right to handle the job in-house. With several hundred thousand donors and a budget in excess of $20 million, that might be the case. However, if you've gotten that far, you've probably long since figured out that you benefit from hiring not just one but perhaps several outside consultants to provide a steady stream of new ideas and to keep your staff on their toes.

Although neither the very biggest nor the smallest organizations may need outside consultants to manage their direct mail fundraising programs, most of the rest probably do. Chances are, that includes you.

Here, then, are a few guidelines to follow as you look around in search of a direct mail fundraising firm that's right for you.

Selecting the Right Consultant

There's no license required to hang out a shingle as a direct mail fundraising consultant. There's no test to pass, no certification procedure. And you won't find many of us in the Yellow Pages.

A national organization has established a code of ethics for the profession and a mechanism to enforce it: the Association of Direct Response Fundraising Counsel (ADRFCO). For a listing of members and other information, contact ADRFCO, 1612 K Street, N.W., Suite 510, Washington, DC 20006–2802; phone (202) 293-9640, fax (202) 887-9699, e-mail: ADRFCO@aol.com.

A great many of the companies that offer direct mail management, creative, or consulting services to public interest organizations are engaged in some *other* business; they may be printers, computer service bureaus, advertising agencies, list brokers, public relations consultants, or design firms. By and large, with some very notable exceptions, the quality of service offered by these groups is low. Often it's "free," and in some cases that's exactly what it's worth.

There are also many solo consultants serving one or a few clients, with little or no staff. In a few cases, they're refugees from the constraints imposed by their earlier jobs at larger firms and may offer a *range* of previous experience. Most, however, gained their principal experience in *one* direct mail fundraising program, typically as staff for a nonprofit organization or political campaign or in commercial direct response marketing. These consultants may offer services ranging from copywriting alone, to full-service management and consulting, to data entry. Some are brilliant fundraisers, but skill levels vary widely among the solo consultants.

Among the dozens of established consulting firms, only a handful of which are more than ten years old, the level of skill and breadth of experience also vary. These firms are often highly specialized geographically, politically, and by issue. Some work exclusively for nonprofit or political clients; many pay the bills by taking commercial assignments (for which fees are typically much higher). Some work with a broad range of clients; others emphasize one or a few special markets or issue. Most serve fewer than a dozen organizations at any one time. In most cases, the total staff numbers twenty persons or less.

With such a variety of choices, then, how can you select the consultant that's right for *your* organization?

As you start the process, you're likely to rely heavily on what you can learn of the firms' reputation and experience. Some may clearly be unsuitable because their track record is unimpressive or is based on issues and organizations that seem irrelevant, whereas others may clearly be inadequate to the task of meeting your diverse needs. That will help you narrow the field down to a manageable number of three or four prospects. But then the choice is likely to get tougher.

You might start by requesting sample mailing packages from each of the finalists. Then *read* them. You'll learn a lot. (If they won't send samples, you'll learn something from that, too.)

Naturally, you should also ask for references or a client list, or both. If you follow up with phone calls to the consultants' references, you'll learn a lot from that.

But even after all that, you may still face a difficult choice. Here are the *real* issues to consider at that point:

• *Understanding.* Do you and the consultant speak the same language? Regardless of whether the firm has direct experience with the issues your organization addresses, do you believe the consulting staff understands what you're about and the values that motivate your constituents? Will they be able to present your programs in fundraising appeals that are honest, accurate, and effective?

• *Range of services.* Does the consultant have the experience and the resources to do the *whole* job and do it right? If a firm doesn't offer all the services you need, does it have well-established relationships with other vendors who do?

• *Contract terms.* Is the consultant offering you attractive financial incentives, such as capital to finance your program or a guarantee that you'll make a profit, or offering to accept only a percentage of the returns in compensation? Any or all of these incentive arrangements *may* be legitimate, but they bear an extra-careful look because they're also commonly used by crooks. And there are a few of those in the direct mail field, as there are in any other.

• *Creativity.* Will the consultant create specially tailored packages for your direct mail fundraising program or apply formulas (and recycle packages) that have proven successful for other organizations? Winning formulas on which successful agencies have been built include such things as sweepstakes offers and extremely inexpensive prospect package formats. There's no such thing as a "right" or a "wrong" way to look at this question, but it's important stylistically and it may have financial implications. To launch a sweepstakes or use some other tested but controversial formula may be cost-effective, but it may also undermine your support from your board or major funders—or even risk the ire of regulatory authorities. Just be sure you know what you're getting into.

• *Decision making.* Who will make the key creative and financial decisions, you or the consultant? Does the firm want you to write a check and leave them alone? Or will you be entering into what is effectively a partnership, with the firm making recommendations and you or your staff making the real decisions at every crucial point along the way?

• *Accessibility.* Just because a firm is located in your city doesn't mean you'll get the attention you deserve. Regardless of geographic location, are you convinced that the consultant will be available to answer your questions and address your concerns in a timely fashion? Will you get service or a runaround? Will your telephone calls be answered? Will you have opportunities for periodic strategy and creative meetings?

• *Compensation.* Aside from the management or consulting fees the firm will charge you, what other fees will you be paying? Will the consultant mark up printing and other vendor bills, receive all the list rental revenue, or even receive title to your donor or membership list? The proposed fees may look a whole lot lower than they really are. Look at the whole compensation package before you conclude that one firm is less expensive than another.

If these considerations don't do the trick, there's one more that may decide the question once and for all:

> Which of the consultants you're considering is likely to best understand your strategy and to design—then implement—the most effective direct mail fundraising program to help you reach your goals?

If you find the right firm, you may be squarely on track toward your strategic goals. Now all you have to do is figure out how to work with the consultant you've selected.

Managing a Consultant

As a client of a direct mail fundraising firm, you can exert considerable control in four ways:

1. *Creative responsibility.* You have to expect—and you should insist on—being involved in the fundamental creative decisions. It's your responsibility as much as the consultant's to develop a marketing plan that meets your organization's long-term strategic needs and to devise marketing concepts for individual mailings that fairly reflect the overall strategy. No matter how much you may rely on your consultant for solid advice on both creative and technical matters, you (or a key staff member) must maintain an overview of the program on a continuing basis.

2. *Management style.* If you've hired a firm to manage your direct mail fundraising program, let them do the job. Ask questions, insist on signing off on all major decisions, but don't micro-manage their work, as though you don't need the firm's help except to serve as messengers between you and the printshop. You've got better things to do than to second-guess their segmentations or argue constantly about type sizes or ink colors. If over an extended period they haven't produced acceptable results, or you just don't like the way they represent you to the world, fire them and find another firm.

3. *Planning and scheduling.* If direct mail is going to work for you, you'll have to mail again and again on a reliable, consistent schedule. This means you'll have to resist the perfectionist temptation to rewrite or redesign every appeal or to insist on waiting an extra few weeks before the last trickle of test results confirm a decision to roll out a new package. Occasionally, caution and extra attention to detail are important enough to delay a mailing *but not very often.* One of the most impor-

tant things your direct mail consultant can do for you is to help you work out a long-term mailing schedule—and stick to it. If they're missing maildates right and left, and it's not your fault, then it's time to reexamine the relationship.

4. *Trust.* Your consultant is not the enemy. Although it's important that financial aspects of the relationship be conducted at arm's length and with all due consideration for what is legal and proper, it's counterproductive to nit-pick every bill and question every minor departure from the mailing budget. If the company is taking advantage of you or consistently overspending by significant amounts, by all means talk to them. It may be time to look for an alternative. As a response to such situations, distrust isn't a constructive alternative. It can be demoralizing for a consultant to face the third degree about every minor decision, and ultimately *you'll* pay the price.

The relationship between you and your direct mail consultant is a two-way proposition, and you're responsible for making the most of it because you're footing the bill. But in many ways, the burden will be on the company you hire. Not only will your consultant be managing the work they've contracted to do for you; they'll also have to manage their relationship with *you*.

Managing a Client

Whether called a client consultant, account executive, program coordinator, or something else entirely, the person within your consultant's firm who is in charge of the overall management of your account should be responsible for the following items, as drawn from the Client Consultants' job description at Mal Warwick & Associates, Inc.:

Strategic Planning and Analysis

- Be familiar with the terms of the client's contract and with the provisions of any proposal or marketing plan.
- Review the long-term direct mail schedule on a monthly basis, updating it at least quarterly, and obtain the client's approval for each update.
- Analyze and review the results of each mailing, with particular attention to testing data, so you're sure they're reflected in the design of future mailings.
- Take the fullest possible advantage of your clients' donor lists with frequent and varied donor renewal and special appeal programs specially tailored to the client's program.
- Prepare timely statistical reports for the client, and help interpret the data.

Copywriting and Package Design

- Initiate creative meetings or focus groups to determine marketing strategy.
- Develop a marketing concept for each mailing, and work with the copywriter and designer to ensure that the concept is properly executed and that the resulting package adequately reflects the client's program as well as budgetary limitations.
- Take full advantage of potential marketing opportunities through aggressive package and price testing.

Management and Coordination

- Stay in close contact with the client, and discuss plans and program performance as often as needed but at least monthly.
- Obtain and keep on file timely client approvals for budget, copy, art, and donor file segmentations.
- Be aware at all times of the status of production work and list acquisition on every project in order to certify that schedules are being met (or to notify the client in advance if they're not).
- Seek to ensure that the client's mailing list is properly maintained and managed, that caging, cashiering, and donor acknowledgment services are adequately performed, and that useful and accurate reports to track each mailing are generated and delivered.
- Maintain close communication with the telephone fundraising firm, computer service bureau, or other major program vendor.

Financial Oversight

- Draft, monitor, and update the budget for each mailing.
- Monitor each client's payments to head off financial problems before they develop.

Overall Marketing and Management

- Take advantage of new opportunities for the client, whether they result from changing events reported on the evening news, changing circumstances in clients' organizations, or changing patterns in the returns from direct mail campaigns. (I tell our Client Consultants that they're not obligated to come up with brilliant ideas three times a week but that I do expect them to gain enough of a feel for their clients' work that they can sense when it's important to talk about making major changes.)
- Pay close attention to clients' mailing programs: identify and avoid major errors or problems, even if that means stopping work on a mailing that might lose the

client money, delaying a maildate to head off significant design or production problems, or testing a new package because the old one isn't meeting the program's goals.

If you're lucky enough to find a consultant who'll do all this for you—and if you cooperate fully—you'll be well on the way to getting the most from your direct mail fundraising program.

With skill, patience, adequate investment, and a little luck, you'll be able to derive full value from your organization's resources and multiply your impact. By making the right strategic choices and using state-of-the-art direct mail techniques to further your strategic goals, you'll become part of a revolution that has already started to change the face of American society.

Answering the Arguments Against Direct Mail

Direct mail may be wrong for your organization if you or other central figures such as key board members, staff, or the candidate cannot swallow the unconventional logic on which the whole system is based—a set of principles and mechanisms that prompt some people to think of direct mail as somehow immoral. Here are my answers to some of the most common arguments against the use of direct mail.

Argument 1: "Direct Mail Fundraising Provides Few Benefits"

One memorable afternoon early in my direct mail fundraising career, in a walnut-paneled Wall Street board room, I sat at a massive conference table across from a prominent former Cabinet member, engaged in one of the more frustrating conversations of my life to that point. I was visiting him with the founder of a public interest group that the man supported enthusiastically. We hoped he'd agree to become the honorary cochair of an intensive donor acquisition campaign, based on the results of an encouraging initial test mailing. After our lengthy presentation, here's the gist of what he said: "Let me see if I understand this correctly. You want me to put my name on a letter asking people to send $25 checks to my favorite charity—*so you can send out more letters?*"

Some feel this question poses difficult ethical issues for public interest organizations. To address them, let's review a few of the basic realities of direct mail fundraising.

First, a well-planned and creatively executed direct mail fundraising program will ultimately raise a good deal of money for an organization committed to direct mail as one component of a long-term development campaign. At the same time, the direct mail program will give thousands—perhaps hundreds of thousands—of people the opportunity to support a public interest group or charity they might otherwise be unaware of.

It's true that initial returns from a direct mail program will be plowed back into producing and mailing more fundraising letters. Over time, however, the funds reinvested in direct mail will be a small percentage of the money earned by the program, and the rest of the money will be available to pay for the activities the group was set up to accomplish. As the years go by, the initial investment in direct mail may come to seem minuscule by comparison with the dividends it produces.

Every fundraising program costs money, and a certain percentage of the returns from every fundraising effort goes to cover its costs, whether it's a benefit event, a newsletter, a T-shirt, or a direct service. Because a direct mail program may require a large initial investment, continuing reinvestment, and a long-term commitment, it appears that the bulk of the proceeds are simply used to generate more letters. If this were true, no nonprofit would continue its direct mail program. Obviously, to be useful, direct mail fundraising must sooner or later raise money to fund the organization's operations.

Furthermore, consider that direct mail donor acquisition is the most cost-effective and sometimes the *only* feasible way for a nonprofit to build a broad financial base, expand its operations, and ensure its long-term survival.

Argument 2: "Direct Mail Misleads Donors"

Some people feel it isn't right to ask the public to give by mail unless the organization discloses fully how it will spend every penny raised through the mail. As I was told in that board room, "Those $25 checks aren't going to be used to meet anyone's human needs. They're going to pay for more letters! I say it's immoral unless we *tell* people that's what their contributions are going to be used for."

The underlying principle here seems to be that if a fundraising letter asks people to send money to "Save the Whales," the public has the right to assume that every dollar they send will go directly to that specific purpose. That's just silly. No office runs without overhead, and virtually no nonprofit runs without fundraising. A portion of every dollar raised—in any manner—must go to pay rent, telephone bills, office staff, and, yes, even further fundraising. Why should direct mail be singled out for scrutiny? A direct mail fundraising program can't be reduced to a formula. Numbers can be misleading unless you're looking at the big picture, because the numbers change over time—sometimes very rapidly.

Singling out the costs of direct mail also tends to distort its wider effects. A direct mail fundraising program must be seen in context because it contributes in a great many ways to the overall effort. For example, gifts from major donors probably won't be counted in the proceeds of a direct mail fundraising program, even if the program first made them aware of the organization's work. Thus public disclosure about the *direct* costs and benefits of the direct mail fundraising program will obscure rather than illuminate the reality.

And there are some other important considerations when thinking about public disclosure issues. For example, if costs and benefits are to be spelled out, it should be in the context of the organization's finances as a whole, rather than taking the direct mail program out of context. Existing law already provides for financial disclosure to the public, since charities' tax returns are available through the IRS, and in many states their financial statements may be obtained through charities' registration offices.

Public disclosure of fundraising costs and proceeds is a very blunt weapon with which to attack the tiny minority of fraudulent charities and consultants. Invariably, overlapping boards of directors, sweetheart contracts, or demonstrably fraudulent claims in the fundraising programs of these organizations will provide a much easier route to the heart of the matter.

Freedom of speech is another applicable principle here. In fact, the U.S. Supreme Court has rejected on the basis of First Amendment rights the most stringent disclosure and reporting requirements legislated by the states. This freedom, in turn, encourages innovation, which may be the public interest sector's greatest contribution to American society.

With all this said, let me make absolutely clear that I believe direct mail must always tell the truth. No reputable direct mail consulting firm will work for any organization it feels isn't delivering on its promises. Ultimately, I'm convinced, donors will respond more generously to the truth than to exaggerated or distorted claims.

Argument 3: "Direct Mail Fundraising Kills Millions of Trees"

Now let's take a look at an entirely different argument used to question the ethics of direct mail fundraising. It crops up in cocktail party conversations from time to time and in donors' letters to some environmental organizations: "You people are cutting down millions of trees to send out God-knows-how-many letters nobody wants to receive. You should be ashamed of yourselves!"

I confess I do not feel an overwhelming sense of shame in the face of this argument, but it does warrant a response. Quite apart from the fact that there are much worthier targets of ecological zeal, chiefly, lumber companies who devastate the land by clear-cutting forests, for several reasons the argument is off the mark.

First, direct mail is used by public interest groups and charities because it's cost-effective, that is, it consumes fewer resources than alternative methods of fundraising and communications. Many nonprofit organizations could not exist without large-scale direct mail fundraising programs. Others would need to curtail programs serving millions of Americans.

There are just two ways for most organizations to communicate with their supporters: (1) using paper or (2) using electronic means. Television, radio, fax, the telephone, e-mail, and the World Wide Web may all have roles to play in a fundraising or donor communications program, but they're no substitute for letters. Until we become a paperless society, nonprofits will have to go on using the mails to do their jobs. After all, no one's proposing to abolish the post office to save trees.

Direct mail fundraising packages account for a *very* small portion of the paper output of the U.S. economy. According to the U.S. Postal Service, nonprofits collectively mailed 990,005 pounds of bulk mail in 2002. (That accounted for less than 10 percent of all bulk mail, and you can be sure it didn't require cutting down millions of trees to make less than one million pounds of paper.) The *New York Times* and the *Los Angeles Times* together have average daily circulation of about two million, as you can see on the Web site maintained by the Northwestern University Media Management Center. The papers' Sunday circulation is higher, but let's take two million as a base, to be conservative. If you've ever tried hefting one of these papers, you know they weigh a lot—averaging about one pound thirteen ounces each, according to the reference desk of the Berkeley Public Library. Multiply two million by one pound thirteen ounces, or 1.81 pounds, by 52 weeks, and what do you get? One hundred eighty-eight million, two hundred forty thousand pounds. Add another six days per week for each of these newspapers at an average weight of six ounces: another 234,000,000 pounds. The sum of these two numbers is 422,240,000 pounds, or nearly half the total *yearly* weight of all nonprofit direct mail! And that's just *two newspapers*—out of the nearly 1,500 that are published.

Does this mean I'm suggesting that we should all cancel our newspaper subscriptions? Not at all! I mean to show that (1) direct mail fundraising is not the major environmental factor so many people just assume it is but is in fact a minor factor at best, and (2) paper is still an indispensable medium of communications in our era, like it or not.

Argument 4: "Direct Mail Is an Invasion of Privacy"

I don't know about you, but I have more friends than I can count who become positively livid at the mere mention of direct mail. (Somehow, we still manage to be friends, but only by avoiding the topic of direct mail.) They profess to believe—well, all right, they believe—that it is improper if not downright immoral that they are forced to receive unsolicited mail. In fairness, their anger usually encompasses catalog merchants and credit card purveyors as well as fundraisers, but to them it's all "junk mail."

It puzzles me that any reasonably intelligent grown-up could become unhinged over this issue. After all, this "problem" can be quickly and easily solved by recycling unwanted mail or (heaven forbid!) depositing it in the trash, which is precisely what happens to so much of it. So why the fury?

Privacy is precious, of course, and most Americans view it as a constitutional right. But shouldn't we all reserve our anger for those who genuinely invade our privacy? For example, most of America's financial institutions thrive on the basis of intimate personal information about all of us that's freely traded in the marketplace. Identity theft is becoming a concern for more and more Americans, precisely because so much sensitive personal information is so readily available through public channels, chiefly over the Internet. Granted, this sort of thing is generally well hidden from us, and a piece of mail in a mailbox is a tangible thing that is hard to overlook. But does that seem to be an appropriate object of anger?

Unfortunately, this is an emotional matter. Logic has nothing to do with it, so there is no way I can refute the argument using only words. A little TLC seems to be called for.

● ● ●

I hope I've successfully refuted the arguments against direct mail and given you the ammunition you need when one of these misconceptions crops up in conversation. But you be the judge!

Fundraising Ratios
and Other Deceptions

onventional wisdom holds that the best way to measure your organization's efficiency is to look at the percentage of your income spent on overhead and fundraising. The popular press, the charitable "watchdog" agencies, and our own ingrown instincts all tell us this is the right way to determine whether you're doing a good job of running your nonprofit organization. As the argument goes, if you spend more than 10 or 20 cents to raise a dollar—a "fundraising ratio" of 10 to 20 percent—then there must be something wrong with you.

Well, that's bunk.

The fundraising ratio is a meaningful measurement for America's biggest charities: the Red Cross, the Salvation Army, UNICEF, Goodwill Industries, CARE, the American Cancer Society. All these groups are decades-old, command instant name recognition, and have large development departments with the talent and the resources to use every conceivable means to raise money and can make the most of every dollar spent on fundraising. Each of them raises more than $300 million per year. But applying the same simplistic criteria to young public interest groups or charities with budgets a hundredth or a thousandth the size usually makes no sense at all.

In exceptional cases where fraud or flagrant mismanagement is suspected, an extremely high fundraising ratio *may* be an early warning signal. An organization that's spending 95 cents to raise every dollar after three or four years of extensive direct mail promotion is clearly not worthy of donors' support. A closer look may reveal that the organization is promising a miraculous cancer cure and working out of a third-floor walkup and a post office box, and that the organization's founder and $200,000-a-year executive director is the brother-in-law and former employee of its direct mail consultant. But even though fraudulent charities have existed since a charitable impulse moved some far-sighted noble to give away the first shekel, they are uncommon today. It's a tragic mistake to hobble thousands of sincere and effective public interest organizations with rules designed to inhibit a few bad actors. Moreover, where fraud is likely, an unusually high fundraising ratio is probably just one of many grave and obvious problems.

If charitable donors were to limit their gifts to the handful of the nation's more than one million nonprofit tax-exempt organizations that meet these conventional criteria for nonprofit performance, charities would be few and far between. Groups springing up to meet new needs or simply to keep the old agencies honest would die as quickly as they were born. That's because only an organization with a truly secure funding base can fulfill these extravagant regulatory fantasies.

When a few phone calls and a lunch meeting with a wealthy donor can produce a multi-million-dollar gift or bequest, fundraising costs are minimal when expressed as a percentage of the proceeds. Much the same goes for an organization with a large, loyal following of donors who can be counted on to renew their support year after year. In either case, the fundraising ratio is likely to be low.

But a small, less well-established group or one just starting out to address a newly emerging need is not likely to be in a position to achieve the same results with such little effort. It may take several years of repeat giving and continuous cultivation before you can *count* on getting gifts from a donor.

Fundraising is hard work and for *most* nonprofits expensive, especially at the beginning. Partly because many so-called authorities keep beating the drum for the most restrictive definitions of acceptable fundraising practices, relatively few donors will give more than token sums to any but the best-established, blue-ribbon charities. To smaller and newer organizations, gifts are typically much less generous. And obtaining them can take a great deal of time and money. People tend not to trust what they don't know.

To show the contrast, let's look at two hypothetical nonprofit organizations:

Charity A

Founded thirty years ago, Charity A has an annual budget of $12 million, which it obtains in the following manner:

Trustees and major donors	$4,000,000
Bequests and planned giving programs	$2,000,000
Income from endowment (established 15 years ago)	$2,000,000

Foundation and corporate support	$2,000,000
Direct mail and telephone fundraising (from 30,000 donors)	$1,000,000
Sale and licensing of products and services	$1,000,000
Total Income Budget	$12,000,000

Organization B

Founded three years ago, Organization B has a $2 million budget, which it meets as follows:

Foundation support	$900,000
Direct mail and telephone fundraising (from 20,000 donors)	$600,000
Trustees and major donors	$400,000
Sale of products and services	$100,000
Total Income Budget	$2,000,000

It's entirely possible that Charity A and Organization B could each be spending $1 million per year on fundraising and overhead. For Charity A, this represents one-twelfth of its budget, or *8 cents* on the dollar. For Organization B, $1 million is half its revenue, or *50 cents* on the dollar—more than six times as high a fundraising cost as that of Charity A. Does that make Charity A six times "better" than Organization B?

Not on your life!

Leave aside for the moment the possibility that the $11 million that Charity A has left over to spend directly on its programs might just be going down the drain on misguided or irrelevant projects, getting socked away in fatter and fatter "reserve" funds, or even keeping a passel of unimaginative people at work in featherbedding jobs. After all, Organization B could just as easily have misbegotten priorities or incompetent staff. Let's just look a little closer at the *income* side of the ledger. The contrast is dramatic:

- Organization B's work with major donors is just beginning. It's had few opportunities to identify or cultivate major donors or to establish a program of planned giving and bequests, much less an endowment fund. These are Charity A's *principal* sources of financial support, but they took years to develop.
- Nearly half of Organization B's $2 million budget is contributed by foundations. For Charity A, which receives grants worth more than twice as much, foundation and corporate support is only one-sixth of its total funding. Most foundations—and particularly corporate philanthropies, which may have stockholders to worry about—favor name-brand charities. Money attracts money.

- With its name less well established and its merchandising program in its infancy, Organization B's income from the licensing and sale of products is only a tenth as great as Charity A's. Name recognition usually takes time to establish, and familiarity sells products as well as programs.

The real measure of a nonprofit organization's effectiveness is the cost of the *results* it gains. By that yardstick, many nonprofits with enviable fundraising ratios are singularly ineffective when compared to some of the scrappy, innovative, grass-roots organizations with which I'm familiar—ventures that rarely are able to raise a dollar for less than 35 or 40 cents.

Another big contrast between Charity A and Organization B lies in their direct mail and telephone fundraising programs:

- For Charity A, raising money from 30,000 direct mail donors, a great many of them of long standing, is a very profitable proposition. To replace those five or six thousand lost by attrition each year requires little new investment in donor acquisition. The full cost of Charity A's direct mail program may be no more than $250,000. An overall revenue-to-cost ratio of four- or even six-to-one is not at all unlikely in a mature program of this sort.
- Organization B's fast-growth direct mail strategy looks a lot different. In its second year of aggressive donor acquisition, Organization B might even be spending on direct mail *more* than the $600,000 it's raising.
- Charity A's direct mail program obviously emphasizes the cultivation and *resolicitation* of loyal, long-term donors. For Organization B, direct mail and telemarketing are tools to meet a different and more costly challenge: to identify and recruit new donors.

How does Organization B get to be like Charity A? By doing precisely what it's now doing, that is, methodically building and cultivating its donor base year after year after year.

As you can see clearly in this example, direct mail is only *one* of a great many fundraising tools that charities and public interest organizations can employ in the service of their strategies to make the world a better place. In fact, for all but a handful of nonprofits and political campaigns, a large-scale direct mail program makes little sense in the absence of other fundraising efforts, especially on the high end of the donor scale. For example, Organization B's expensive, fast-growth strategy will really start paying off only when its development program includes major gift opportunities such as Charity A's.

Nonprofit organizations spring into existence to fill unmet needs, to challenge old concepts, and to espouse new ideas. It's no accident that many nonprofits have such a tough time raising funds; what they advocate is downright unpopular.

But even organizations that meet universally acknowledged needs and altogether avoid controversy are likely to face an uphill battle getting their fundraising programs up to a level of efficiency that allows for a consistently low fundraising ratio and still provides for necessary growth.

To do so takes *time*. After people, issues, and money, time is the fourth dimension of fundraising. It's often unseen and rarely appreciated. But no fundraising program may be fairly evaluated without a full understanding of this most precious of commodities. I hope that the central role of time in direct mail fundraising has become clear in the pages of this book.

Direct Mail Fundraising in the Thirteenth Century?

If you think Richard Viguerie, Jerry Huntsinger, Roger Craver, or any other living human being invented direct mail fundraising, guess again. I knew it came into existence a lot earlier than World War II. I just didn't know how much earlier. Now I believe I know.

Friends and colleagues competed to pass along to me the world's first example of a direct mail fundraising letter. I thought I'd hit the jackpot last year when writer Adam Hochschild presented me with a photocopy from the "Minute Books of the Society for Effecting the Abolition of the Slave Trade"—minutes of the meeting of October 7, 1788. The handwritten letter reproduced in those minutes reads in full as follows:

> Sir,
>
> The Funds of the Society instituted for the abolition of the Slave Trade being nearly exhausted, the Committee being of the opinion that the prosecution of the business will require a Sum equal to if not exceeding the amount of the Subscriptions already received in order to defray the necessary expenses of the Parties who are disposed to give their evidence before the House of Commons feel it incumbent upon them again to make application to the liberality of the Public & have directed their

Secretary Mr. John Frederick Garling to solicit on their behalf the renewal of your Subscription to facilitate the completion of an object so important to the Interests of Humanity.

By Order of the Committee,

Granville Sharp, Chairman

In its formality, the 114-word single sentence of that solicitation has a distinctly quaint character. Imagine my surprise, then, to receive a much older but far more contemporary-sounding direct mail appeal, sent to me by San Francisco Bay Area fundraising consultant Lisa Hoffman. Lisa works with the San Francisco Zen Center, and there she encountered a translation of an appeal sent to Buddhist monks throughout Japan in 1235 by Eihei Dogen, monk of the Kannondori Monastery. (The letter was translated by Michael Wenger and Kazuaki Tanahashi.) The letter begins:

> We respectfully make this announcement to all buddhas in the ten directions, sages and monks in the heavenly and human worlds, the eight types of beings in the dragon realm, generous men and women. We wish to construct a training hall with small donations from people's pure heart.

Now, how's that for targeting the audience? "Eight types of beings in the dragon realm" as well as "generous men and women"?
The letter continues after two paragraphs of references to Buddhist duty:

> For some years ever since I returned to Japan from China, I have vowed to establish a monastery. But there has not been a place suitable to support monks' formal practice using bowls and robes. Now we have acquired an excellent place. . . . Although it is still covered with weeds and not yet functioning, we plan to build a training monastery there . . .
>
> We urgently need a Monks' Hall right now. We plan to build one seven ken square [70-feet-square], with no interior walls. We will set up long platforms to reside on, where we will practice day and night without fail . . .

It's difficult to find a better example in contemporary fundraising letters of a specific justification for the need for money. And did you notice the urgent note in the copy?

The letter continues by noting the great impact the new monastery can have on the practice of Buddhism and how it represents the latest expression of a centuries-old tradition, then offers this note about donor recognition:

> We will acknowledge gifts by installing the donors' names in the center of the sacred image. The myriad syllables of the seed wisdom will honor the donors and everyone.

The monk's letter closes on a lyrical note, waxing poetic about the celestial scope of the project:

> Those who attain the way in this hall will be guiding masters of the assembly. Truly they will be knowledgeable and reach not only the human realm but transform beings in the heavenly realm and in the dragons' palace. Those in the realms of magic and darkness will also listen. Thus this dharma wheel transmitted from Shyakyamuni Buddha can reach everywhere.

How could you possibly resist such a compelling appeal?

Reading List and
On-Line Resources

The following is a list of twenty-nine books about direct mail fundraising, fundraising in general, and direct marketing. I've found them all to be helpful in understanding and applying the principles of fundraising and their application to direct response. I am immodestly including several of my own books.

The Twenty-Nine Most Useful Books

1. Burk, P. *Thanks! A Guide to Donor-Centred Fundraising.* Toronto: Burk & Associates, Ltd., 2000. Based on intensive market research in Canada, this book is a sharp slap in the face to any fundraiser who believes it's possible to dispense with donor acknowledgments.

2. Burk, P. *Donor-Centered Fundraising: How to Hold On to Your Donors and Raise Much More Money.* Toronto: Burk & Associates, Ltd., 2003. This book, like its predecessor, is based on intensive donor research, but this time in the United States.

3. Burnett, K. *Relationship Fundraising.* (2nd ed.) San Francisco: Jossey-Bass, 2002. This classic, recently revised and updated by the dean of direct mail fundraising in Europe and the United Kingdom, compellingly states the case

for relationship fundraising and sets the tone for truly successful long-term donor development programs.

4. Burnett, K. *Friends for Life.* London: The White Lion Press Limited, 1996. This sequel to Burnett's original book includes illuminating case studies.

5. The Center on Philanthropy at Indiana University, *Giving USA 2003: The Annual Report on Philanthropy for the Year 2002.* Indianapolis: AAFRC Trust for Philanthropy, 2003.

6. Flanagan, J. *Successful Fundraising.* (2nd ed.) Chicago: Contemporary Books, 2000. This is simply the best and most comprehensive treatment of fundraising for community organizations; probably the best-selling fundraising book of all time.

7. Grace, K. *Beyond Fund Raising: New Strategies for Nonprofit Innovation and Investment.* New York: Wiley, 1997. This book addresses the need for the non-profit sector to go beyond fundraising and understand and apply development principles.

8. Huntsinger, J. *Eighty-Six Tutorials on Creating Fundraising Letters and Packages.* Ashland, Va.: Emerson Publishers, 2000. Huntsinger has holed up on his farm in Virginia to make money by (what else?) writing fundraising letters, but his sagacity about writing for response lives on in this three-inch-thick workbook chock full of examples.

9. Johnston, M. *Direct Response Fund Raising: Mastering New Trends for Results.* New York: Wiley, 2000. This is a handy guide to contemporary thinking about new techniques in direct response fundraising.

10. Kuniholm, R. *The Complete Book of Model Fund-Raising Letters.* Englewood Cliffs, N.J.: Prentice Hall, 1995. Of a shelf full of books that feature sample and model fundraising letters, this is the best I've seen.

11. Lautman, K., and Goldstein, H. *Dear Friend: Mastering the Art of Direct Mail Fund Raising.* (2nd ed.) Washington, D.C.: The Taft Group, 1990. This intro-ductory book on direct mail is very well done; emphasizes the technical side of the craft rather than the strategic.

12. McKinnon, H. *Hidden Gold: How Monthly Giving Will Build Donor Loyalty, Boost Your Organization's Income, and Increase Financial Stability.* Chicago: Bonus Books, 1999. Written by one of the world's leading practitioners of monthly giving programs, this book lays it all out, from soup to nuts; edited by yours truly.

13. Nash, E. *Direct Marketing*. New York: McGraw-Hill, 2000. The industry's "how-to" classic has been completely updated with new chapters on the Internet and global marketing.

14. Ogilvy, D. *Ogilvy on Advertising*. New York: Crown Publishers, 1983. This is one of several extraordinary books by the late, great David Ogilvy, who was in many ways the godfather of direct mail fundraising for his lifelong emphasis on long, information-packed copy.

15. Panas, J. *MegaGifts*. Chicago: Pluribus Press, 1984. This is one of a slew of beautifully written books by one of the most prolific and perceptive writers in the field of fundraising.

16. Rich, P., and Hines, D. *Membership Development*. Gaithersburg, Md.: Aspen Publishers, 2002. This is a comprehensive discussion of all aspects of building a successful membership development program.

17. Robinson, E.M.M. *The Nonprofit Membership Toolkit*. San Francisco: Jossey-Bass, 2003. Here is a comprehensive treatment of membership development techniques as used by small and medium-sized nonprofit organizations in the United States.

18. Stern, G. J. *Marketing Workbook for Nonprofit Organizations*. St. Paul, Minn.: Amherst H. Wilder Foundation Publishing Center, 1990. This book is a wonderful resource to assist the nonprofit sector in the marketing planning process.

19. Stern, G. J. *Marketing Workbook for Nonprofit Organizations Volume II: Mobilize People for Marketing Success*. St. Paul, Minn.: Amherst H. Wilder Foundation Publishing Center, 1997. This sequel to Stern's popular *Marketing Workbook* includes complete instructions, examples, and detailed worksheets to help mobilize nonprofit organizations toward focused promotion campaigns.

20. Stone, R., and Jacobs, R. *Successful Direct Marketing Methods*. New York: McGraw-Hill, 2001. Regarded as the bible of direct marketing by generations of marketers, this is a thoroughgoing approach to the principles of the craft.

21. Tempel, E. (ed.). *Hank Rosso's Achieving Excellence in Fund Raising*. (2nd ed.) San Francisco: Jossey-Bass, 2003. A fresh take on what the late Hank Rosso called "the gentle art" of fundraising, this compendium of tightly edited articles on all major aspects of fundraising is edited by the director of the nation's preeminent academic center on philanthropy.

22. Trenbeth, R. *The Membership Mystique*. Rockville, Md: The Fund-Raising Institute, 1986. This classic, first book on membership development by the late Dick Trenbeth is long out of print but still well worth reading, if you can find a copy in a library.

23. Vögele, S. *Handbook of Direct Mail*. Cambridge: University Press, 1992. The good Herr Doktor wrote this book in German, and it shows in the clumsy English translation, but the wisdom embedded in these pages is worth the digging and the puzzlement; Vögele's "Dialogue Method" forms the basis of much of the practice of successful contemporary direct mail fundraisers.

24. Warwick, M. *The Five Strategies for Fundraising Success*. San Francisco: Jossey-Bass, 2000. Based on the strategic concept introduced in Chapter One of this book, this is the only effort I've encountered in print to devise a theoretical construct to analyze the role of fundraising in nonprofit development.

25. Warwick, M. *How to Write Successful Fundraising Letters*. San Francisco: Jossey-Bass, 2001. Several others have written how-to books on this topic, but no others are currently in print. I can recommend this one to you.

26. Warwick, M. *Testing, Testing, 1, 2, 3*. San Francisco: Jossey-Bass, 2003. This is the only book now in print on the subject of testing for direct mail fundraising; includes actual detailed results from more than three hundred tests.

27. Warwick, M., Hart, T., and Allen, N. (eds.). *Fundraising on the Internet*. (2nd ed.) San Francisco: Jossey-Bass, 2002. Appearing in 1995, the first edition of this book was the first ever to be published on the subject (just three years after the public debut of the World Wide Web); rather than a true second edition this is a completely new treatment of the topic and remains the only attempt to cover it in a comprehensive way.

28. Warwick, M., and Hitchcock, S. *Ten Steps to Fundraising Success*. San Francisco: Jossey-Bass, 2002. Here's a workbook that includes dozens of checklists and worksheets that may be used to implement a strategic planning process based on the theory developed in *Five Strategies*.

29. Wunderman, L. *Being Direct: Making Advertising Pay*. New York: Random House, 1996. Wunderman, known as the pioneering father of direct marketing, tells his own story of how his visionary marketing techniques transformed the advertising industry and will shape the interactive marketplace of the future; a good read and full of insight.

The Eleven Most Useful Periodicals

Among the many periodicals published for fundraisers, nonprofit executives, and direct marketers, these eleven have proven themselves consistently the most helpful in my work in direct mail fundraising for public interest organizations. I'm including my own newsletter because it is the only one devoted exclusively to direct response fundraising.

1. *The Chronicle of Philanthropy,* 1255 Twenty-Third Street, N.W., Washington, DC 20037. Biweekly except for the first two weeks in July and the last two weeks in December, $69.50 annual subscription; the single best source of current news and opinion about fundraising and the nonprofit sector.

2. *Contributions,* P.O. Box 338, Medfield, MA 02052, www.contributions magazine.com. 6 issues per year, $40 annual subscription; includes a regular column on direct mail by my colleague, Steve Hitchcock; informative tabloid-style magazine and a good source of information about newly published books on fundraising.

3. *Direct,* Box 4949, Stamford, CT 06907–0949. 16 issues per year, $85 annual subscription; occasionally carries an article featuring an outstanding direct mail fundraising program.

4. *DM News,* 19 West 21st Street, New York, NY 10010, www.dmnews.com. 48 issues per year, $49 annual subscription; a controlled circulation publication offered free to a fixed number of qualified U.S. subscribers meeting certain criteria; a waiting period of up to two months for new subscriptions; mostly about commercial direct marketing but covers direct mail fundraising from time to time as well and offers free e-news on-line.

5. Newsletter of the DMA Nonprofit Federation, 1111 19th Street, N.W., Suite 1180, Washington, DC 20036, nonprofitfederation@the-dma.org. Excellent for members; focuses on direct response fundraising.

6. *Give & Take: News and Ideas for Development Executives of Nonprofit Organizations,* Robert F. Sharpe & Co., Inc., 6410 Poplar Avenue, Suite 700, Memphis, TN 38119, www.rfsco.com. Published monthly by Bob and Tim Sharpe, specialists in legacy giving, and reflects that focus; promotional in purpose (Sharpe and Co. sells planned giving newsletters) but always features well-written and informative articles of substance on topics related to legacy giving; available in HTML format on-line as well as in print.

7. *Grassroots Fundraising Journal,* 3781 Broadway, Oakland, CA 94611, www.grassrootsfundraising.org. 6 issues per year, $32 annual subscription; a bimonthly magazine published by the legendary Kim Klein, one of the nation's most gifted fundraisers for community-based social change organizations, frequently featuring articles whose wisdom transcends the limitations of small, local nonprofits.

8. *Inside Direct Mail* (incorporating *Who's Mailing What!*), North American Publishing Company, 401 North Broad Street, Philadelphia, PA 19108-1001. 12 issues per year, $195 annual subscription, US$235 in Canada. For years, *Who's Mailing What!* reflected the colorful and always interesting views of its founder and editor, direct mail copywriter Denny Hatch, writing from his home in Connecticut. Denny sold the company years ago, and it's now being published by a largely new crew in Philadelphia. It's gotten slick and much less interesting but is still useful for the professional engaged in direct mail of any kind; features fundraising packages from time to time.

9. Mal Warwick's Newsletter: *Successful Direct Mail, Telephone & Online Fundraising,* Strathmoor Press, Inc., 2550 Ninth Street, Suite 103, Berkeley, CA 94710-2551, www.malwarwick.com. 6 issues per year, introductory subscription $49.95, US$69 in Canada; free issue available on-line at my Web site.

10. *Professional Fundraising,* Subscription Department, 39-41 North Road, London N7 9DP, UK. Twice a month except for single issues in December and January, $75 annual subscription for an individual, $90 for a charity, $110 for an institution; lively and informative about fundraising issues and practices in the U.K.; no special focus on direct response.

11. *The NonProfit Times,* 120 Littleton Road, Suite 120, Parsippany, NJ 07054-1803. 24 issues per year, free subscriptions only for full-time U.S. nonprofit executives, $65 annual subscription, US$89 in Canada.

The Eight Most Useful On-Line Resources

1. changingourworld.com A site maintained by a subsidiary of one of the world's largest advertising agencies, the Omnicom Group, that offers fundraising and philanthropy services.

2. clickz.com A well-developed commercial site that features a wealth of information and insight about on-line marketing.

3. donordigital.com A lively site that features current examples of state-of-the-art on-line fundraising, marketing, and advocacy; edited by Donordigital's extremely knowledgeable president, Nick Allen, and vice president, Madeline Stanionis; sign-ups available for Donordigital's free electronic newsletter.

4. gilbert.org Site of The Gilbert Organization developed by e-mail maven Michael Gilbert; publishes a respected free, very useful weekly, "Nonprofit Online News: News of the Online Nonprofit Community."

5. www.canadianfundraiser.com Sign-ups available for the free "Canadian Fundraiser E-News," which devotes itself to matters Canadian but often has provocative articles about broader fundraising topics of interest to others as well.

6. www.levison.com Written by Ivan Levison, a brilliant copywriter who makes a living largely by writing for high-tech companies; a free monthly newsletter on copywriting, both direct mail and e-mail, that is often directly pertinent to the challenges we face in writing fundraising appeals; newsletter can be ordered.

7. www.malwarwick.com Includes more information about direct mail and other aspects of direct response fundraising than anything else on the World Wide Web today; sign-ups available for free monthly electronic newsletter, "Mal Warwick's Successful Fundraising Online," which features some of the material included in my print newsletter but is mostly original material.

8. yesmail.com A commercial site that focuses on "permission marketing" and offers a free bimonthly e-newsletter, "Email Insider."

References

Burk, P. *Thanks! A Guide to Donor-Centred Fundraising.* Toronto: Burk & Associates, Ltd., 2000.

Burk, P. *Donor Centered Fundraising: How to Hold On to Your Donors and Raise Much More Money,* Burk & Associates, Ltd., 2003.

Burnett, K. *Relationship Fundraising.* (2nd ed.) San Francisco: Jossey-Bass, 2002.

Craver, R. "Green Pages." Co-Op America. *Fund Raising Management,* 1989.

Huntsinger, J. *Fund Raising Management,* 1989.

McKinnon, H. *Hidden Gold: How Monthly Giving Will Build Donor Loyalty, Boost Your Organization's Income, and Increase Financial Stability.* Chicago: Bonus Books, 1999.

Ray, P. H., and Anderson, S. R. *The Cultural Creatives: How 50 Million People Are Changing the World.* New York: Harmony Books, 2000.

Warwick, M. *Five Strategies for Fundraising Success.* San Francisco: Jossey-Bass, 2000.

Warwick, M. *How to Write Successful Fundraising Letters.* (rev. ed.) San Francisco: Jossey-Bass, 2001.

Warwick, M. *Testing, Testing, 1, 2, 3: Raise More Money with Direct Mail Tests.* San Francisco: Jossey-Bass, 2003.

Warwick, M., Hart, T., and Allen, N. (eds.). *Fundraising on the Internet: The ePhilanthropy Foundation.Org's Guide to Success Online.* (2nd ed.) San Francisco: Jossey-Bass, 2002.

Index

.

I Want to Hear From You!

Once you've read this book, I want to hear from you. I want to know if you take issue with something in these pages. If your experience with direct mail fundraising has taught you a lesson I haven't learned, I want you to tell me about it. The same goes if you have illuminating facts at your fingertips or fascinating stories about direct mail fundraising or important arguments I've ignored.

Please contact me at Mal Warwick & Associates, Inc., 2550 Ninth Street, Suite 103, Berkeley, CA 94710; e-mail: mal@malwarwick.com, and check out my Web site at www.malwarwick.com.

I'll do my best to answer you. And someday, perhaps, I may immortalize your contribution in a further revised edition of *Revolution in the Mailbox*.

Thank you for your support.